Reason Unbound

A volume in the SUNY series in Western Esoteric Traditions

David Appelbaum, editor

Reason Unbound

On Spiritual Practice in Islamic Peripatetic Philosophy

MOHAMMAD AZADPUR

SUNY
PRESS

Published by State University of New York Press, Albany

Printed in the United States of America

For information, contact State University of New York Press, Albany, NY
www.sunypress.edu

Production by Diane Ganeles
Marketing by Michael Campochiaro

Library of Congress Cataloging-in-Publication Data

Azadpur, Mohammad.
Reason unbound : on spiritual practice in Islamic peripatetic philosophy / Mohammad Azadpur.
p. cm. — (Suny series in western esoteric traditions)
Includes bibliographical references and index.
ISBN 978-1-4384-3763-7 (hardcover : alk. paper)
ISBN 978-1-4384-3762-0 (pbk. : alk. paper)
1. Islamic philosophy. I. Title.

B741.A985 2011
181'.07—dc22 2011004136

10 9 8 7 6 5 4 3 2 1

Contents

Acknowledgments vii

Introduction: Islamic Philosophy and the Crisis of Modern Rationalism 1

Chapter 1: Beyond Orientalism and Academic Rationalism: A Critique of the Standard Readings of Islamic Philosophy 7

1.1. Philosophy as Practice of Spiritual Exercises 8
1.2. Standard Readings of Islamic Philosophy 12

Chapter 2: To the Things Themselves: Corbin and Heidegger on Phenomenological Access 21

2.1. Phenomenology According to Henry Corbin 23
2.2. Heidegger's Phenomenology 24
2.3. Two Contemporary Approaches to Heidegger's Phenomenology 28
2.4. Back to Corbin 35

Chapter 3: From the Things Themselves to Prophecy: Philosophical Cultivation in Islamic Peripateticism 39

3.1. The Ethical Foundations of Islamic Philosophy 40
3.2. Alfarabi's Appropriation of Islamic Ethics 42
3.3. Alfarabi's Philosophical Appropriation of Islamic Prophetology 45
3.4. The Reception of the Notion of Active Intellect in the Islamic Philosophical Tradition 49
3.5. Alfarabi on Religion and Politics 52
3.6. Avicenna on Philosophical Felicity 53
3.7. Avicenna on Intellectual Prophecy 60

Chapter 4: Disciplining the Imagination: Intellect, Imagination, and Prophecy 65

4.1. Prophetic Imagination 65
4.2. The Beautiful and the Sublime 71
4.3. Before and After Kant 72
4.4. Avicenna on the Poetic Cultivation of Imagination 75

Chapter 5: The Theologian's Dream: Imagination and Intellectual Heresy 81

5.1. Ghazali on Dreams 82
5.2. Ghazali and Avicenna on the Interpretation of Prophetic Symbols 86
5.3. Ghazali's Charge of Heresy Against Islamic Peripatetics and Averroes' Reply 89

Chapter 6: On Human Finitude, Conscience, and Exemplarity: A Comparison between Islamic Philosophy and Phenomenology 95

6.1. Being-Towards-Beyond-Death: On the Immortality of the Soul in Islamic Peripateticism 96
6.2. Conscience and the Active Intellect 105
6.3. Paradigms of emulation: Divine Exemplars and Existential Heroes 108

Conclusion: Importance of Islamic Peripateticism for Modern Philosophy in the West and Its Impact on Later Islamic Philosophy 111

1. Islamic Peripateticism and the Predicament of Modern Western Philosophy 111
2. Peripateticism in Later Islamic Philosophy 113

Notes 123

Bibilography 157

Index 169

Acknowledgments

The production of this book was assisted by several grants from San Francisco State University (SFSU), specially a Presidential Award that gave me a semester's leave (when I wrote it all down for the first time) and a summer stipend (when I worked through this project in Tehran's Iranian Institute of Philosophy). I would like to express my thanks to Ghulāmriḍā A'vānī, who kept the doors to the Iranian Institute of Philosophy open for me. I benefited greatly from conversations with him, and also with Ghulāmḥussain Dīnānī and my friend, Muḥammad Esmā'ili, who showed exemplary Persian hospitality and made the institute's library available to me. I also benefited from the advice and comments of a number of my colleagues at San Francisco State. They include Jerry Needleman, Jim Royse, Anatole Anton, Pamela Hood, Shirin Khanmohammadi, and Mohammad Salama. Jim, Anatole, and Mohammad read through the whole manuscript and made valuable suggestions. San Francisco State's Humanities dean, Paul Sherwin, supported me intellectually and financially throughout my career at SFSU, and to him I owe a special debt of gratitude. I am also grateful to Abdulaziz Sachedina, Minoo Moallem, Vincent Cornell, and Mehdi Aminrazavi, who gave me helpful advice at different stages of this project. I also should mention my graduate students Todd Gullion, Mehdi Rajabzadeh, Kirk Templeton, Melissa Smart, Saja Parvizian, Cecily Driscoll, and last—but not least—John MacWillie. They read parts of this manuscript and helped in making it make sense. Todd read and heard about this project ever since his undergraduate years at SFSU, and his struggles with and responses to this material have always inspired me. John subjected the manuscript to a thorough editorial review and his suggestions were always fair and constructive. Of course, I should say that I am solely responsible for the imperfections of this work.

Above all, I must acknowledge the patience, encouragement, and forbearance of my family, especially my wife, Avissa. She patiently tolerates my eccentricities and gives me great joy. My daughter, Kimia, is a blessing and like the true alchemical agent, she improves everyone who comes into contact with her. I also should mention my gratitude to my parents, who tease me for not pursuing a more lucrative career, and frankly sometimes I wonder if things could have been better, but then when the fatigue of teaching and writing wears off, I thank God for the life of the mind.

Introduction

Islamic Philosophy and the Crisis of Modern Rationalism

This volume examines the modern reception of Islamic philosophy and its importance (and implications) for a critique of modern Western philosophy. In an essay titled "Orientalism and the Study of Islamic Philosophy," an eminent scholar of Islamic political philosophy, Muhsin Mahdi, extends the crisis identified and labeled by Edward Said as "Orientalism" to the academic approach to Islamic philosophy. Mahdi accepts Said's diagnosis that the problematic sense of "Orientalism" arises from "a dynamic exchange between individual authors and the large political concerns shared by the three great empires—British, French, and American—in whose intellectual territory the writing was produced."[1] This so-called dynamic exchange is, according to Said, "the corporate institution for dealing with the Orient—dealing with it by making statements about it, authorizing views of it, describing it, by teaching it, settling it, ruling over it."[2] In other words, Orientalist discourse is the systematic academic discipline of dominating, controlling, and managing the so-called Orient for the sake of the Western imperial political agenda. The Orient, in this account, is not the Far East, but rather primarily refers to what we call the Middle East, and for Said principally the *Islamic* Orient. His conclusion is that, as a result of the Orientalist discourse, Islam "has been fundamentally misrepresented in the West."[3]

In Chapter 1, I identify the Orientalist moves of some of the prominent modern scholars of Islamic philosophy and trace them to what Mahdi astutely identifies as the underlying philosophical predicament of Orientalist discourse (i.e., the discourse that succumbs to Imperialist pressure). Mahdi admits that the recent literature critical of Orientalism has shown that "Oriental studies of Islam and Islamic civilization have been founded on a mixed bag of religious, cultural, ideological, ethnic (in some cases even racist), and scientific prejudgments and practical political interests."[4] In other words, "these studies are guided by irrational motives and political interests."[5] Mahdi asserts that there is no escape from this predicament and that there is an underlying crisis of rationalism tainting modern scholarship wherein the so-called modern rationalism is "in many ways . . . dogmatic and irrational."[6] Said also acknowledges the philosophical root of the Orientalist quandary: "The real issue is whether indeed there can be a true representation of anything." Said denies that such a representation is possible; therefore, "we must be prepared to accept the fact that a representation *eo ipso* is implicated, intertwined, embedded, interwoven with a great many other things besides the 'truth,' which is itself a representation."[7]

Rejecting the possibility of true representations jeopardizes Said's attempts to diagnose "Orientalist" symptoms of Oriental studies, as it would be impossible to accuse such studies of falling short of "truth." Said is aware of this problem and circumvents it by arguing that we should aim for methodological self-consciousness.[8] In other words, we should acknowledge the complexity of "irrational" factors that constitute a representation and refuse to camouflage our representations as "truths." I agree with Mahdi that Said's "methodological self-consciousness" is only a beginning and "must lead to a search for a genuine form of rationalism."[9] Mahdi writes: "Understanding the reasons for the limited scope and humanly unsatisfying character of modern rationalism, and the search for a more wholesome unity that satisfies both the rational and imaginative or poetic aspects of man's life, are tasks that are still before us."[10] These are tasks that Mahdi himself does not carry out. However, he does provide a clue as to how to proceed in performing them; he maintains that the study of premodern rationalism, including Islamic philosophy, can "be of some use" in dealing with the development of a full and complete account of rationalism.[11] In this text, I draw on the work of principal Islamic Peripatetic philosophers (*mashshā'īyūn*)[12] in order to elucidate and challenge the boundaries of modern reason. As a result, I believe some of the false dualisms afflicting mainstream modern philosophy (e.g., reason vs. nature, reason vs. spirituality, and reason vs. imagination) will weaken their grip on us.

By "the principal Islamic Peripatetic philosophers," I mean Abū Naṣr Muḥammad Fārābi (Alfarabi) [d. 950] and Abū 'Alī Ḥussain ibn Sīnā (Avicenna) [d. 1037] upon whose work the core edifice of Islamic philosophy is constructed. Following Michael Marmura, I maintain that Alfarabi was, properly speaking, the architect of this edifice.[13] But I also agree with Roger Arnaldez when he calls the early period of Islamic philosophy "Avicennan," presumably due to the realization and completion of this edifice in the work of Avicenna.[14] I also consider the debate initiated by the influential theologian, Abū Ḥāmid Muḥammad Ghazzālī (Ghazali) [d. 1111], in critiquing Alfarabi and Avicenna, and the rebuttal of Ghazali offered by the twelfth-century Muslim Peripatetic Abū al-Walīd ibn Rushd (Averroes) [d. 1198]. These exchanges contribute to the clarification of the Peripatetic intellectualism. This is not to deny the importance of their predecessors—for example, Abū Yūsuf Ya'qūb ibn Isḥāq al-Kindī (al-Kindi) [d. 873] and his school as well as the early Ismaili thinkers, such as Abū 'Abdullah Muḥammad ibn Aḥmad al-Nasafī (d. 942) and Abū Ya'qūb al-Sijistānī (d. circa 974)—who sought, in various ways, to reconcile Islam and Greek philosophy. This work, however, is not an examination of the history of the rise of Islamic philosophy. Rather, what I am seeking to accomplish is the recognition of the importance of Islamic Peripateticism in the formulation of an antidote to the dualisms troubling mainstream modern philosophy.

In the first chapter, I ground my search for the role of intellect in Islamic Peripatetic philosophy by questioning the received account of philosophical activity as the production of abstract rational discourse. For this, I draw from Pierre Hadot's insightful readings of Greek philosophy wherein Hadot advances the view that, for the Greeks, philosophy was primarily the practice of spiritual exercises aimed at the transformation of the self and the acquisition of wisdom.[15] I accept this account, which flies in the face of the dominant yet sterile understanding of philosophy as rational discourse, and propose that Hadot's thesis (about the nature of philosophical inquiry among the Greeks) provides a novel way of interpreting Islamic philosophy as an inheritor of the Greek philosophical tradition.

In Chapter 2, I develop the corollary to the above account of Greco-Islamic philosophy as an overcoming of the modernist's divide between reason and world through an account of moral knowledge as involving a cultivated sensitivity to relevant features of the world.[16] In this account, claims to knowledge, as active exercises of our acquired concepts, are answerable to a world that is experienced by means of an involuntary actualization of those same concepts. This account of knowledge can be generalized and contains important consequences for the crisis-ridden modern foundationalism (and its opponents who deny the rational bearing of the world on the mind).[17] In this regard, I contend that Heidegger's phenomenology anticipates and embraces a version of this overcoming of the divide between mind and world.[18] More pointedly, it was this aspect of Heidegger's view that led his disciple, Henry Corbin, to Islamic philosophy. I draw on the relevant writings of Corbin and Heidegger to illuminate just how this phenomenological insight is anticipated by the Islamic Peripatetic tradition. In the third chapter, I expand on the ways in which the phenomenological debunking of the mind–world dualism is available in the texts of the Islamic Peripatetics. For the latter, the world is always already intellectually shaped (through the emanations of the Active Intellect). The philosopher is tasked with overcoming the inertia that prevents us from getting things right. In their concern with philosophy as a practice of spiritual exercises aiming at the things themselves, Islamic Peripatetics and their modern European counterparts are in alliance with the Greeks in their focus on the emulation and realization of a human exemplar as the standard of wisdom.[19] This relationship to an exemplar is not a mere moral discipleship; rather it is constitutive of the philosophical activity as such—the transformation of the self for the sake of knowledge. However, the Muslim Peripatetic philosophers differ in the significance they assign to the power of prophecy in their accounts of philosophical exemplars and their disciples. This unique Muslim Peripatetic account of the philosophical exemplars follows from the Islamic tradition's explanations of the revelations of Prophet Muhammad. The Islamic Peripatetic account of prophecy is, in turn, responsible for what Mahdi identified as the harmony of the rational and the imaginative aspects of human life that, in this context, has legal, ethical, intellectual, and spiritual dimensions.

In Chapters 4 and 5, I explore the Islamic theory of imagination and its place in the prophetology distinctive of Islamic philosophy. In developing the details of the cultivation of the imagination advanced by the Islamic philosophers, I delineate the poetic appropriation of the art of spiritual hermeneutics (*ta'wīl*) to account for the cultivation of the theoretical dimension of the intellect. Beginning with Avicenna, a significant moment in the Islamic cultivation of the soul involves the interpretation of imaginative symbolism. This hermeneutics aims to free the interpreter from the grip of the mundane and culminates in an experience of the divine. I relate this aspect of Islamic philosophy to a strand in modern European philosophical exploration of the faculty of the imagination and the analytic of the concept of the sublime. For this comparison, I consider the seminal aesthetic writings of Kant, Hegel, and Heidegger as well as the work of some of their prominent readers and commentators.[20]

The modern accounts of the sublime explicate that of which this term is predicated either as located beyond the reach of imagination (Kant and his followers) or as a relic of an era that failed to recognize the full capacity of human imagination (and therefore the Hegelian sublation of the sublime in the beautiful). I maintain that Islamic Peripatetics, following Avicenna, develop an engagement of the sublime that bypasses the Kantian paradox (imagining the unimaginable) without succumbing to the historicizing of the sublime (*pace* Hegel). Shihāb al-Dīn Yaḥyā Suhrawardī, a prominent expositor of this alternative, which is a subject matter of my conclusion, advances the Avicennan account of the poetic imagination by assigning to the perfected imagination the role of a cognitive faculty that brings into view the objects of an imaginal realm (*'ālam al-mithāl*), between the spiritual and the physical.

In Chapter 6, before turning to the later tradition of Islamic philosophy, I offer a critique of Heidegger's phenomenology from the perspective of Islamic Peripatetic philosophy. I show that Islamic Peripatetics extend the domain of the practice of spiritual exercises beyond Heideggerian "authenticity"; as a result, they unfold new vistas of theoretical experience and endow the philosopher with exceptional dignity and freedom.

In the conclusion, I show that the later Islamic philosophers continue the projects of the Periaptetics and make original contributions to the philosophical enterprise advanced by their predecessors. To illustrate this point, in addition to Suhrawardi's writings, I discuss the salient work of the greatest of the later Islamic philosophers, Ṣadr al-Dīn Muḥammad Shīrāzī (Mulla Sadra), and the schools and the traditions that trained him and those that were subsequently influenced by his contribution.

Chapter 1

Beyond Orientalism and Academic Rationalism

A Critique of the Standard Readings of Islamic Philosophy

This chapter begins with a critique of several modern readings of the Islamic Peripatetic tradition with the intention of framing a more accurate and fruitful approach to thinking about that tradition that, in turn, can answer the central concern of this work (i.e., the elaboration of a genuine, autonomous philosophy). This strategy requires beginning with asking what constitutes philosophy. For example, Islamic philosophers inherited something from the Greeks that they called *al-falsafa,* derived from the Greek word *philosophia.* What was that something? It is my contention that the standard, modernist interpretation of what Muslims inherited from the Greeks involves a fundamental misunderstanding. These modernist historians of Islamic philosophy consider Greek philosophy to be comprised of systems of rational knowledge formulated by different philosophers or schools of philosophy. But I adopt Pierre Hadot's view that the Greeks, in their own conceptualization of what constituted their philosophic project, saw philosophy as primarily the practice of spiritual exercises aimed at the transformation of the self and the acquisition of wisdom. And it is my contention that this is how "Islamic" Peripatetic philosophers understood what they inherited from the Greeks. If this point is substantiated, then it is not hard to similarly see Islamic Peripateticism as an Islamic practice of philosophical spiritual exercises. Of course, to justify this argument much more needs to be said. What is critical is understanding that what makes the philosophical way of life advanced by Islamic philosophers unique is the appropriation of this Greek tradition into a legacy of Islamic prophetology. But before I attend to this assertion I need to establish the groundwork of what constituted Greek philosophy in the view of Hadot and how, if that interpretation is correct, it is in a fundamental contradiction with the modernist reading of Islamic philosophy. In the following chapter, I elucidate just how such an Hadot-like argument can be read from an Islamic perspective (as was accomplished in part by Henry Corbin—a former student of Martin Heidegger). Then in Chapter 3, I weave these strands together in a re-reading of Islamic Peripatetic philosophy.

1.1. Philosophy as Practice of Spiritual Exercises

Pierre Hadot, throughout his later writings, especially in *Philosophy as a Way of Life*, revives the ancient distinction between philosophical discourse and philosophy itself in order to criticize the condition of modernist scholarship on ancient philosophy. He writes: "historians of philosophy pay little attention to the fact that ancient philosophy was, first and foremost, a way of life. They consider philosophy as, above all, philosophical discourse."[1] By philosophical discourse, Hadot means the production of a "systematic explanation of the whole of reality."[2] By contrast, for Hadot's ancient Greek philosopher, philosophy is a way of life—not in the service of producing a work as a rational account of reality—rather the goal is to transform oneself, to become wise.[3] Philosophers, as lovers of wisdom, are in training for wisdom[4] and wisdom is not contained in a philosophical treatise, but is a condition of the human soul, its authentic condition, that is. The philosopher "knows that the normal, natural state of man should be wisdom, for wisdom is nothing more than the vision of things as they are, the vision of the cosmos as it is in the light of reason, and wisdom is also nothing more than the mode of being and living that should correspond to this vision."[5] The significance (for ancient philosophers) of the production of systematic philosophical works was in its pedagogical role for the training of the soul for wisdom. Philosophy yielded systematic texts,

> in order that it might provide the mind with a small number of principles, tightly linked together, which derived greater persuasive force and mnemonic effectiveness precisely from such systematization. Short sayings summed up, sometimes in striking form, the essential dogmas, so that the student might easily relocate himself within the fundamental disposition in which he was to live.[6]

This, of course, does not exhaust the significance of rationally systematized philosophical treatises. One could think of other functions: For instance, attending to a tightly argued and systematic treatise assists the philosopher in transcending the limits of the uncultivated self bound in its service of the appetites, mundane desires, and social conventions.[7] Regardless, the aim is wisdom (i.e., the mode of being that sees things as they are).

Hadot's account of ancient philosophy as primarily a way of life or, as he says elsewhere, "the practice of spiritual exercises,"[8] accentuates the centrality of ethics in the ancient philosophical enterprise. Famously, ethics concerns the good life (i.e., how one should live), and most modern moral philosophers construe this concern as directing us to the agent's actions and the articulation of the requirements determining the rightness or the wrongness of those actions. These philosophers divide into deontologists and teleologists, depending on their preference for the intrinsic goodness of acts or human interests and desires, respectively. Although there are those espousing hybrid theories as well, they all share a concern for calculating the propriety of *actions*. It is in this regard that modern philosophy's *act-centered* ethics should be contrasted with the ancient *agent-centered* virtue ethics where the focus turns on the agent's character. Thus, virtue ethicists inquire into the cultivation of those character traits that allow the agent to lead the good life.[9] In other words, the moral agent does not resort to an algorithm (deontological, consequential, or a hybrid) to figure out what to do. The cultivation of relevant character traits enables the agent to perceive the good in each particular circumstance and to pursue it.

In "Radical Virtue Ethics," Kurt Baier, a contemporary moral philosopher, aims to reconcile act-centered moral theories and virtue ethics through what he calls the moderate thesis: "The moderate thesis regards contemporary ethics as lamentably incomplete but not radically wrongheaded. For it thinks that the question it has tried to answer is logically independent of, or indeed, logically prior to the questions neglected."[10] The moderate thesis, according to Baier, considers act-centered theory as logically independent of virtue ethics. Nevertheless, it perfects virtue ethics by answering a logically antecedent question, namely, "What morally speaking ought we to do?" According to Baier's moderate thesis, virtue ethics, without the analytical lens of an act-centered moral theory, would be blind to its own theoretical foundations.

The approach exemplified by Baier's reconciliation of act-centered moral theory and agent-centered virtue ethics has motivated some to read the Greek philosophers and their Islamic successors as committed to a similar project. For example, in "Medieval Islamic Philosophy and the Virtue of Ethics," Charles Butterworth argues "Plato and Aristotle are in fundamental agreement about the hierarchical relationship between virtue and ethics, that is, about the subordination of ethics to virtue. For ethical conduct to be sound, it must be guided by correct opinion or even knowledge of virtue."[11] Correct opinion and knowledge of virtue, for Butterworth, are moral-theoretical foundations for the proper moral habits, that is, the ability to engage in right (i.e., ethical) action. For Butterworth, the difference between the ethical views of Aristotle and Plato amounts to the rigor of the theory presupposed for right conduct. Plato advocates for knowledge of the good, whereas Aristotle is "content to proceed according to generally accepted opinion."[12] Given this view, Butterworth asserts the exact opposite of the claim that I take Hadot to be making. For example, Butterworth writes, "Fārābi follows Plato . . . and constantly argues that we must acquire theoretical knowledge of the way things are before we can develop the deliberative and moral virtues."[13]

Hadot's reading of the ancients implies the antithetical thesis that ancient ethics does not need theoretical foundations.[14] For Hadot, virtue ethics, in that it is concerned with the formation of character constituting the good life, forms the foundation of the philosophical orientation of ancient thought. Ancient theoretical discourse is grounded in philosophical practice. Even Aristotle, whose account of the highest good as the contemplation culminating in thought thinking itself often is invoked to establish the dependence of practice on theory, situated theory in the context of the ethical cultivation of the soul. "It is sometimes claimed that Aristotle was a pure theoretician, but for him, too, philosophy was incapable of being reduced to philosophical discourse, that is, to the production of a body of abstract knowledge. Rather, philosophy for Aristotle was a quality of the mind, the result of an inner transformation."[15] In other words, for Aristotle and other ancient philosophers, theoretical discourses are subsidiary to the act of philosophy as the cultivation of practical and theoretical virtues.

In this regard for the cultivation of theoretical virtue, there is a relevant exchange between Hadot and Michel Foucault worthy of closer scrutiny. Foucault's later writings contain his explorations of the ancient fascination with the Socratic care of the self and are greatly indebted to Hadot's pioneering work.[16] Foucault's reading of the ancient spiritual exercises, however, limits them to their purely ethical function (i.e., the cultivation of practical virtues). "Paul Veyne has reported the following exchange with Foucault: "One day when I asked Foucault: 'The care of the self, that is very nice, but what do you do with logic, what do you do with physics? He responded: 'Oh, these are enormous excrescences!' "[17] Hadot had his hesitations about Foucault's underestimation of the significance of theoretical spiritual exercises. In this I agree with Hadot that Foucault's rendition of spiritual exercises is tailored to modern sensibilities—to what Hadot refers to as a "new form of Dandyism"[18]—and therefore brackets the ancient goal of going beyond the self[19] and attaining what Arnold Davidson, similarly following Hadot, calls the (theoretical) awareness of the place of the self in a cosmic whole.[20] For example, Hadot's focus on Stoic physics as a spiritual exercise illuminates the exteriorizing moment in philosophical cultivation.[21] This exteriorizing moment places the theorizing philosopher alongside a world that shows itself as it is, not one that is in the service of the various frameworks that relativize our knowledge.[22] In other words, physics, for Hadot, is not a mere blemish, but an essential moment in philosophical *askēsis*, one that we should not want to conceal under the Dandyist powder.

Hadot's own position, despite its advance over the Foucaultian version, suffers from a similar limitation that comes out when he expresses hesitation about the place of Plotinus' accounts of mystical experiences within the broader cosmic dimension of self-cultivation: "[T]he phenomenon of mysticism which is so striking in Plotinus," remarks Hadot on his own intellectual development, "continues to intrigue me. Yet as I grow older, Plotinus speaks to me less and less. . . . From 1970 on, I have felt very strongly that it was Epicureanism and Stoicism which could nourish the spiritual life of men and women of our times, as well as my own."[23] Of course, one should pay attention to the spiritual life of one's contemporaries, but that should not come at the cost of suspending one's concern with relevant phenomena (which may not be in vogue). Islamic Peripatetic philosophy, as seen in the following, draws heavily from the cosmological and the mystical dimensions of Plotinian Neoplatonism and this influence is instrumental in the articulation of the distinctive Islamic philosophical prophetology. I return to this question in the next chapter when I draw on the work of Henry Corbin to remedy the limitations of Hadot's position and to situate the importance of Islamic Peripateticism in relation to modern philosophy.

1.2. Standard Readings of Islamic Philosophy

Having sketched the outlines of an alternative reading of the purpose and significance of Greek philosophy, I offer a critique of the views of some prominent scholars of Islamic philosophy who have written on the Muslim inheritance from the Greeks. This critique is informed by Hadot's account of ancient philosophy, because Hadot's work—despite his underestimation of the philosophical significance of mystical experience and inattention to the tradition of Islamic philosophy—is extremely useful in unveiling the assumptions that obfuscate the genuine sense of philosophy in the Islamic tradition.

Richard Walzer, a prominent scholar of the Greek heritage of Islamic philosophy, maintains that Islamic philosophy continued and preserved the Greek philosophical discourse. Walzer's "Islamic philosophers" draw on the translated Greek philosophical texts and compose works that are a fusion of the views of their Greek predecessors. In this vein, "genuine" philosophy ultimately is advancing original theses in "rational terms," in topical categories, and Walzer is adamant that no such original thesis is to be found in the works of Islamic philosophers. In the case of Alfarabi, for instance, Walzer maintains that the latter's theory of prophecy may contain an original synthesis of Greek views on "imitation" and imagination, but he cannot help committing an *ad ignorantiam* and argues that "I have not been able to find precise evidence for it in extant Greek texts although it is obviously of Greek origin."[24] Later, I discuss some Greek predecessors of this account of imagination; nevertheless, this does not mean that Alfarabi adopted this notion from those Greek sources as there is no evidence that they were available to him. In his zeal to find Greek sources of all the interesting views of Alfarabi, Walzer overlooks the explanation that Alfarabi arrives at his account of imagination independently. Borrowing Edward Said's approach, there is a trace of Orientalism in Walzer's views. Specifically, Orientalists argue for the superiority of the Western culture (that of the colonizers),[25] and Walzer's exaggerated effort to attribute all originality in Islamic philosophy to its Greek sources implies that the golden age of "Oriental" philosophy was not anything other than a replica of the Greek original. Therefore, we lose nothing if we bypass Islamic philosophy and focus our attention on the Greeks, the so-called founders of "Western" philosophy.

It also is important to observe that Walzer's philosophical Orientalism is itself premised on the view that philosophy, as such, is the production of rational and systematic treatises. Walzer's Greeks take the credit for the conception of philosophy as the production of rational systems and the later Europeans are credited for advancing these systems. Muslims, in this picture, play the role of the transmitters, who lacked the rational prowess and the requisite creativity to build on the Greek heritage.[26] Walzer's philosophical Orientalism in conjunction with his commitment to the account of philosophy as production of philosophical discourse blinds him to the ways the Muslim philosophers sought to reconcile ancient Greek practice of philosophy with their own religious commitments and practices. As a result, Islamic philosophy is construed as the mere repository and transmission belt of ancient theories (for the later Europeans).[27]

Muhsin Mahdi, a leading scholar of Islamic political thought, challenges Walzer's reading of Alfarabi and advances a reading that gives prominence to Alfarabi's political thought. Walzer, as we have seen, asserts that Alfarabi's philosophical view is a mere replica of the Greek material, but then he argues, in keeping with the passage in the previous paragraph, that Alfarabi's innovation (which is not a philosophical innovation) results from his use of Greek sources to rationalize Islamic doctrines. Mahdi recoils from Walzer's Orientalism[28] and emphasizes the political dimension of Alfarabi's writings. Mahdi maintains that Alfarabi's major treatises (i.e., *On the Perfect State* and *Political Regime*) are "models to guide future legislators in establishing new cities. Models of this kind . . . are artful productions created by the teachers of legislators with an eye to general habits, character, opinions, and conditions, and these the legislator will adjust further with a view to a particular city under particular conditions."[29] According to Mahdi, a novel aspect of Alfarabi's thought is that it lays the theoretical foundation for political programs in the postclassical age, a period dominated by revealed religions.

On the one hand, I agree with Mahdi that Alfarabi's philosophy contains a philosophical grounding of the postclassical state. But also I contend that Mahdi's analysis overlooks the significance of virtue ethics in Alfarabi's philosophy. This deficiency comes into view when Mahdi wants to explain Alfarabi's inclusion in his political treatises of significant portions devoted to cosmology and psychology.[30] For this explanation, Mahdi implicitly invokes Socrates' strategy in the *Republic.* In order to define what a just individual is, Socrates declares that it is easier to define justice in the city and then, by establishing an analogy between the city and the individual, arrive at the definition of justice in the person. Socrates' strategy accords with his later contention that justice is primarily an attribute of persons and characters, and then only derivatively a property of laws, the social structure of the city-state, or the quality of our actions (*Republic,* 442a–445e).[31] Mahdi, however, considers this argument only in so far as philosophical psychology relates to political science.[32] He concerns himself with the parallels between the structure of the soul and that of the city, while overlooking the purpose of the argument, that is, the supply of insights for the fundamental Socratic concern for the ethical cultivation of the person.

In the subsequent chapters, I develop an account of this concern and its unique form in Islamic Peripatetic philosophy. But before turning to this important issue, I explore more of the problematic features of the modern reception of Islamic philosophy.

Oliver Leaman, a contemporary scholar of Islamic philosophy, diagnoses another manifestation of Orientalism in the position advanced by Mahdi's teacher, Leo Strauss.[33] Strauss, in *Persecution and the Art of Writing*, attributes the "collapse" of philosophy in the Jewish and the Islamic traditions to the conflict between reason and religious practice. He argues that philosophy prospered in the West precisely because Christian theology, the rational defense of Christian dogma, allowed philosophical discourse an important role in the education of the clerics.[34] Strauss assumes that there is a collapse of rationalism in the East, as the tenets of philosophy are incompatible with those of Islam and Judaism. Consequently, in his view, Jewish and Islamic traditions of philosophy become disfigured, because philosophers had to *conceal* Greek philosophical theories in their texts so as to avoid persecution by the irrational practitioners of faith who constituted the majority of the society. As a result, Muslim and Jewish philosophers simply restated what they inherited from the Greeks and their major contribution was developing an art of writing that contained their accounts of Greek philosophy in disguise (so as to avoid persecution).[35]

Strauss's Orientalism, like its counterpart in Walzer, presupposes the notion of philosophy as the production of rational knowledge. The identification of this assumption helps explain more of the details of Strauss's position. Philosophy comes into conflict with religion, in Strauss's reading, because it involves rational reflection on the nature of things and religion is concerned with practice based on revealed doctrines, that is, doctrines that are presumably impervious to rational scutiny. Perhaps the most striking evidence for Strauss's conclusion is his assertion that philosophy, after being passed on to the West, prospered under the protection of Christian theology.[36] However, according to Hadot, it was precisely under these conditions that philosophy proper was marginalized:

> With the advent of medieval scholasticism, however, we find a clear distinction being drawn between *theologia* and *philosophia*. Theology became conscious of its autonomy *qua* supreme science, while philosophy was emptied of its spiritual exercises which, from now on, were relegated to Christian mysticism and ethics. Reduced to the rank of a "handmaid of theology," philosophy's role was henceforth

> to furnish theology with conceptual—and hence purely theoretical—material. When, in the modern age, philosophy regained its autonomy, it still retained many features inherited from this medieval conception.[37]

Strauss applauds Christian theology's appropriation of philosophy, because, and this is quite important, he does not see ethics and the practice of spiritual exercises as constitutive of ancient Greek philosophy. For him, philosophy is the manufacturing of rational knowledge, and, under the tutelage of Christian theology, it comes into its own (perhaps for the first time). But even if it does so, ironically, and presumably unbeknownst to Strauss, it is at the cost of changing its essence. It goes without saying that Strauss completely misses the particular character of Islamic philosophy, as a reconciliation of the practice of ancient philosophy and that of Islam.

Sarah Stroumsa's reading of political *falsafa* in "Philosopher-King or Philosopher-Courtier? Theory and Reality in the *Falāsifa*'s Place in Islamic Society" and Joel Kraemer's interpretation in "The *Jihād* of the *Falāsifa*" belong in the same category as Strauss's account. Kraemer argues that

> the *Falāsifa* diverge radically from true Islamic doctrine on substantive questions concerning the nature of the best polity and the purpose of justified warfare. I present this divergence as a cardinal example, or test case, demonstrating the fundamental alienation of the *Falāsifa* from the ultimate aspirations of the society in which they lived and a parade instance of their artful accommodation to the Islamic lexicon by means of a hermeneutic and rhetorical reinterpretation of root concepts.[38]

Kraemer suggests that philosophers suffered alienation from the Islamic political climate, and consequently used Islamic terminology to craft a camouflage for their philosophical ideals. Like Strauss, Kraemer uses the philosophical ideal articulated by the *falāsifa* to paint the Islamic context as oppressive to a philosophically motivated individual. Stroumsa echoes the same concern when she asserts "the existence of a pronounced tendency to alienation in the writings of Islamic medieval philosophers, in the east as well in the west."[39] Kraemer and Stroumsa identify an *inessential* conflict between the Islamic doctrines and philosophical doctrines and as a result they miss out on the *essential* correspondence between Islam and philosophy at the level of ethics and the practices of self-cultivation. This oversight blinds their understanding of the *falāsifa*'s proper relationship to their Islamic milieu.

Such an approach to Islamic philosophy—relying, as it does, on the understanding of ancient Greek philosophy as the production of rational discourse and tainted with an Orientalist bias—is not restricted to European and American scholars. The Moroccan Scholar, 'Abed al-Jabri, in *Arab-Islamic Philosophy*, argues that philosophy *qua* "production of rational knowledge" declined in the Islamic world because of the influence of Persian Gnosticism. For al-Jabri, the Arabic Islam was an ideology "committed to the service of science, progress and a dynamic conception of society."[40] As a result, it embraced Greek rationalism. However, Persian anti-rationalism (i.e., Gnosticism) gave rise to an assault on the Arabic tradition and resulted in its decline.[41] Implicit in al-Jabri's argument is a call to disengage the Gnostic, especially the Shi'i, element from the Islamic heritage and facilitate a renaissance of Arabism, which is nothing other than Islam at the service of reason and the European ideas of progress. For al-Jabri, the borders of the Orient have shifted further to the east but the same prejudices are present in his view. Because it flies in the face of historical evidence, Al-Jabri's view is especially awkward. It is well known that the Persian Shi'i world encouraged the pursuit of philosophy. The flowering of philosophy in the Safavid dynasty and its cultivation in the Shi'i seminaries to this day testify to the problematic nature of al-Jabri's account of the nature of philosophy and its history in the Islamic world.[42]

As already seen in the case of Muhsin Mahdi, assigning primacy to the production of rational knowledge in defining the Greek philosophical heritage need not always accompany the Orientalist attitude. For example, Oliver Leaman holds a similar view. As seen, he rejects Orientalism, while also affirming Greek philosophy as "the acme of rationality."[43] Leaman writes: "The main purpose of philosophy is to understand arguments, and to assess those arguments and construct new arguments around them."[44] He does not argue that Muslims were barbarians and opposed to reason (a favorite assumption of some of his Orientalist counterparts); rather he maintains that, in the Islamic context, Greek philosophy was challenged by a number of other rational modes of discourse. These included Islamic theology, theory of language, and jurisprudence. Leaman argues that these modes of rational discourse had already entered the Islamic cultural scene before philosophy came along. Now this view makes some sense of the resistance offered to philosophy by a theologian and jurist such as Ghazali, but it is still problematic, because it misses out on the significance of philosophy as a way of life and the Islamic appreciation and appropriation of this significance.[45] So, for Leaman, Islamic philosophy is Islamic just as any other production of rational knowledge in an Islamic context is Islamic: "Perhaps the best way of specifying the nature of Islamic philosophy is to say that it is the tradition of philosophy which arose out of Islamic culture, with the latter term understood in its widest sense."[46] This reading is aligned with those that define *falsafa* as that species of philosophy (understood as radically other than what constitutes a religious activity) cultivated in the Islamic civilizations under the patronage of Arab rulers and by scholars who are culturally Muslim. And because these scholars want to maintain the autonomy of philosophy against the perceived encroachments of religion, they prefer to translate *al-falsafa* as Arabic philosophy[47] or even Muslim philosophy.[48] To be fair, Leaman admits that Islamic philosophy, when it comes to its own, "involves study of reality which transforms the soul and is never separated from spiritual purity and religious sanctity."[49] Here, Leaman recognizes the significance of Islamic philosophy as the practice of cultivating and transforming the soul, but he does not see its continuity (in this regard) with its Greek past *and* its genuine uniqueness.

Perhaps one of the most notable proponents of the view that Islamic philosophy involves the practice of transformative spiritual exercises is Seyyed Hossein Nasr. In "The Meaning and Concept of Philosophy in Islam," Nasr claims that "[t]his conception of philosophy as dealing with the discovering of the truth concerning the nature of things and combining mental knowledge with the purification and perfection of one's being has lasted to this day wherever the tradition of Islamic philosophy has continued and is in fact embodied in the very being of the most eminent representatives of the Islamic philosophical tradition to this day."[50] Nasr calls the practice of spiritual exercises "the purification and perfection of one's own being" and insists that it is constitutive of Islamic philosophy. Nasr also recognizes that the Greeks, especially the Platonists and Hermetico-Pythagoreans, underscored the relation between the theory and the practice of philosophy.[51] But for him, Peripateticism de-emphasizes that relation and one of the virtues of Islamic philosophy proper is the overcoming of the Peripatetic distortion.[52] For Nasr, the move away from Peripateticism occurs in the later writings of Avicenna, especially in what remains of *al-Ḥikma al-mashriqiyya* (*Eastern Philosophy*), in which Avicenna decries the follies of the Peripatetics and declares his commitment to an approach to philosophy that draws from non-Greek sources.[53]

Nasr sees in this a revival of perennial wisdom, which involves an alliance between theory and spiritual exercises. He is adamant about the importance of ascetic self-purification and self-discovery for the true notion of philosophy:

> Philosophy [without spiritual exercises] becomes sheer mental acrobatics and reason cut off from both intellect and revelation, nothing but a luciferan instrument leading to dispersion and ultimately dissolution. It must never be forgotten that according to the teachings of *sophia perennis* itself, the discovery of the Truth is essentially the discovery of one's self and ultimately of the Self . . . and that is the role of philosophy.[54]

Islam, in Nasr's view, is an expression of perennial wisdom, as it is essentially an association of theory and practice, truth and spiritual exercises, *ḥaqīqa* (truth) and *ṭarīqa* (the way). So, according to Nasr, philosophy in the Islamic tradition comes into its (perennial) own when it overcomes the Peripatetic pressures toward pure theory and recognizes the inseparability of truth and spiritual exercises. Nasr, then, connects Avicenna's *al-Ḥikma al-mashriqiyya* to the tradition inaugurated by Suhrawardi's *Ḥikmat al-ishrāq* (*Philosophy of Illumination*). In the latter, the account of theory as spiritual practice is central and continues to be so in the later Islamic philosophical tradition mainly because of Suhrawardi's influence.

Although I agree with Nasr that certain Islamic philosophical traditions (including Suhrawardi's Illuminationism) were based on a rejection of aspects of Peripateticism, I deny his claim that the Peripatetics divorced theory from practice.[55] It is likely, as I mentioned earlier, that Aristotle's emphasis on thought thinking itself as the highest activity occasions such a reading of his work and that of his successors. A good dose of Aristotelian ethics, however, can help overcome this reading, as it becomes apparent that for Aristotle—and the successors who took this central text seriously—cultivation of the soul and its excellence is presupposed for the life of contemplation, and the latter is, *qua* life, a practice.[56] In other words, it seems that Nasr appreciates neither the reach of Aristotle's virtue ethics beyond the practical to the theoretical nor the impact of Aristotelian ethics on Islamic philosophy.[57] Once we allow Hadot's thesis that all schools of ancient philosophy are focused on the practice of spiritual exercises and that rational discourse is only ancillary to practice, then Nasr's assumption that Islamic philosophy comes into its own only in establishing a necessary connection between spiritual practice and theory becomes suspect. My contention is that we have to be more precise and identify the particular *way* in which Islamic philosophers consider theory as a spiritual exercise. In Chapter 3, I show that this identification is established by Islamic prophetology,[58] and the Islamic Peripatetics Alfarabi and Avicenna are the early proponents of this prophetology.

Chapter 2

To the Things Themselves

Corbin and Heidegger on Phenomenological Access

In Chapter 1, I borrowed from Pierre Hadot's insights into the nature and purpose of ancient Greek philosophy to highlight the continuity between the ancient Greek understanding of philosophy as a way of life and the focus on spiritual practice found in Islamic philosophy. Although Hadot himself did not address the Islamic tradition of philosophy, Henry Corbin, another French philosopher and scholar working somewhat earlier than Hadot, did discover Islamic philosophy through his early training, of all things, as a phenomenologist. What is both surprising and fascinating about Corbin's intellectual path is the importance of the connection he made between spiritual practice in the Islamic philosophical enterprise and the phenomenological work he had already completed.

In this chapter, I concentrate on Corbin's interest in the parallels between phenomenology and Islamic philosophy. This project is valuable in several ways: First, it resists the idea that the centrality of spiritual practices belongs to an early phase of philosophy and is of mere antiquarian interest. As I show in this chapter, the primacy of the cultivation of the self is a paramount feature not only of ancient Greek philosophy as well as Islamic philosophy but of phenomenology as well. In this way, this project also disrupts the sense that studying Islamic philosophy is a mere historical curiosity, that is, the idea that Islamic philosophy has no connection with contemporary trends in philosophy. Second, phenomenology claims to overcome the divide between reason and nature that haunts the modern tradition of philosophy. Islamic philosophy, as a premodern tradition, does not suffer from such an anxiety as it does not recognize a rift of this sort. Therefore, a comparison with phenomenology on the issue of access to things themselves helps to articulate a genuine form of rationalism immune to dependence on irrational "Givens" as the ground of our claims to knowledge. Third, this project underscores just how the ethical training of the philosopher facilitates theoretical knowledge. Phenomenology helps in seeing how the apparent partition between practical virtue and knowledge is overcome and in this sense, I consider how the focus on the practical cultivation of the self in Islamic philosophy prepares one for scientific and metaphysical speculations. Finally, tracing Corbin's transition from Heidegger's phenomenology to Islamic philosophy also is useful in bringing into focus the philosophical significance of relevant religious phenomena. Modern secularism's rendition of religious and mystical experiences as extraneous to the philosophical project is (as we have seen) apparent in the later work of Hadot.[1] Similarly, Heidegger's phenomenology also circumvents these religious phenomena. Corbin's censure of this secularist tendency provides the platform for my meditations in the following chapter, in which I investigate the prominence of prophetic religion in the Islamic Peripatetic framework.

In this chapter, I sketch the influence of phenomenology on Corbin, the principles of Heidegger's account of phenomenology, and how the interpretations of two contemporary philosophers (Dreyfus and McDowell) amplify the significance of the interpretation that Corbin gave to the phenomenological experience. I show that what all of these philosophers share is the aim of getting at the things themselves and through the working out of this process, the phenomenon (i.e., the being of beings) that makes possible all others (while concealing itself) also must be disclosed. The access to the things themselves and their being is mediated by the refinement of the inquirer. This brings us back at once to the philosophical spiritual exercises and allows for a more profound engagement of their significance.

In the next chapter, I engage the Islamic Peripatetics, Alfarabi and Avicenna, and show a similar concern with the cultivation of the inquirer preceding phenomenological access. I explore the nuances of the Islamic account of the care of the soul and find it centered on a prophetology and its derivative notion of religion. Later, I trace these concerns to the differences between the conceptions of the human being and its cultivation that are operative in Heideggerian phenomenology and Islamic philosophy. Heidegger defines the being of the human as finite (i.e., a being-towards-death) and draws on cultural exemplars to bring the individual to authenticity. Islamic Peripatetics, on the other hand, take the human being to be immortal, a being-towards-beyond-death, and appeal to divine exemplars for the individual's salvation. I follow the analyses that lead Alfarabi and Avicenna to assert the immortality of the soul and show that these thinkers are not merely advocating a dogmatic hypothesis. In fact, their attention to relevant psychological and spiritual evidence indicates the advantage of their approach to the human being and its care.

2.1. Phenomenology According to Henry Corbin

Corbin began his philosophical career as the first translator of Heidegger into French.[2] Many years later, in 1966, on the eve of the first Western colloquium on Shi'i Islam at the University of Strasbourg, Corbin confided to Seyyed Hossein Nasr that he used to drive through Strasbourg, when he was younger, to get to Freiburg, "to seek knowledge at the feet of"[3] his mentor, Heidegger. But he no longer desired to travel that path, as he had found such contentment in Islamic philosophy which he could never hope to find in Heidegger's "limited and truncated"[4] philosophy. Corbin's turn to Islamic philosophy occurred in the 1930s when Louis Massignon, the author of the famous *Passion of al-Ḥallāj*, gave him a work by the twelfth-century mystic and philosopher, Suhrawardi, with the comment, "I think there is something in this book for you."[5] In 1939, Corbin went to Istanbul and stayed there for six years, during which he published nothing while he immersed himself in the study of Suhrawardi and Islamic philosophy. In 1946, he refounded his career, and in the thirty-two years before his 1978 death, divided his time between Paris and Tehran studying Islamic philosophy.

Phenomenology, according to Corbin, "consists in 'saving the appearance,' saving the phenomenon, while unveiling the hidden which shows itself beneath this appearance."[6] The phenomenologist, according to Corbin, refuses to explain phenomena by forcing them under general theories. Rather, he recognizes that phenomena must be seen as they are in themselves, and in this process the phenomenon that makes possible all others (and conceals itself) should also be unveiled. In this process of unveiling and getting at the things themselves, phenomenology draws our attention to "the indissoluble link between *modi intelligendi* and *modi essendi*, between modes of understanding (*comprendre*) and modes of being. The modes of understanding are essentially a function (*essentiellement en fonction*) of the modes of being. Any change in the mode of understanding is necessarily concomitant with a change in the mode of being."[7] This phenomenological link is explicated in what Corbin calls the "triumph of hermeneutic as *Verstehen*, meaning that that which we truly understand is only what we experience and undergo, what we suffer in our very being. Hermeneutics does not consist in deliberating upon concepts, it is essentially the unveiling (*dévoilement*) of that which is happening within us."[8] To properly understand this principle of phenomenological hermeneutics, it is necessary to explicate relevant aspects of Heidegger's *Being and Time*. Through the analysis that follows, I show that the modes of being (e.g., the modes of our passions, suffering, and toil) concern the character of the knower. In other words, to get at the things themselves, to understand, presupposes an education and refinement of the inquirer. This brings us back at once to the philosophical spiritual exercises and allows for a more profound engagement of their significance.

2.2. Heidegger's Phenomenology

In order to understand what Corbin "discovered" in Heidegger as a portal to the Islamic tradition, I have to briefly explain relevant concepts of Heidegger's project. Corbin's rendition of the link between the modes of being and those of understanding is grounded in Heidegger's phenomenological method. As does Corbin, Heidegger distinguishes between phenomenological philosophy and the positive sciences (including the positive study of history).[9] Clarifying this distinction requires the working out of the concept of interpretation (*Auslegung*), as discussed in §32 of *Being and Time*. According to Heidegger,

> in interpreting, we do not, so to speak, throw a "signification" over some naked thing which is present-at-hand, we do not stick a value on it; but when something within-the-world is encountered as such, the thing in question already has an involvement which is disclosed in our understanding of the world, and this involvement is one which gets laid out by interpretation. (*SZ* 150; *BT* 190–91)

In other words, for Heidegger, interpretation appropriates its subject matter in the disclosure of relations that are constituted by our practical involvements in the world. This interpretative appropriation (*Zueignung*) is an effort at making explicit that which is implicitly understood in these pragmatic involvement relations. Interpretation generates, in Heidegger's construct, a form of discourse.

As a result, Heidegger distinguishes between hermeneutic and apophantic modes of discourse. The apophantic discourse does not always keep the relation of its subject matter to the involvement relations in view.

> In its function of appropriating what is understood, the "as" no longer reaches out into the totality of involvements. As regards its possibilities for articulating reference-relations, it has been cut off from that significance which, as such, constitutes environmentality. The "as" gets pushed back into the uniform plane of that which is merely present-at-hand. (*SZ* 158; *BT* 200)

Once the appropriating of what is understood is severed from the involvement relations, the entity appears as "present-at-hand." Put otherwise, the entity or the object of discourse, in the apophantic discourse, appears in itself and by itself as present-at-hand. It is this present-at-hand appearance of entities that makes possible the correspondence theory of truth. Thus, in Heidegger's model, assertions, as positive knowledge claims, are items in the apophantic mode of discourse. An articulation of involvement relations can become a present-at-hand assertion when it comes up for confirmation. In confirmation, the proposition as the immanent present-at-hand entity is said to correspond to the object as the transcendent present-at-hand entity. In this context, it becomes possible to say that the transcendent entity exists; it has a being separate from the observer, possessing its own attributes and properties. Heidegger organizes the various modes of discourse in the following passage:

> Assertion and its structure (namely, the apophantical "as") are founded upon interpretation and its structure (viz., the hermeneutical "as") and also upon understanding—Dasein's disclosedness. (*SZ* 223; *BT* 266)

Heidegger, as we have already seen, maintains that an assertion involves an interruption of the practices making up the involvement relations. Assertion can sever its object from its involvement context and treat it as a thing that belongs to other things of a particular species or type, subject to laws determining the objects of a particular mode of inquiry (e.g., the various positive sciences). Hermeneutic discourse, on the other hand, appropriates its subject matter in its practical context, and ultimately, there is a mode of assertion and knowledge that can be true to the hermeneutic context,[10] but before getting to that it is necessary to bring to the fore the relevant features of the human being that are presupposed for any interpretation.

Heidegger begins *Being and Time* with a phenomenological analysis of the being of man (i.e., Dasein) as the being who understands being (*SZ* 11–12; *BT* 32). His purpose in using this unusual terminology is to avoid the pitfalls of traditional philosophical psychology, the study of the soul:

> Dasein's ontico-ontological priority was seen quite early, though Dasein itself was not grasped in its genuine ontological structure, and did not even become a problem in which this structure was sought . . . Aristotle says . . . "Man's soul is, in a certain way, entities." . . . Aristotle's principle, which points back to the ontological thesis of Parmenides, is one which Thomas Aquinas has taken up in a characteristic discussion. . . . He does this by invoking an entity which, in accordance with its very manner of Being, is properly suited to "come together with" entities of any sort whatever. This distinctive entity . . . is the soul (*anima*). (*SZ* 14; *BT* 34)

The "soul" is unique in that it is that being in the light of which other beings show themselves. The problem with the traditional accounts of the "soul" is that they treat it as a present-at-hand entity among other present-at-hand entities. With this assumption, "Being-in-the-world does not as such get conceived" (*SZ* 59; *BT* 85). The soul's absorption in the world (i.e., its being-in-the world) provides for and can obfuscate its transparency and access to other beings. Heidegger's hermeneutics of the soul (i.e., Dasein) aims to articulate the structures of the context of human practices (i.e., the involvement relations) and because these structures affect the soul's access to beings, he refers to his inquiry as *fundamental* ontology.[11]

Heidegger's fundamental ontology culminates in an examination of Dasein's self-understanding. This examination, in turn, is an interpretation of Dasein's projection of a self in terms of its various possibilities. A possibility, however, is not an end in the sense of a product, a being, but an end as the for-the-sake-of-which of Dasein's self-projection. As already in the world, Dasein is in truth, it knows how to be itself; yet this primordial truth is obfuscated by Dasein's falling away from its primordial for-the-sake-of-which. However, Dasein's lot in life is that it is not in immediate possession of its primordial purpose and must unover it.[12] Therefore, Dasein is either authentic [*eigentlich*], understanding itself in terms of its primordial for-the-sake-of-which, or inauthentic. An authentic Dasein casts its being in terms of its *own* self as the "for-the-sake-of-which." Dasein's "uncritical" projection of its being in terms of an unowned "for-the-sake-of-which" accounts for Dasein in the inauthentic mode. Heidegger writes:

> Proximally and for the most part the self is lost in the "they." He understands himself in terms of those possibilities of existence which "circulate" in the "average" public way of interpreting Dasein today. (*SZ* 383; *BT* 435)

Authenticity, as the process of taking over (owning) one's roles critically, implies that one is not in the grip of this or that "public" or idiosyncratic ideal. Rather the authentic individual adjusts himself to the demands of the particular situation: he acts appropriately (does the right thing) (*SZ* 307–8; *BT* 355). As a result, the authenticity of Dasein makes possible a genuine encounter with things themselves and not as things that appear through the mold of available public or idiosyncratic ideals. In *Being and Time,* Heidegger writes: "To have a science 'of' phenomena means to grasp its objects in such a way that everything about them which is up for discussion must be treated by exhibiting it directly and demonstrating it directly" (*SZ* 35; *BT* 59). In a phenomenological encounter that reaches to things themselves, things appear in their relevant contexts, and the inquirer is free of interpretive constraints that distort those contexts.

> The achieving of phenomenological access to the entities which we encounter, consists rather in thrusting aside interpretive tendencies, which keep thrusting themselves upon us and running along with us, and which conceal not only the phenomenon of such "concern," but even more those entities themselves, as encountered of their own accord in our concern with them. (*SZ* 67; *BT* 96)

These interpretive tendencies (which result in the blocking of phenomenological access) are caused by Dasein's inauthenticity, its appropriation of phenomena for the sake of public or idiosyncratic possibilities of being. Authenticity frees Dasein from such interpretative constraints and authenticity makes the ideal of phenomenology possible (*SZ* 28, 34; *BT* 50, 58).

An authenticity that is won through a hermeneutics of Dasein will result in knowledge of the things themselves. Heidegger insists that this knowledge is not a feature of the present-at-hand assertions of positive sciences. He writes,

> Being-in-the-world, as concern, is *fascinated* by the world with which it is concerned. If knowing is to be possible as a way of determining the nature of the present-at-hand by observing it, then there must first be a *deficiency* in our having-to-do with the world concernfully. When concern holds back [*Sichenthalten*] from any kind of producing, manipulating, and the like, it puts itself into what is now the sole remaining mode of Being-in, the mode of just tarrying alongside. . . . [*das Nur-noch-verweilen bei* . . .] This kind of Being towards the world is one which lets us encounter entities within-the-world purely in the *way they look* (*eidos*), just that; on the basis of this kind of Being, and as a mode of it, looking explicitly at what we encounter is possible. (*SZ* 61; *BT* 88)

As tarrying alongside, Dasein is free from the prejudices that frame the entities it observes. Liberating the self from these prejudices through the achievement of authenticity, Dasein is capable of "dwelling autonomously [*eigenständigen*] alongside entities within-the-world. In this kind of '*dwelling*' [*Aufenthalt*] as a holding-one's-self-back from any manipulation or utilization, the perception of the present-at-hand is consummated" (*SZ* 61; *BT* 89). This knowledge (i.e., "the consummation of the perception of the present-at-hand") is not achieved through the apophantic approach of positive sciences, and the present-at-hand entities here are not necessarily the entities broached by such sciences. The present-at-hand here are things themselves as they show themselves, and the inquiry that allows us to dwell by them autonomously, to tarry alongside them, is phenomenology.[13] Moreover, the hermeneutic method of this phenomenology involves a self-understanding that is a self-constitution, a self-cultivation that removes Dasein's opaqueness and allows it to see, to let "entities which are accessible to it be encountered unconcealedly in themselves" (*SZ* 147; *BT* 187).

2.3. Two Contemporary Approaches to Heidegger's Phenomenology

In his presidential address to the American Philosophical Association, "Overcoming the Myth of the Mental: How Philosophers Can Benefit from the Phenomenology of Everyday Life," Hubert Dreyfus interprets Heidegger as an antagonist to the kind of position I have attributed to him (i.e., Heidegger) thus far. Dreyfus's polemic is directed against John McDowell's realist claim that the mind reaches all the way out to the things themselves. In a lecture delivered at the Eastern APA ("What Myth?"), McDowell replies to Dreyfus's charges, also drawing from Heidegger. A consideration of the exchange between these two important analytic philosophers and sensitive readers of Heidegger deepens our understanding of Heidegger's phenomenology.

Before addressing Dreyfus's critique and McDowell's reply, a brief account of McDowell's realism, the trigger for this exchange, is necessary. McDowell's realism is formulated, in part, as a response to Wilfrid Sellars's influential attack on the "Myth of the Given." In his "Empiricism and the Philosophy of Mind," Sellars criticizes the approach of certain forms of empiricism to the problem of justifying perceptual beliefs, a critique which has had considerable influence on late twentieth-century philosophy. According to Sellars, some forms of empiricism rest on a claim that perceptual beliefs can only be justified by a certain kind of foundational mental state: direct perceptual awareness. Such states are foundational in that they are the ultimate court of appeal for all perceptual beliefs and presuppose no other beliefs.[14] Sellars rejects the empiricist notion of presuppositionless foundations and contends that the justification of perceptual beliefs is a matter of their relation to other beliefs in the public practice of asking for, and giving, reasons.[15] Sellars develops powerful arguments, which he traces to the philosophy of Kant, to show that the empiricist appeal to presuppositionless sensory foundations is flawed, because it is in the grip of the "Myth of the Given" (i.e., the absurd notion that raw, nonconceptual deliverance of the senses can stand in the logical relation of justification to a belief).[16] Sellars is correct to object that the empiricist's appeal to presuppositionless sensory foundations to justify our perceptual beliefs is problematic, in that such an appeal is in the grip of the "Myth of the Given." The Sellarsian rejection of mythological justifications of perceptual beliefs, however, offends our ordinary intuitions concerning our claims to know that which we have directly perceived. Those who are not already in the grip of a theory do, after all, suppose that such knowledge claims are justified by the impact of the world on them and not by the coherence with other entrenched beliefs. McDowell maintains that this "see-sawing" can be ended by rejecting the shared premise.[17] He argues that our representations of the world are not merely given, but rather are produced by the involuntary exercise of the same conceptual capacities that are voluntarily exercised in the production of perceptual beliefs.[18] In other words, he concedes to the backers of the empiricist Given that perceptual beliefs can be justified by items that are not beliefs, but such items, contrary to the mythological view of them, are conceptualized. More precisely, the world, as we experience it, is already conceptualized, because we are initiated into the conceptual space through our traffic with the world and others like us. Therefore, the world's impacts on our senses put us in immediate contact with the world by actualizing our conceptual capacities independently of our volition. As a result, our sensory experience can justify our perceptual beliefs. McDowell also concedes to Sellarsian coherentists that all justification must be grounded in conceptualized states, but he rejects the coherentist thesis that all conceptualized states that play a role in justification are beliefs. This puts him in a position to reject the Myth of the Given while preserving the intuition that our perceptual beliefs are justified by our experience of the world.[19]

Dreyfus diagnoses a problematic form of Aristotelianism in McDowell's nuanced balance between empiricism and coherentism.

> To suggest how impingements received from nature can be conceptual through and through without the mind imposing meaning on a meaningless Given, McDowell introduces an account of Aristotle's idea of second nature: "Human beings are . . . initiated into . . . the space of reasons by ethical upbringing, which instills the appropriate shape into their lives. The resulting habits of thought and action are second nature."
>
> McDowell then generalizes Aristotle's account of the production of second nature: "Imposing a specific shape on the practical intellect is a particular case of a general phenomenon: initiation into conceptual capacities, which include responsiveness to other rational demands besides those of ethics."
>
> The phenomenon McDowell has in mind is clearest in phronesis, usually translated "practical wisdom." He tells us: "Practical wisdom is the right sort of thing to serve as a model for the understanding, the faculty that enables us to recognize and create the kind of intelligibility that is a matter of placement in the space of reasons."[20]

Dreyfus correctly observes that McDowell's account of initiation into the space of reasons is a generalization of Aristotle's account of the cultivation of the practically wise person, the *phronimos*. The ethical training of the *phronimos* endows him with an appropriate conceptual repertoire. When faced with a particular situation requiring moral consideration, the impact of the particulars on the sensibility of the *phronimos* draws the relevant concepts into operation. The *phronimos* then perceives the good and acts immediately for its sake. For McDowell, as perhaps for Aristotle, all knowledge is to be understood on the model of the ethical knowledge of the *phronimos*. Dreyfus, however, believes that McDowell's position reacts excessively to the Myth of the Given. Dreyfus invokes Heidegger's phenomenology as exemplifying the proper response to the Given:

> But, according to Heidegger, most of our ethical life consists in simply seeing the appropriate thing to do and responding without deliberation, as when we help a blind person cross the street or when, after years of experience, we unreflectively balance, case by case, the demands of our professional and personal lives. As Aristotle says: "Phronesis . . . involves knowledge of the ultimate particular thing, which cannot be attained by systematic knowledge but only by 'perception.' " Heidegger thus claims that Aristotle's account of phronesis does not assume, as McDowell does, that ethical expertise can be conceptually articulated. On the contrary, phronesis shows that socialization can produce a kind of master whose actions do not rely on habits based on reasons to guide him. Indeed, thanks to socialization, a person's perceptions and actions at their best would be so responsive to the specific situation that they could not be captured in general concepts.[21]

Dreyfus reads phronetic expertise as a kind of mastery that is outside the space of reasons. In other words, Dreyfus, vis-à-vis Heidegger's phenomenology, wants to resuscitate the Given; he calls it a meaningful Given to contrast it with what he calls "the bare Given" of the empiricists. A consideration of the full impact of Dreyfus's problematic philosophical commitments in his reading of Heidegger is beyond the scope of this work, but it suffices to say that for Dreyfus, it would not make sense to make too much of Heidegger's references to the authentic Dasein's seeing the things themselves. Even if we were to entertain Heidegger's references to an encounter with things themselves, we would have to understand it in a pragmatic way without concern for the intelligibility of things themselves.

McDowell's reply to Dreyfus rescues the notion of the phenomenological access to things themselves. First, he draws attention to Dreyfus's misappropriation of Heidegger in placing phronetic perception outside the conceptual space:

> Dreyfus cites from Heidegger the claim that the "pure perceiving" that is the characteristic accomplishment of the *phronimos* "no longer falls within the domain of *logos*." Dreyfus reads this as a formulation of the contrast he assumes, between the situation-specificity of the kind of competence exemplified by *phronēsis*, on the one hand, and, on the other, conceptual rationality conceived as situation-independent.[22]

But McDowell maintains that Heidegger, following Aristotle, does not think of the realm of *logos* as the realm of situation-independent rationality.

> There is no call to foist such an idea on Heidegger. The word "*logos*" can accept many different interpretations. Aristotle explains the "perception" of the *phronimos* partly in terms of a comparison with theoretical intuition, which immediately grasps indefinables (things of which there is no *logos*). On a more charitable interpretation, Heidegger is picking up on that comparison. The domain of *logos* in Heidegger's remark is not, as Dreyfus thinks, the space of reasons, the domain of conceptual articulation. Contrary to what Dreyfus implies, the domain of conceptual articulation includes thoughts that are not intelligible in abstraction from particular situations, so that interpretation of "the domain of *logos*" would not secure the contrast Heidegger wants with the "pure perceiving" of the *phronimos*. The domain of *logos* that is relevant to Heidegger's point is the domain of the definable, which is not the same thing at all.[23]

For McDowell's Heidegger (and Aristotle) conceptuality extends beyond the domain of the situation-independent rationality; it reaches all the way to the world. McDowell's earlier ethical writings have contributed to the making of this point. In "Virtue and Reason," for example, McDowell illustrates his account of the conceptuality of the world by explaining how a kind person acts in response to a particular situation requiring kindness:

> A kind person can be relied on to behave kindly when that is what the situation requires. Moreover, his reliably kind behavior is not the outcome of a blind, non-rational habit or instinct, like the courageous behavior—so called only by courtesy—of a lioness defending her cubs. Rather, that the situation requires a certain sort of behaviour is (one way of formulating) his reason for behaving in that way, on each of the relevant occasions. So it must be something of which, on each of the relevant occasions, he is aware. A kind person has a reliable sensitivity to a certain sort of requirement that situations impose on behaviour. The deliverances of a reliable sensitivity are cases of knowledge; and there are idioms according to which the sensitivity itself can appropriately be described as knowledge: a kind person knows what it is like to be confronted with a requirement of kindness. The sensitivity is, we might say, a sort of perceptual capacity.[24]

For McDowell, the virtuous person perceives the relevant moral features of a situation and responds appropriately. He has knowledge, that is, gets things right when he confronts a moral requirement inscribed, so to speak, in the specific situation. The label of knowledge is not conferred here as a courtesy, as one would to Dreyfus's Dasein who reacts without deliberation to situations through appropriate programming. The virtuous person has acquired the proper set of concepts, and the particulars he experiences draw upon the relevant concepts to show themselves.[25]

Heidegger's account of attentiveness to the things themselves—which is won through a cultivation of the self such that opaqueness is removed—also implies conceptual articulation at the level of particulars. This point comes through in Heidegger's account of existential sight as a perception of the situation-dependent intelligibility of things themselves:

> "Seeing" does not mean just perceiving with the bodily eyes, but neither does it mean pure non-sensory awareness of something present-at-hand in its presence-at-hand. In giving an existential signification to "sight," we have merely drawn upon the peculiar feature of seeing, that it lets entities which are accessible to it be encountered unconcealedly in themselves. (*SZ* 147; *BT* 187)

The existential sight is available when the person is delivered from interpretative constraints, and is able to let the entity draw on the relevant conceptual abilities and show itself. This sight is won through the attainment of virtue, as it is only the virtuous (i.e., authentic) Dasein who is able to encounter unconcealed entities by holding back "from any kind of producing, manipulating, and the like" and putting himself in "the mode of just tarrying alongside, . . . which lets us encounter entities within-the-world purely in the way they look" (*SZ* 61; *BT* 88).

To sum up, consider this passage from *Being and Time*: "The meaning of phenomenological description as a method lies in interpretation . . . through which the authentic meaning of Being and also those basic structures of being which Dasein itself possesses, are made known to Dasein's understanding of Being" (*SZ* 37; *BT* 61–62). Bringing the existential strutures of Dasein to view, by means of a hermeneutic Dasein analytic, allows the phenomenologist to seize resolutely on his possibility for authenticity, which, in turn, removes the illusions that block the transparent encounter with the things themselves and their being.

The unveiling of entities within-the-world comes about when the inquirer attains authenticity (i.e., liberation from ossified theoretical and practical constraints). Once he attains authenticity, he dwells autonomously alongside entities within-the-world. Following a suggestion of McDowell, I interpret authenticity on the model of *phronēsis*, practical wisdom. Dasein is authentic when it does not merely submit to the roles it is assigned publicly; rather, the authentic Dasein takes over its roles critically. In doing so, its perception of the entities is no longer obscured by a derivative self-understanding. Dasein's authentic self-understanding liberates it from interests that interfere with its clear-sighted encounter with the things themselves. Like Aristotle's *phronimos*, the authentic Dasein allows the entities to draw on its conceptual repertoire and show themselves. Heidegger suggests that authenticity, choosing to be itself (i.e., autonomous), is an *existentiell* matter, that is, it has to do with the way a human being lives his life: "The question of existence never gets straightened out except through existing itself" (*SZ* 12; *BT* 33). Heidegger's hermeneutics of Dasein, however, is concerned with the *structure* of existence. Heidegger claims that the concern for authenticity "does not require that the ontological structure of existence should be theoretically transparent" (*SZ* 12; *BT* 33). In other words, the acquisition of the ideal human existence does not indicate that one can successfully engage in the analysis of the structure of human existence. However, seizing on the possibility of the *philosophical* life (and its specific path to authenticity), the philosopher analyzes the structure of existence on the way to authenticity (*SZ* 13; *BT* 34). Existence grounds the essence of Dasein (*SZ* 42; *BT* 67), and its analysis prepares the way for a state of Dasein in which it has access to phenomena in general and phenomenon in its technical phenomenological sense, that is, that which is hidden and lets beings show themselves (*SZ* 35; *BT* 59). Here, we should be aware of the precariousness of the claim to authenticity. Heidegger's involvement with the Nazis and his atrocious treatment of his colleagues, as the rector of Freiburg University, fail the test of authenticity and virtue.[26] It should be kept in mind that Heidegger's analytic of existence does not presuppose the inquirer's ethical excellence; it aims to provide the inquirer with a preparatory self-understanding that may motivate authenticity.

2.4. Back to Corbin

Seyyed Hossein Nasr recalls asking Corbin about the Perso-Arabic equivalent to "phenomenology." Corbin replies that "phenomenology" means "*kashf al-maḥjūb*, 'the casting aside of the veil,' which is a fundamental method of expounding the truth in Sufism."[27] Corbin, however, seems to go beyond Heidegger and his efforts to unveil entities as they are in themselves:

> [T]o save the reality demands the same procedure: *kashf al-maḥjūb*, to detach, to unveil that which reveals itself while remaining hidden in the *phainomenon*. I said just now that this is what phenomenology is. . . . It is a matter of leading the observer to a point where he allows himself to see what it is that lies hidden. This essentially is what hermeneutic is.[28]

What Corbin means—when he maintains that phenomenology and its Islamic counterpart, *kashf al-maḥjūb*,[29] lead the observer to see what is hidden—does *not* exceed Heidegger's account. For Heidegger, as we have seen, phenomenology is that project that aims to present the individual with the choice of authenticity and its consequent unveiling of the phenomena (if one accepts the challenge of authenticity). The technical, phenomenological conception of phenomenon, however, concerns that phenomenon which accompanies and makes possible all that shows itself (i.e., phenomenon in its ordinary sense) [*SZ* 31; *BT* 54–55]. For Heidegger, the phenomenon, in the specific sense, is available to Dasein (i.e., a modified version of the traditional "soul"[30]).

Corbin's phenomenological commitment to unveiling the phenomenon, as that which is hidden and makes possible all appearances, should not imply that there are no significant differences between Corbin and Heidegger. For Corbin, unveiling the hidden is, more precisely, an inquiry aiming to "illuminate how, in understanding itself, the human presence situates itself, circumscribes the *Da*, the *situs* of its presence and unveils (*dévoile*) the horizon that has hitherto remained hidden."[31] Thus, Corbin, in contrast to Heidegger, takes mystical and prophetic experiences very seriously and grounds his phenomenology on the phenomena in these experiences. Moreover, Corbin does not take Dasein to be a Being-towards-Death (*Sein-zum-Tode*),[32] it is a being whose finality is not death, but a "Being-towards-Beyond-Death." He maintains, "so long as the 'resolute decision' (*décision-résolue*) remains simply 'free for death,' death presents itself as a closure and not as an *exitus*. Then we can never leave this world. To be *free for beyond death*, is the anticipation and the making of the future as an *exitus*, the *way out* of the world towards other worlds."[33] The account of Dasein as Being-towards-Beyond-Death is not indicative of Corbin's prior commitment to an elaborate religious ontology, rather it is a position that is won through a full deliverance from prejudices (and prior commitments). The complete execution of the phenomenological preparation should culminate, according to Corbin, in the continuation of the process of unveiling beyond the finality of death, and via the hermeneutics of prophetic symbols, to other worlds.[34]

Corbin agrees with Heidegger that an ethical preparation is required for the phenomenological access to the things themselves and their being, but he thinks that philosophical spiritual exercises should not be restricted to this preparation. Earlier, we saw Corbin celebrating the "triumph of hermeneutics as *Verstehen*, meaning that that which we truly understand is only what we experience and undergo, what we suffer in our very being. Hermeneutics does not consist in deliberating upon concepts, rather, it is the unveiling of that which is happening within us."[35] This is the core principle of phenomenological hermeneutics: Knowledge presupposes a transmutation of the soul, an ethical cultivation that brings the inquirer to the condition of transparency such that things show themselves as they are in themselves. Corbin, however, believes that Heidegger draws narrow limits to the execution of this principle. By contrast, Corbin traces his own discovery of the spiritual dimension of this principle to the notion of *significatio passiva* in the hermeneutics of young Luther: "divine attributes cannot be understood (*modus intelligendi*) except in relation with ourselves (*modus essendi*)."[36] In *The Man of Light in Iranian Sufism*, Corbin gives a broader account of the history of this principle:

> We already hear it in Empedocles: "Fire can only be seen by fire." In the *Corpus Hermeticum* (11.20) where the Nous declares to Hermes: "If you do not make yourself like God, you cannot understand God." In Plotinus (*Enneads* VI, 9, 11): "The principle can be seen only by the principle." In the West it leads us from Meister Eckhart to Goethe.[37]

This history of the hermeneutic principle should not obscure its prevalence in the ancient philosophical tradition,[38] in the form of theoretical philosophy as a practice of spiritual exercises and the transmission of this tradition to the Islamic philosophers. In other words, we should not, *pace* Corbin, just look for Hermetic thinkers and traditions in the Islamic spirituality (e.g., the Illuminationists, the Sufis, and Isma'ilis[39]) to see the hermeneutic principle at work. This principle also is available in the work of Peripatetic thinkers such as Alfarabi and Avicenna.

In the next chapter, I examine the primacy of ethical cultivation in Islamic Peripatetic philosophy with a focus on how this ethical preparation results in the philosopher dwelling autonomously (i.e., tarrying) alongside entities within-the-world and consummating the perception of them. More precisely, I show how the cultivation of virtue brings about theoretical knowledge of the worldly entities. Islamic Peripatetics, however, do not cease the spiritual exercises at this point. They reach beyond mundane, practical concerns to a spiritual quest for intimacy with the Divine.

Chapter 3

From the Things Themselves to Prophecy

Philosophical Cultivation in Islamic Peripateticism

Drawing on the previous chapter's discussion of Corbin's critique of Heidegger's phenomenological account of the being of man, in this chapter I turn to the Islamic Peripatetics to show that not only do they presuppose the practical cultivation of the soul for philosophical inquiry, but the ways in which they also extend the reach of spiritual exercises to the cultivation of the theoretical intellect. I submit that the recognition of the philosophical primacy of an ethical training immunizes the notion of the soul in Islamic philosophy to the critique that Heidegger launches against traditional philosophical psychology. The soul is not merely given; it should be constructed through a rigourous ethical training. Moreover, the Peripatetic recognition of the primacy of ethics brings to view the dependence of the theoretical encounter with present-at-hand entities on the orientation of the self in the context of human involvements with the world. Here, the world is not a mere nexus of causal interactions; rather it is infused with the intelligibility that purposiveness generates. The things in the world show themselves when the person attains virtue (i.e., an understanding of and an alignment with the unconditional purpose, the good). Finally, the Islamic philosophical program continues beyond the tarrying alongside of present-at-hand entities (in the context of their involvement relations) to theoretical enlightenment and encounters with spiritual beings. This is to say that the primacy of ethics in the Islamic Peripatetic tradition does not terminate the practice of spiritual exercises. The further executions of spiritual exercises opens intellectual vistas and spiritual experiences that surpass the limits of Heideggerian ontology.

3.1. The Ethical Foundations of Islamic Philosophy

To demonstrate the primacy of the practice of spiritual exercises in the Islamic Peripatetic tradition, I begin with a passage from Alfarabi's *Taḥṣīl al-sa'āda* (*The Attainment of Happiness*), which is classified as an introductory text to the study of philosophy.[1] However, I should emphasize that the primacy of the practice of spiritual exercises is also a feature of the work of earlier philosophers in the Islamic tradition, such as al-Kindi[2] and Abū Bakr Muḥammad ibn Zakariyā Rāzī.[3] This is in keeping with the thesis I advanced in Chapter 1 that the Arabic reception of ancient Greek philosophy did not obfuscate the centrality of the ethical cultivation of the self in Greek thought. However, as my aim here is to elucidate the centrality of the practice of spiritual exercises in the Peripateticism of Alfarabi and Avicenna, I begin with *The Attainment of Happiness* where Alfarabi lays out the conditions for the proper engagement in theoretical philosophy:

> As for mutilated (*al-bitrā'*) philosophy: the counterfeit (*al-zawr*) philosopher, the vain (*al-buhraj*) philosopher, or the false (*al-bāṭil*) philosopher is the one who sets out to study the theoretical sciences without being prepared for them. For he who sets out to inquire ought to be innately equipped for the theoretical sciences—that is, fulfill the conditions prescribed by Plato in the *Republic*: he should excel in comprehending and conceiving that which is essential. Moreover, he should have a good memory and be able to endure the toil of study. He should love truthfulness and truthful people, and justice and just people; and not be headstrong or a wrangler about what he desires. He should not be gluttonous for food and drinks, and should by natural disposition disdain the appetites, the *dirhem*, the *dinar*, and like. He should be high-minded and avoid what is disgraceful. He should be pious, yield easily to goodness and justice, and be stubborn in yielding to evil and injustice. And he should be strongly determined in favor of the right thing.[4]

Alfarabi's account of the ethical cultivation of the self is continuous with the ancient Greek understanding of philosophy as the practice of spiritual exercises, and it constitutes what Moraux calls prephilosopical morality (*vorphilosophische Sittlichkeit*), that is, the propaedeutic to the proper practice of theoretical philosophy.[5] More precisely, the acquisition of justice, that is, the perfection and balance of the soul, paves the way for the intellectual labors of theoretical inquiry in that such a (Platonic) preparation allows the individual to resist goals and distractions extraneous to the relevant problems of thought and action. A virtuous person, the potentially true philosopher, in the words of Alfarabi, excels "in comprehending and conceiving that which is essential."

Alfarabi distinguishes the true philosopher, the one who has attained virtue before engaging in theoretical inquiry, from the vain, the false, and the counterfeit philosophers. "The vain philosopher is he who learns the theoretical sciences, but without going any further and without being habituated to doing the acts considered virtuous by a certain religion (*milla*) or the generally accepted noble acts" (*Taḥṣīl al-sa'āda,* 96–97; trans. 48). The vain philosopher is not virtuous; he is ruled by his appetites and inclinations (*Taḥṣīl al-sa'āda,* 97; trans. 48). Through time, he loses what he had learned and recedes into ignorance (*Taḥṣīl al-sa'āda,* 96–97; trans. 48–49). The counterfeit philosopher also loses what theory he learns, as he is naturally unfit for philosophical inquiry (*Taḥṣīl al-sa'āda,* 96–97; trans. 48). He may learn some theory for purposes such as advancement in his practical objectives, but theoretical inquiry is not his main calling. The false philosopher, finally, is he who acquires the theoretical sciences without achieving the utmost perfection so as to be able to introduce others to what he knows (*Taḥṣīl al-sa'āda,* 96; trans. 48). The false philosopher is not like the counterfeit or the vain in that he lacks the requisite natural constitution or the proper cultivated habits. Rather, he falls short of perfection, because he "is not yet aware of the purposes for which philosophy is pursued" (*Taḥṣīl al-sa'āda,* 97; trans. 49). In other words, the false philosopher doesn't pursue philosophy for the happiness intrinsic to philosophizing, but for the sake of conceptions of happiness that are publicly available, for example, honor, recognition, and power (ibid.).

Alfarabi writes that engaging in acts considered virtuous by a religion advances philosophical inquiry (*Taḥṣīl al-sa'āda,* 96; trans. 48). If anything, as with Heidegger, preoccupation with these matters is a sign of inauthenticity, as they involve succumbing to public ideals. The historical context for Alfarabi's claim suggests that he may have the Islamic religious life in mind when he discusses the religious cultivation of virtue. So it will be useful to take a look at Islamic ethics, especially as it bears on the issue of virtue.

3.2. Alfarabi's Appropriation of Islamic Ethics

For a characterization of the Islamic ideal of virtue, let us turn to Seyyed Hossein Nasr's characterization of the Islamic tradition. In his more recent work, *Islam: Religion, History, and Civilization,* Nasr writes:

> The *Shari'ah* [Islamic law] is like the circumference of a circle, each point of which represents a Muslim who stands on that circumference. Each radius that connects every point on the circumference to the center symbolizes the *Tariqah,* and the center is the *Haqiqah,* which generates both the radii and the circumference. The whole circle, with its center, circumference, and radii, may be said to represent the totality of the Islamic tradition.[6]

The Islamic law, as a set of act-centered deontological injunctions, provides a *starting point* for the achievement of moral excellence or virtue that characterizes the state of the person who has attained intimacy with the center—*ḥaqīqa,* that is, the divine truth. Islamic ritual practices—*ṭarīqa* (i.e., the way)—are a *portal* to being-in-truth (another way of characterizing the state of the virtuous person).

Falzlur Rahman, in "Some Key Ethical Concepts of the Qur'an," posits another terminological triad at the foundation of the ethical perspective in the Qur'an and another way of looking at the relations of virtue. This triad is *islām, īmān,* and *taqwā,*[7] which are well-known Islamic terms. *Islām* means surrender to God, *īmān* means faith in (or commitment to) God, and *taqwā* refers to the state of religious virtue. Rahman maintains that "those who have faith must cultivate *taqwā* and must do *islām* or surrender to God's Law . . . while *īmān* is rooted in the inner life of the individual, *taqwā* includes *īmān* and results in action, and *islām* is that overt activity that expresses *īmān* and *taqwā*."[8] *Taqwā* is the state of the accomplished believer, and in it the inner and the outer, the psychological (i.e., the cultivation of the soul) and the communal (i.e., submission of the agent to the public law—the *sharī'a*), are reconciled. This reconciliation implies that the individual is able to recognize the good without the need for a legal enforcement. "[T]he basic function of *taqwā* is to allow man to correctly examine himself and to see the right from wrong."[9]

However, Fazlur Rahman does not discuss the way *īmān* and *islām* can make the state of *taqwā* possible, which is what Toshihiko Izutsu does in the *Ethico-Religious Concepts in the* Qur'an. Drawing from chapter 49 ("*al-Ḥujurāt*"), verses 14 and 15, Izutsu argues that *islām* (from the verb *aslama,* which means literally "to submit") is ambiguous. On the one hand, it denotes "the very first step in the faith, a shallow belief which has not yet penetrated deep into the heart."[10] On the other hand, Izutsu—drawing from al-Bukhārī—claims that *islām* denotes the whole of the religion as stated in chapter 3 ("*Āl 'imrān*"), verse 19: "Verily the religion in the sight of God is *Islām*."[11] According to Izutsu, the narrower sense of *islām,* as the first in the ethical triad mentioned above, is deepened in *īmān,* that is "belief." Belief names the stage where the person has embraced the divine guidance and has conditioned his inner life so as to be in accord with the divine will. *Taqwā,* as the culmination of the Qur'anic ethical progress, is rendered by Izutsu as the "fear of God" and he interprets it literally: "It is, originally at least, the emotion of fear."[12] Izutsu implies that *taqwā* was introduced to break the haughtiness and humble the pride of the pre-Islamic Arab.[13] I find this explanation problematic and I agree with Fazlur Rahman that "the element of fear conveyed by this term has a very complicated nature and the only translation that will do justice to it is perhaps 'the fear of responsibility' which is very different from a fear someone might have, say of a wolf, or a fear that a guilty person might have of the police."[14] This "fear of responsibility" fits well with the sense of *taqwā* as the virtuous person's wonder and trepidation before the sublimity of the good that he has learned to recognized in particular situations. The "awe" before the good silences the motivations competing with the good (i.e., the reasons for acting for the sake of anything other than the good). The person with *taqwā* recognizes the good, is overcome by awe, and acts for the sake of it.

Conjoining this discussion of the Qur'anic ethics with the earlier account of the Islamic tradition that I extracted from the work of Nasr, we can see the following rough outline of an Islamic approach to moral progress. Submission (*islām*) to the law initiates the process of moral growth by preventing the agent from obsession with the gratification of biological and conventional needs and desires. Instead the initiates learn to frame action by appeal to divinely sanctioned moral rules (*sharī'a*). The observance of *ṭarīqa,* the body of Islamic ascetic practices, begins the supererogation needed to produce *īmān*—the accord of the agent's inner life with the divine will. Practicing the *ṭarīqa* continues the cultivation begun by the law and removes the pressure of any desire, need, or feeling that might prevent a response appropriate to the intrinsic good of a situation. Ultimately, the cultivated Muslim has attained the balance (or beauty—*iḥsān*[15]) of the soul, and is able to see, in an unselfish and unbiased manner, the reflection of the divine goodness in each particular situation and act for the sake of it. This is the Islamic state of virtue or *taqwā*.

William Chittick, in *The Heart of Islamic Philosophy*, interprets the triad in a different way:

> Like other religions, Islam addresses three basic levels of human existence: practice, understanding, and virtue: or body, mind, and heart; or to use the well-known Koranic triad, *islām* (submission), *īmān* (faith), *iḥsān* (doing what is beautiful). . . . Islamic practice is rooted in the Sunnah or model of the prophet, who demonstrated how the Koran could be applied to everyday life. Islamic understanding is rooted in investigating the objects of faith that are identified by the Koran—God, the angels, the scriptures, the prophets, the Last Day, and the "measuring out" (*qadar*) of good and evil. Islamic virtue is grounded in the attempt to find God present at all times and in all places, just as the prophet found him present.[16]

My reading of the triad replaces Chittick's account of "understanding" with supererogatory ascetic practices, such that the outward obedience to God's law (*islām*) acquires an internal dimension; it becomes second nature, as it were. This is a better reading of the term *īmān* because, in Chittick's account, faith (*īmān*) becomes, paradoxically, a matter of intellectual practices. As a result, in my account, *iḥsān* is not seen as a mysterious quality of the soul (i.e., "virtue of the heart")[17] but involves the ability to recognize and understand the reflection of divine goodness in each particular situation so that one acts for its sake. Therefore, in my reading, *iḥsān*, *pace* Chittick, involves understanding and is an intellectual quality.[18]

Alfarabi's account of the relation between philosophy and religion reflects my rendition of the Islamic paradigm of religious development. For Alfarabi, philosophy lies at the core of the centripetal process of religious development of *islām, īmān, taqwā*. Religion makes that core accessible to the multitude through imaginative representation.

> Now when one acquires knowledge of the beings or receives instruction in them, if he perceives their ideas themselves with his intellect, and his assent to them is by means of certain demonstrations (*al-borhān al-yaqīnī*), then the science that comprises these cognitions is *philosophy*. But if they are known by imagining them through similitudes (*al-amthāl*) that imitate them, and assent to what is imagined of them

> is caused by persuasive method (*ṭarīq al-iqnāʿ*), then the ancients call what comprises these cognitions *religion.* (*Taḥṣīl al-saʿāda,* 88–89; trans. 44)[19]

As the multitude lacks the practical and the theoretical training required for the philosophical commerce with truth (*ḥaqīqa*) resulting in felicity, religion is drawn on to bring it into a relationship with truth. Religion provides imaginative similitudes, imitations, in order to persuade people of matters that are demonstrable philosophically (*Taḥṣīl al-saʿāda,* 89; trans. 44). Some of these similitudes have to do with the conditions necessary for recognizing the intelligible (practical and theoretical) features of objects; these conditions are embodied in the laws (*al-nawāmis*) (*Taḥṣīl al-saʿāda,* 91; trans. 45)[20] and the virtuous practices (*al-afʿāl al-fāḍila*) (*Taḥṣīl al-saʿāda,* 96; trans. 48). Because "[i]n everything of which philosophy gives an account based on intellectual perception or conception, religion gives an account based on imagination" (*Taḥṣīl al-saʿāda,* 89; trans. 44), the philosophical laws and practices are reflected in religious laws and practices (the *sharīʿa* and the *ṭarīqa* in the particular case of Islam). The latter, in turn, constrain the ordinary person and train him for access to the core, the *ḥaqīqa.* For Alfarabi, the persuasive imitations of religion are a function of the perfected imagination of the philosopher-lawgiver.[21] In this, there is a further specification of Alfarabi's position in the teachings of Islam.

3.3. Alfarabi's Philosophical Appropriation of Islamic Prophetology

According to Islamic sources, Prophet Muhammad possesses three major attributes. First, he has *risāla;* he is a *rasūl* (i.e., he carries a message). This is the feature of the Prophet that has to do with his mission as the conveyer (messenger) of the divine law (*sharīʿa*). Second, he has *nubuwwa;* he is a *nabī* (i.e., a prophet), and this has to with his task as the conveyer of a path (*ṭarīqa*), a set of practices to bring the faithful closer to God. Finally he has *walāya,* i.e., as a *walī,* he is intimate with God and therefore, privy to the inner mystery of God (*ḥaqīqa*). Now, *walāya* and *nubuwwa* are necessary for all prophecy, but *risāla* is not. In the Islamic tradition, a very select number of other prophets are considered to have all three of these attributes, among whom Jesus and Moses, along with Muhammad, figure prominently. In a chapter on prophetology in his *History of Islamic Philosophy,* Corbin uses the following metaphor: "the *risāla* is like the shell, the *nubuwwa* is like the almond, and the *walāya* is like the oil within the almond."[22] The *risāla* concerns the exoteric aspect of Prophet Muhammad's mission, *nubuwwa* has to do with the esoteric—it goes beyond concern about communal behavior and social justice, it provides insight into unknown mundane and spiritual phenomena—and *walāya* concerns the esoteric of the esoteric (*bāṭin al-bāṭin*) (i.e., the truth unveiled to one who is in truth).

Corbin maintains that Alfarabi's philosophical position is influenced by Shi'i Islam,[23] and it is therefore useful—in this regard—to explore briefly the prophetology of early Shi'i Imamism. Mohammad Ali Amir-Moezzi, in *The Divine Guide in Early Shiism,* points to the following salient aspects of the early Imami doctrine:

> The exoteric side of Truth is manifested through lawgiving prophecy, bringing to the mass of humanity (*'āmma*) a Sacred Book that descended from Heaven (*tanzīl*); Muhammad is both prototype and the end of this first aspect. The esoteric side of the Truth is revealed through the mission of the imams (*walāya*), accompanying each prophetic mission, bringing to the elite believers (*khāṣṣa*) the only true interpretation (*ta'wīl*) of the Holy Book; together the twelve imams, but in particular Ali, who is considered the father of the eleven others, are the plenary manifestation of this second aspect [of Truth]. Fatima, called the "Confluence of Two Lights" (*majma' al-nūrayn*), reflects the "place" where the two aspects of prophecy intersect. Of course, the prophet (*nabī*) also has knowledge of the esoteric side of religion; he is thus also *walī,* but he reserves his esoteric teachings for his imam(s) exclusively; on the other hand, the imam is never considered a prophet.[24]

It follows that the Islamic tradition is a reflection of Prophet Muhammad's qualities. At the center of the prophetic qualities and the reflecting tradition is Truth, *ḥaqīqa,* as theophany, and the prophet's message is to lead (i.e., remind) the faithful through the various aspects of Islam (the *sharī'a* and *ṭarīqa*) to the inner core (*ḥaqīqa*), where they achieve intimacy with the Divine. The achievement of the inner enlightenment or *taqwā,* on the other hand, is only possible through the earlier submission (*islām*) to the Islamic law and observance of the prescribed practices leading to inner purity (*īmān*). In Shi'i Islam, the guidance of the imams, as the companions of the inner truth (*ḥaqīqa*), is superadded to the basic regime. The imams are those who, in the absence of the prophet, guide the faithful to intimacy with God. They are the possessors of *ta'wīl,* the spiritual hermeneutics of the revelation. *Ta'wīl,* literally going to the beginning (*awwal*), begins with the knowledge of the apparent (e.g., the physical world) and traces it to its source. The aim is to cultivate the soul and its intellectual faculty beyond mere involvement with the bodily or the conventional. *Ta'wīl*, to use the terminology introduced earlier, presupposes the submission to the *sharī'a* laws and the practices of *ṭarīqa* and cultivates the theoretical faculty, culminating in intimacy (*walāya*) with the divine (*haqīqa*). Of course, the state in which that intimacy is attained is *taqwā*, the subtle intellection of the good that is freed of conditional worldly concerns. This implies that the objects perceived by the subtle intellect appear as they are in themselves and not under the distortion of mundane objectives. Such authentic vision sees things in the way they relate to the divine attributes, and the one who possesses this vision is compelled to act in the way that advances the divine purpose, the good.[25]

The question that I want to pursue here concerns the way this Islamic articulation of the human ideal maps onto Alfarabi's exemplary human, the true philosopher. To that end, I turn to Alfarabi's account of the happiness of the true philosopher in his major work containing a unified presentation of his philosophical position, *Mabādī ārā' ahl al-madīna al-fāḍila* (*On the Perfect State*).[26] For Alfarabi, the faculty of practical reason (*al-quwwa al-nāṭiqa al-'amaliyya*) is subservient to the theoretical reason (*al-quwwa al-nāṭiqa al-naẓariyya*). "The rational faculty is partly practical reason and partly theoretical reason; practical reason is made to serve the theoretical reason" (*al-Madīna al-fāḍila*, 208-09). The perfection of practical reason—the acquisition of Aristotelian *phronēsis*—involves the excellence in actions directed toward the present and the future particulars (*al-juz'iyyāt*) [*al-Madīna al-fāḍila*, 218–19]. In other words, one learns to perceive and respond to the *universal* features of particulars, for example, ethical intelligibles (which motivate the person to act without reference to purposes beyond themselves). The function of theoretical reason is to contemplate and understand the intelligibles, including the transcendent intelligibles (*al-ma'qūlāt al-mufāriqa*) [*al-Madīna al-fāḍila*, 224–25], presumably by recognizing that which is common to the sensory representations and how they are different from each other. Alfarabi is insistent that the purpose of this contemplation is to bring the human being to felicity: "Theoretical reason, however, is not made to serve anything else but to bring man to felicity (*al-sa'āda*)" [*al-Madīna al-fāḍila*, 208–9]. It follows that theoretical reason brings man to felicity, *in the first instance*, by understanding ethical intelligibles embodied in the particulars, so that the properly habituated person recognizes their demands and submits to them (*al-Madīna al-fāḍila*, 208–9).

The human being holding the highest degrees of happiness (*a'lā darajāt al-sa'āda*) has conjoined with the Active Intellect, the most proximate transcendent intelligible and intellect (*al-Madīna al-fāḍila*, 198–203):

> When this [i.e., perfection] occurs in both parts of his rational faculty, namely the theoretical and the practical rational faculties, and also in his representative faculty (*al-quwwa al-mutakhayyila*), then it is this man who receives Divine Revelation, and God almighty grants him Revelation (*waḥy*) through the mediation of the Active Intellect (*al-'aql al-fa'āl*). . . . Thus he is . . . a wise man and a philosopher and an accomplished thinker who employs an intellect of divine quality, and through the emanation from the Active Intellect to his faculty of representation a visionary prophet: who warns of things to come and tells of particular things which exist at present. *This man holds the most perfect rank of humanity and has reached the highest degree of felicity*. . . . This is the sovereign over whom no other human being has any sovereignty whatsoever. (*al-Madīna al-fāḍila*, 244–47)

The highest felicity, the one toward which the true philosopher aims, is the conjunction with the Active Intellect. If this conjunction is accompanied by a perfected imagination, then the philosopher also is a prophet,[27] a person whose perfected imagination receives intelligible forms from the Active Intellect, the giver of forms, *and* from the senses. The modification of the imagination by the revelations of the Active Intellect allows for "prophecy of present and future events and . . . prophecy of things divine" (*al-Madīna al-fāḍila*, 224–25). At the peak of prophecy, the perfect man attains a divine-like status, and—just as God who, in His absolute goodness, emanates His mercy upon creation—the perfect person reaches out to his fellow human beings and legislates laws to improve their lot.[28] Therefore, we should not overlook Alfarabi's insistence that the philosopher-prophet is also a lawgiver, a skillful orator (a further feature of a perfected imagination) who knows how to guide people toward the achievement of happiness (*al-Madīna al-fāḍila*, 246-47). These attributes of the true philosopher, the supremely happy human, correlate directly to *walāya*, *nubuwwa*, and *risāla*. *Walāya*, as intimacy with truth (*ḥaqīqa*), is the state of practical *and* theoretical perfection. In this state of perfection, one is removed from mundane concerns and receives intellectual emanations from the Active Intellect. *Nubuwwa* corresponds to the state of imaginative reception of emanations from the Active Intellect.

In other words, the *nabī* (one who has *nubuwwa*) receives prophetic insight (i.e., sees the future and the past and has visions of the spiritual entities) and can communicate the intellectual insight (received from the Active Intellect) in symbolic form to the uncouth in order to initiate him into contemplation. *Risāla*, finally, corresponds to the state of ultimate perfection and felicity, when the perfected person dispenses goodness to the multitude (not just to a select few—as in the case of the *nabī*) in the form of religious laws. In this reading of Alfarabi's account, the prophet of Islam would be one such person, that is, a philosopher-prophet-lawgiver.

3.4. The Reception of the Notion of Active Intellect in the Islamic Philosophical Tradition

In order to ward off the charge that Alfarabi's account of prophecy as conjunction with the Active Intellect is a mere philosophical camouflage of dogmatic religious assumptions, I want to present a brief account of its philosophical genealogy and clarify the relevant contributions of the Islamic Peripatetics. In his *De Anima*, Aristotle puts forward the notion of a transcendent Active Intellect. He maintains that "in fact mind, as we have described it, is what it is by virtue of becoming all things, while there is another which is what it is by virtue of making all things: this is the sort of positive state like light; for in a sense light makes potential colours into actual colours" (430a14–17).[29] The Active Intellect or the productive mind (*nous poiētikos*) is explained through the contrast with the mind as passive (*pathētikos*), that is, the conforming mind (430a25). In the *Metaphysics*, Aristotle characterizes thinking as an activity (*energeia*); it is an act that has its end in itself (1048b18–30). This thinking is not thinking through a problem, as the latter kind of thinking is a movement (*kinēsis*); it has its end, purpose (i.e., the solution), outside of itself and when it reaches it, it comes to a termination (1048b18–30). Thinking as an activity has the end, that is, purpose—having thought the thinkable—in itself, and it can go on indefinitely (1048b23–25). Active Intellect is essentially activity (*energeia*) (*De Anima*, 430a17–19). Therefore, it is separate and productive of its objects. The ordinary intellect—the conforming mind—is kinetic: Its object—the thinkable—is external to it, but through inquiry it acquires the thinkables and *becomes* its objects (430a15–16). As such, its movement approaches activity, and it achieves closeness to the separate Active Intellect. In a way, the Active Intellect shines like light on the passive mind and its objects, illuminating the passive mind into activity. This notion of a separate Active Intellect becomes an important aspect of the psychology of the Islamic Peripatetics.[30]

But Islamic Peripatetics Platonized the account of the transcendent Active Intellect given by Aristotle and his Hellenic followers. Aristotle had rejected Plato's account of the existence of intelligible objects in a realm of their own as well as Plato's claim that knowledge is precisely the intellectual perception of these transcendent objects. He had maintained that forms do not exist independently of objects, but that they can be separated from them only in thought (*De Anima*, 427–29). Alexander Altmann has observed that in the Islamic Peripatetic tradition:

> the [Aristotelian] denial of self-subsistent Forms (even though assumed to reside in some supernal hypostasis) enforces a shift of the object of ultimate knowledge to a different plane. Instead of the supernal Forms it is now the separate intellects to which the quest for ultimate felicity is directed. These separate intellects or intelligences are not the essences of the sensible things, as the Platonists maintained, but conceived as simple, i.e., immaterial substances of an ontological order.[31]

The Forms (intelligibles), for Muslim Peripatetics, inhere essentially in separate intellects making up the immaterial spiritual order, and only accidentally in the human intellect and the objects manifesting them. The Active Intellect is one such separate intellect. It is this divine being that infuses the human soul and the sensible world with intelligence and intelligibility; it is the angelic giver of forms (*wāhib al-ṣuwar*) (*al-Madīna al-fāḍila,* 406).[32] In other words, Active Intellect is, for Islamic Peripatetics, not just the Aristotelian actualizer of the human intellect; it is also the divine being that infuses the sensible world with intelligibility; it is the giver of intelligibles in the manner of Plato's Demiurge in the *Timaeus* (29e–30c)[33] and Plotinus' cosmic Intellect.[34] Therefore, union with the Active Intellect means that one receives intelligibles directly from the source as well as through an engagement with the sensible intermediaries.[35] This is a view that has Platonic antecedents. In the *Protagoras,* Plato sets forth the view that the elements of the political art (i.e., respect and justice) are a gift of Zeus, mediated by the divine messenger, Hermes (323b–d). In the *Meno,* he presents the argument that the politician's excellence is a divine gift (99c), and this view forms the backdrop to the *Republic*'s allegory of the cave where the solitary philosopher returns from dwelling in the intimacy of the divine light to the cave of human existence and, under ideal conditions, rules over it (520a). In the *Laws*, the Cretan leader, Minos, is presented as receiving instructions from Zeus (624a).

A good example of the Islamic synthesis of Platonism and Aristotelianism in the account of prophetic inspiration is the reception of the so-called *Theology of Aristotle*. Although doubts were expressed about its authorship, this text—which is a paraphrase of Plotinus' last three *Enneads*—contributed immensely to the development of an Islamic spiritual dimension in philosophical psychology. In a particularly influential portion of the *Theology*—*Enneads* IV, 8, 1—Plotinus describes the philosopher's solitary journey, which culminates in his union with the divinity and then ends by his return to the limited human domain.[36] In the *History of Islamic Philosophy*, Corbin writes that in this Ennead "the mystical philosophers [including Alfarabi and Avicenna] found both the exemplar of the Prophet's celestial assumption (*mi'rāj*) . . . and the exemplar of the vision which crowns the efforts of the divine Sage, the Stranger, the Solitary."[37] Alfarabi, for instance, employs the Arabic paraphrase of *Enneads* IV to argue that both Aristotle and Plato considered the purification of the soul as connecting it with the intellect and therefore with the Creator (*Ḥakīmayn* 71–72; trans. 164–65). In such a unity, "divine matters are known" (*Ḥakīmayn* 71; trans. 164).[38]

It is not too difficult to garner support for Corbin's testimony as to the prominence of the prophetic exemplar in the Islamic Peripatetic account of the perfection of the individual. A central feature of the Islamic proclamation of faith is the belief in the prophecy of Muhammad. Prophet Muhammad is a prophet, as we have seen, because he was inspired by the angel of revelation, Gabriel, who made him recite the Qur'an in the interval of twenty-three years. These recitals contain the divine wisdom (*ḥaqīqa*), the divine path (*ṭarīqa*) to reach that wisdom, and the foundations of the law (*sharī'a*) to constitute the community of Muslims, literally those who submit to the will of God and His wisdom. Alfarabi's works represent one of the earliest attempts to connect the Islamic notion of prophecy to the Peripatetic account of the perfect man as the intimate of the Active Intellect.[39] In *Kitāb al-sīyāsa al-madaniyya* (*The Political Regime*), Alfarabi identifies the Active Intellect (*al-'aql al-fa'āl*) with Islam's angel of revelation (*al-Madīna al-fāḍila*, 406). Walzer, in his commentary on *On the Perfect State*, writes: "To know the true meaning of the Active Intellect is . . . essential, according to al-Fārābi, to an adequate understanding of one of the most fundamental Muslim articles of faith, the transmission of eternal truth to mankind through a man of overwhelming mental power—a philosopher-prophet-lawgiver" (ibid.).

3.5. Alfarabi on Religion and Politics

It is important to recognize that for Alfarabi, even before conjunction with the Active Intellect, emanations from the Active Intellect are bestowed on all human intellects. These common emanations allow for the cultivation of the intellect (*al-'aql*) from the potential (*bi-l-quwwa*) to the actual (*bi-l-fi'l*), and they are made up of the imperatives and principles that allow the human individual to free himself from illusion and error and achieve clarity about the intelligibles, which are (*qua* potential) veiled in darkness and come to light with the aid of the Active Intellect. These principles are broken into three categories: productive, ethical, and physical/metaphysical (*al-Madīna al-fāḍila*, 202–05); the second and third among them can be contained in true religions (i.e., those established by the philosopher-prophet-lawgivers).[40] Alfarabi's claim that "philosophy is prior to religion in time" (*Taḥṣīl al-sa'āda*, 90; trans. 45) implies that common religious principles and practices have their source in the teachings of wise legislators. The philosophical contemplation of actual intelligibles—founded on an antecedent ethical training—may advance until the philosopher's intellect becomes the acquired intellect (*al-'aql al-mustafād*). As an acquired intellect, "the intelligible in him has become identical with that which thinks in him" (*al-Madīna al-fāḍila*, 242–43). This is the state in which the intellect is the activity (*energeia*) of thought thinking itself, that is, the intellect contemplates its own contents (i.e., the abstracted intelligibles), by inquiring into their similarities and distinctions. Such a theoretical engagement with its own contents removes the intellect from the material world and brings it closer to the spiritual world (*al-Madīna al-fāḍila*, 198–203), and especially to the most proximate of the spiritual entities, the Active Intellect (which is *essentially* activity [*energeia*]). At this juncture, the philosopher may be endowed with supreme felicity and conjoin with the Active Intellect (*al-Madīna al-fāḍila*, 245–46), and this conjunction results in access to the intelligibles of the Active Intellect and may lead to new legislation and religion (*al-Madīna al-fāḍila*, 244–47).

The virtuous city (*al-madīna al-fāḍila*)—according to Alfarabi—is so organized that it brings the citizens as close as they can be to the condition of ethical excellence. Because Alfarabi lays the emphasis on the individual's struggle for excellence, the inquiry into the virtuous city cannot be a political program per se;[41] it is rather the project of bringing to light and motivating the achievement of a just (virtuous, *fāḍil*) soul. Nevertheless, Alfarabi's synthesis of Platonism and Aristotelianism gives his ethical project a significant political dimension. In Plato's *Republic*, the philosopher seeks solitude to contemplate and acquire contact with the Divine. When he has reached theoretical illumination, he desires to benefit his fellow men. Just as the absolute Good overflows and dispenses his goodness, the perfect human—the likeness of God—also bestows goodness on his fellow citizens. But if the city is corrupt, he shuns it and seeks solitude to contemplate and maintain his virtuous state. He is not less blessed on account of it. In contrast to this Platonic view, Aristotle, in his *Politics*, claims that human beings are by nature political, so participation in a city is necessary for virtue (253a1–3). In the *Nicomachean Ethics*, he launches an even stronger claim: the virtuous person cultivates friendships and engages in political activity (1169b3–1170b20).

Alfarabi follows Aristotle in claiming that philosophical virtue presupposes political activity in a city (*Nicomachean Ethics*, 1177b6–25). Alfarabi's also follows Aristotle when he maintains that the attainmnent of virtue is not the culmination of happiness (*sa'āda*).[42] Rather this happiness requires that one participates in a virtuous city, where the virtuous person can receive cooperation in exercising his virtue. He writes that "felicity in its real and true sense" can only be attained in the excellent city, through the exercise of excellence in a political context (*al-Madīna al-fāḍila*, 230–31).[43] However, in keeping with Plato, Alfarabi maintains that "true" felicity is realized in one's spiritual commerce with the transcendent beings (*al-Madīna al-fāḍila*, 244–45). Such a transaction, for Alfarabi, is mediated through the conjunction with the Active Intellect. It may happen that there is conjunction in the absence of the virtuous city (because conjunction *happens* to one), and as a result the virtuous person may not get to exercise his virtue politically.

3.6. Avicenna on Philosophical Felicity

In the Metaphysics of the major work of his middle period,[44] the *Healing* (*Kitāb al-shifā'*), Avicenna sets forth the conditions for the cultivation of the Peripatetic ideal of conjunction with the Active Intellect. Avicenna adopts, with slight modifications, Alfarabi's privileging of the practice of spiritual exercises. Avicenna follows Plato (and Alfarabi) in distinguishing between the rational, the irascible, and the appetitive parts of the soul. He argues that justice, the balance of the various parts of the soul and the sum of their excellence, is the first step toward the achievement of personal perfection:

> Since the Motivating Powers are three—the appetitive (*al-hahwāniyya*), the irascible (*al-ghaḍabiyya*), and the practical (*al-tadbīriyya*)—the virtues (*al-faḍā'il*) consist of three things: (a) moderation (*al-tawassuṭ*) in . . . appetites . . . (b) moderation in all the irascible passions . . . (c) moderation in practical matters. At the head of these virtues stand temperance (*'iffa*), courage (*shajā'a*), and practical wisdom (*ḥikma*); their sum is justice (*'adāla*), which, however, is extraneous to theoretical virtue (*faḍīla al-naẓariyya*). But whoever combines theoretical wisdom (*ḥikma al-naẓariyya*) with justice, is indeed a happy man (*sa'ad*).[45]

For Avicenna, the acquisition of justice, the excellence and balance of the soul, paves the way for the intellectual labors of theoretical inquiry. Justice comes about through self-control and moderation. These qualities help prevent the person from manipulating and appropriating, that is, from moving for the sake of purposes that lie outside of the situation of action. The just individual recognizes the various goods that motivate his actions, and subordinates them to the practical intellect's preference for the universal good. As such, he attends to that which is good in itself (and not for the sake of another) rather than imposing his own rendition of the good, based on his appetites or passions, on the situation. This is practical wisdom (*phronēsis*). In this state, the practically wise person (the *phronimos*) dwells autonomously alongside entities (to use Heidegger's terminology). The ability of the *phronimos* to see the relevant ethical features of the situation requires the exercise of theoretical intellect[46] and the corresponding notion of intellection (*noiēsis*). This is because theoretical intellect is the faculty that perceives (i.e., intellects) the unity in the multiplicity of an intelligible's material appearances and helps in distinguishing it from and relating it to other intelligibles (*al-Shifā' DA*, 243–47).[47] In *Being and Time*, as we have seen, Heidegger rejects the tradition's account of intellection as based in a primary, nonderivative power of a present-at-hand entity (i.e., the soul) in its theoretical commerce with the world.[48] In the Islamic Peripatetic accounts of the soul's intellectual activity, however, intellection is dependent on the practical and experiential context of human cultivation and the resulting involvements with the world, including the materially embedded intelligibles and intelligences.[49] In other words, intellection presupposes effort and training.

Theoretical wisdom, according to Avicenna, gets its start from the practical virtue of the soul, and its addition to justice (i.e., practical perfection) results in happiness (*sa'āda*) (*al-Shifā' DA*, 50; trans. 183).[50] Theoretical wisdom is the excellence of the intellect in understanding intelligibles. To attain theoretical wisdom, the human intellect should be actualized by acquiring an understanding of the intelligibles through combining and distinguishing potential intelligibles, that is, sensory forms and intentions, using the primary intelligibles. Primary intelligible are easily acquired truths (*al-Shifā' DA*, 49; trans. 184). They provide models of truth for the thinking that distinguishes and relates the sensory forms and intentions. Such thinking is the theoretical practice that prepares the intellect for the reception of the relevant (secondary) intelligibles from the Active Intellect. Once inspired by the Active Intellect, the now actual intellect (*al-'aql bi-l-fi'l*) intellects the intelligibles without having to engage in the preparatory investigation again (*al-Shifā' DA*, 49–50; trans. 185). Conjunction with the Active Intellect provides comprehensive access to the intelligibles, and the now acquired intellect (*al-'aql al-mustafād*) develops a more abstract and systematic understanding by thinking through its own contents.

Dag Nikolaus Hasse challenges the interpretations of Avicenna's views that consider his account of the abstraction and cogitation of the sensory forms only a *'façon de parler'* for emanation of intelligibles from the Active Intellect.[51] According to these interpretations, Avicenna takes knowledge to be a dispensation of the Active Intellect only. Hasse recoils from this approach and argues that "Avicenna insists that intelligible forms ultimately come from the particulars in the imagination and still resemble them."[52] I agree with Hasse's point, but I supplement it with my interpretive strategy that Islamic Peripateticism should be read as privileging an account of the cultivation of the person through spiritual practices. In order to further clarify my strategy, I turn to the psychological part of the *Salvation* (*Kitāb al-najāt*)—written shortly after the *Healing*[53]—where, in a chapter titled "How the Rational Faculties Assist the Rational Soul," Avicenna sets forth in a concise form the four psychological processes that prepare the soul for intellection. The first preparatory process is the isolation (*tajrīd*) of individual universals (*al-kulliyyāt al-mufrada*) from their material embodiments.[54] In this process, the soul exercises the perceptive powers of the animal soul, external (*ẓāhira*) and internal (*bāṭina*) senses (*al-ḥawāss*). The representations of embodied universals provided by the relevant external sensory powers are brought together by the internal faculty of common sense (*al-ḥiss al-mushtarak, binṭāsyā*).[55] The retention of the deliverances of common sense by the faculty of representation (*al-muṣawwara* or *al-khayāl*) enables access to the form (*al-ṣūra*) of the sensed object without need for the presence of the object (*al-Najāt*, 208; trans. 39). The faculty of estimation discovers further relevant features of the object, that is, intentions (*al-ma'ānī*), which are universals essentially free of material attachment although they accidentally happen to be in matter (e.g., good and evil, agreeable and dispensable) (*al-Najāt*, 209; trans. 39). Memory (*al-ḥafiẓa al-dhākira*) stores representations of intentional universals and sensory forms recognized thus by estimation (*al-Najāt*, 202; trans. 31), and imagination manipulates (i.e., synthesizes and analyzes) the psychological representations of forms and embodied universals, that is, intentions (ibid.).[56]

The second and third preparatory processes concern the comparing, combining and dividing of the perceived intentions and sensory forms. In these processes, thinking (*al-mufakira*) is involved. Thinking is the ability which when added to the animal powers brings about the soul which is properly human (*al-nafs al-nātiqa al-insānīya*), that is, a soul that through certain modifications becomes capable of achieving conjunction (*ittiṣāl*) with the Active Intellect (*al-'aql al-fa'āl*). In the second process, thinking is assisted by internal senses in finding the relations of negation and affirmation between the perceived universals and forms (*al-Najāt*, 221; trans. 55). Assisted again by the internal senses, thinking—in what amounts to the third preparatory process—finds (1) the necessary attribution of a positive or negative predicate to a subject, (2) contradictory oppositions, (3) consequence of a positive or negative conjunction, and (4) a positive or negative disjunction without contradictory opposition (ibid.). There also is a fourth process in which animal faculties assist thinking, and it involves the acquisition of "the reports to which the soul gives assent on account of unbroken and overwhelming tradition" (ibid.).

Avicenna's account of thinking is an extension of the Greek notion of *dianoia*, as available to Avicenna in the *Theology of Aristotle*. Avicenna composed an extensive commentary on the *Theology*, titled *al-Insāf* (*Fair Judgment*), of which fragments survive.[57] Peter Adamson, commenting on the Avicennan fragments and the Plotinian text, interprets *dianoia* as "discursive thinking" and maintains that "for Plotinus the soul thinks discursively because it 'unfolds' or divides the pure forms that are in the intellect."[58] Plotinus' account of *dianoia* has Aristotelian and Platonic sources. For Aristotle, *dianoia* functions in separating and combining forms as well as distinguishing true from false and good from evil.[59] In Plato's *Sophist*, the Eleatic stranger tells Theaetetus that "thinking and discourse are the same thing, except that what we call thinking is, precisely, the inward dialogue carried on by the mind with itself without spoken sound" (263e).[60] The inner "silent discourse" should be seen on the model of a Platonic dialogue, where the other is Socrates and the solitary is the interlocutor, the one who must measure up to Socrates' exacting and rigorous examination. Such examination recognizes the genuine combination and conflicts of ideas and sifts truth from falsehood and good from bad. Corbin, in his efforts to explicate the dynamics of the Avicennan account of the soul, identifies the inner solitary dialogue as between the theoretical intellect facing the heavens and an intellect turned toward the body (*al-Shifā' DA*, 47; trans. 183):

> The Self . . . is, "in person," the heavenly counterpart of a pair or a szygy made up of a fallen angel, or an angel appointed to govern a body, and of an angel retaining his abode in heaven. . . . [This pair] individualizes the Holy Spirit into an individual Spirit, who is the celestial *paredros* of the human being, its guardian angel, guide and companion, helper and savior.[61]

Corbin traces the heavenly "intellect" to the Gnostic angelologies of the Abrahamic tradition:

> Whether it be Metatron as the *protos Anthropos* and Active Intelligence, or the Active Intelligence as Holy Spirit and Archangel Gabriel, or as the Holy Spirit and Angel of Humanity in the philosophy of *Ishrāq*, the same figure never ceases to manifest itself to mental vision under this angelophany.[62]

In explaining the account of the inner dialogue in the Persian Sufi tradition, Corbin also identifies the heavenly intellect in the Perfect Nature of Hermeticism: "Hermes is the prophet of Perfect Nature; by initiating him to wisdom, his Perfect Nature taught him how to worship itself, taught him the form of prayer by which to call for it and cause it to appear (a Hermetic *dhikr*); this personal worship is what Hermes transmitted to the Sages."[63] In Heidegger's phenomenology, the inner dialogue is broached, as we will see in the sixth chapter, in the call of conscience, underlying Dasein's move away from the inauthentic absorption in public space (*SZ* 277; *BT* 322). Dasein's inner solitary reticent discourse between the authentic potential of Dasein and Dasein as it is drowned in everydayness raises it out of its lostness in the public space and moves it toward resoluteness and authenticity (*SZ* 277; *BT* 322). The relentless scrutiny of the inner self-discontent frees the self from the grip of mistaken and insufficiently understood beliefs and desires available to him in conventional modes of thought and action. Such a self-assessment situates the thinker in truth, in the way things show themselves in their authentic intelligibility.[64]

In Avicenna's comments on the *Theology*, dialogical thinking is not restricted to "unfolding" the intellect's intelligibles.[65] Avicenna's theoretical intellect is also available as the Socratic other in dialogical thinking (*mufakira*), that is, the voice that challenges the combining and the dividing of the deliverances of sensory powers.[66] As I mentioned earlier, for Avicenna, the intellect, in its potency, already benefits from certain truths imparted by the Active Intellect to human souls. The possession of these truths helps to raise the rational soul from mere conformity to the animal soul's deliverances and their organization to the level of habitual intellect (*al-'aql bi-l-malaka*). The truths available to the habitual intellect are easy to receive and include tautologies such as, "the whole is greater than the part," and "things, which are equal to the same thing, are equal to one another." They serve as models of knowledge and challenge the powers of the soul to think through the forms and intentions obtained by the animal cognitive powers, in order to arrive at the knowledge of the world and the grasp of the intelligibles (*al-Najāt*, 204; trans. 34).

The uncultivated potential intellect, limited to the deliverances of animal powers, interacts with objects in what Heidegger, in *Being and Time*, calls an environment. In an environment, we "manipulate things and put them to use" (*SZ* 67; *BT* 95) for the sake of our animal needs and desires. This brings into view the close alliance between the animal perceptive powers and the animal motivational powers (i.e., the appetitive and the irascible parts) of the soul. For Avicenna, the uncultivated intellect of the soul in the grip of animal perceptive and motive powers acts (and perceives) for the sake of basic sustenance, survival, and worldly success. Avicenna's prerequisite ethical training is the intellect's imposition of a regimentation that trains one to act for the sake of relevant moral intentions in the situation, rather than for the sake of one's animal needs and desires. This recalls Heidegger's account of "dwelling autonomously alongside entities within-the-world" (*SZ* 61; *BT* 89). In this mode of being, as we have seen, the person holds "one's-self-back from any manipulation or utilization" (ibid.) and tarries alongside beings, experiencing them as they are in themselves (*SZ* 60; *BT* 88).

According to Avicenna, the ethical training of the philosopher provides a gateway to the intellectual fulfillment of the individual by curtailing the appetites and passions, allowing the soul to achieve practical wisdom (i.e., to recognize the objective good and act for the sake of it). The practically wise soul perceives the relevant moral intentions enmattered in a situation and engages in action for their sake, rather than for the sake of values imposed on one's actions external to that situation. Therefore, practical wisdom results in actions that have as their ends the unconditional good perceived in the situation of action. This is in sharp contrast to the person's action based on the conditional assessment of the situation for the sake of a good imposed from without (e.g., satisfaction of animal needs). This ability to recognize the intentions (enmattered intelligibles) presupposes the soul's freedom from the animal concerns that determine perception and action. Such freedom is obtained through weakening the hold of animal tendencies through spiritual practices. The practically wise soul then attends to the real and thus empowers the theoretical intellect in its commerce with the deliverances of animal powers. The thinking that is freed from the obfuscation of animal motivations deliberates on the abstracted forms or intentions in a way that their combinations and separations correspond to the way things are in the world rather than to the interpretation we impose upon it. In this way, thinking becomes all things (Aristotle, *De Anima*, 430a14–15). But Avicenna's arguments reach far beyond Heidegger's attempts to gain access to things themselves. Thinking through the forms and intentions *then* results in the attainment of the actual intellect (*al-'aql bi-l-fi'l*), that is, the acquisition of secondary intelligibles based on the primary intelligibles of the potential intellect (*al-Najāt*, 205; trans. 34–35). Intelligibles are unconditional (i.e., universal) and the grasp of secondary intelligibles presupposes reflection on empirical (conditional) concepts and their combinations and distinctions as captured by more general thoughts (and guided by primary intelligibles as models). Such a reflection is a practice that by virtue of its concern with generality purifies thinking of worldly attachments and brings it closer to the Active Intellect. Active Intellect then emanates intelligibles into the intellect of the thinker. Intellection of the secondary intelligibles, through thinking through the forms and intentions, in turn, prepares the ground for the acquired intellect (*al-'aql al-mustafād*), the intellect that has joined with the Active Intellect (*al-Najāt*, 205; trans. 35). On account of this conjunction, the acquired intellect becomes essentially activity (*energeia*), that is, it comes to have its end in itself. In other words, the intelligible form is present in the intellect, the intellect is aware of this presence, thinks through the intelligibles that it contains, and understands the combinations and distinctions.

3.7. Avicenna on Intellectual Prophecy

In the Metaphysics of *the Healing*, as we have seen, Avicenna maintains that the supremely happy person is ethically just, theoretically wise, *and* a prophet. He writes: "[W]hoever, in addition to this [justice and theoretical wisdom], wins the prophetic qualities (*al-khawāṣ al-nabawiyya*), becomes almost a human god. Worship of him, after the worship of God, becomes almost allowed. He is indeed the world's earthly king and God's deputy (*khalīfat Allāh*) in it."[67] In the language of the Psychology of *the Healing*, the prophetic intellect is the acquired intellect. The prophetic intellect (*al-'aql al-qudsī*) has all the intelligibles at its immediate disposal, on account of its conjunction with the Active Intellect (*al-Najāt*, 205–7; trans. 35–38).[68] In his later writings, however, Avicenna seems to distinguish between the prophetic intellect and the acquired intellect. Dimitri Gutas argues that, in his middle period (in which the *Healing* and the *Salvation* were composed), Avicenna puts forth the standard account of intuition (*ḥads*) as "a movement of the Mind [*dhihn*] in its effort to hit spontaneously upon the middle term."[69] Intuiting the middle term, in the terminology of this chapter, is the grasp (i.e., intellection) of the relevant intelligible mediated by combining and separating the deliverances of animal perceptive powers. In the revised view, intuition "is no longer a movement of the Mind for the purpose of tracking down the middle term, but its instantaneous discovery."[70] As a result of this redefinition, Avicenna introduces a second way of acquiring the middle term in addition to intuition. "This is Thinking [*fikr*]."[71] According to Gutas, the motivation for this change is eschatological for it allows "for the possibility for the trained soul to contemplate the intelligibles after death without having to think."[72] Additionally, the revised version of intuition allows for a sharper distinction between the philosopher (possessing acquired intellect) and the prophet. The prophetic intellect would possess the power denoted by the revised "*ḥads*" whereas the philosophical intellect would have to suffer through cultivating his soul to get the middle terms and conjoin with the Active Intellect.

In *On the Proof of Prophecies*, Avicenna spells out the later contrast between intuition and thinking: "That which becomes completely actual does so without mediation or through mediation, and the first is better. This is the one called prophet and in him degrees of excellence in the realm of material forms culminate."[73] This passage contrasts prophetic intellect with the acquired intellect that still requires the mediation of the sensory forms and the theoretical engagement of them for conjunction with the Active Intellect. The prophet, however, intuits the secondary intelligibles immediately, dispensing with preparatory thinking altogether.[74]

Avicenna's philosophers and prophets, like Alfarabi's philosopher-prophets, also possess a powerful imagination enabling them to teach others by expressing their insights figuratively and persuasively.[75] Their utterances can be attractive and provide ways of training the audience to comprehend the esoteric, intellectual meaning. In *On the Proof of Prophecies*, Avicenna writes that the philosophers and the prophets express themselves symbolically:

> It has been said that a condition the prophet must adhere to is that his words should be symbols and his expressions hints. Or, as Plato states in the Laws: whoever does not understand the apostle's symbols will not attain the Divine Kingdom. Moreover, the foremost Greek philosophers and prophets made use in their books of symbols and signs in which they hid their secret doctrine—men like Pythagoras, Socrates, and Plato. As for Plato, he had blamed Aristotle for divulging wisdom and making knowledge manifest so that Aristotle had to reply: "Even though I had done this, I have left in my books many a pitfall which only the initiate among the wise and learned (*al-'ulamā wa al-'uqalā*) can understand."[76]

The philosophers and the prophets benefit from an esoteric and an exoteric dimension to their pronouncements, where the former is reserved for "the wise and learned." Messengers, the prophetic founders of religions, as prophets and like philosophers, must train their audience to be able to understand divinely inspired knowledge. This training begins with ethical guidance. Messengers, however—because they have as their audience the whole of mankind—must convert their guidance to a religio-political program so that the majority can benefit from it. Avicenna finishes the passage above by stating that "[p]olitical guidance (*sīyāsa*), on the other hand, comes easily to prophets; also the imposition of obligations on people."[77] It seems that Avicenna espouses a variation of political Platonism, the view that even though solitary contemplation characterizes the ideal life, the perfect person engages in political activity to diffuse his goodness and bestow it on others. However, the messenger's goodness is extraordinary and enables him to institute a political regime of salvation,[78] whereas the diffusion of goodness in the case of philosophers and ordinary prophets is more modest.

Along with intellectual prophecy and the prophecy of the imagination (which includes lawgiving), Avicenna advocates a third kind of prophecy involving the motive faculty. This is prophecy as the working of miracles (*al-Shifā' DA*; 200–1). In this work, I do not plan to discuss this kind of prophecy, but I address imaginative prophecy and the symbolic expressions of the emanation of the Active Intellect in the following chapter. In Chapter 5, I also consider, in the context of Ghazali's polemics against Islamic Peripateticism, the Peripatetic account of imagination's veridical dreams as a kind of prophecy (*al-Shifā' DA*; 178–80).

According to Aristotle, ethical standards are not abstract moral principles (a view prevalent in the mainstream modern moral philosophy); rather they are given by moral exemplars, the *spoudaios* or *phronimos*, that is, the practically wise person (*Nicomachean Ethics*, 1140a25–28, 1143b21–25). One way the *phronimos* educates is by inviting the adepts to imitate him, and the accounts of human perfection articulated by Avicenna and Alfarabi also articulate an ideal (on par with the Islamic ideal) worthy of emulating, an ideal who is not just an advocate of the laws and the practices of the religion; he also guides the cultivation of the theoretical dimension of the soul. In other words, the Muslim Peripatetic exemplar not only introduces religious laws and rituals as the ethical part of cultivation, he also advocates the cultivation of a theoretical grasp of the truth (*ḥaqīqa*) which the Peripatetics identify at the core of the religion. The emulation of the practices advanced by the prophetic exemplar frees the self from preferences and prejudices that appropriate the knowledge of the world for the sake of extraneous purposes. The Peripatetic free self now attends to the things in themselves and goes beyond the Heideggerian "tarrying alongside," developing his intellect to the point of conjunction with the source of intelligence and the intelligibles (i.e., the Active Intellect). I should also emphasize that the moral and theoretical practices advanced by the exemplar are available to the seeker even without the exemplar. As we have seen, Alfarabi and Avicenna recognize the possibility of the individual's solitary self-disciplining and enlightenment, involving an intellectual inner dialogue. I return to this in Chapter 6.

I now turn to an examination of the Islamic Peripatetic accounts of the faculty of imagination and its spiritual possibilities. Islamic Peripatetic philosophers ascribe a uniquely creative function to imagination that requires a training (supervised by the intellect) and allows for a sensory experience of prophecy. This helps in seeing how Islamic Peripatetics reject the unbreachable divide between the physical and rational, in this case, using the aforementioned account of imagination. In chapter 5, I propose that the Muslim theologian, Ghazali, appropriates the Peripatetic account of imagination to constrain the intellectual aspirations of Islamic philosophy. I defend Islamic Peripatetics against this charge, and maintain that Ghazali's attacks and his charges of heresy suffer from a misunderstanding of philosophy and an impoverishment of the faculty of intellect and its capacities. This misunderstanding anticipates the plight of modern philosophy.

Chapter 4

Disciplining the Imagination

Intellect, Imagination, and Prophecy

Thus far, I have discussed the employment of spiritual exercises in Islamic Peripateticism to the point of the intellect's conjunction with the Active Intellect and the acquisition of intellectual insight. Avicenna considered this conjunction as necessary for prophecy, but the most prominent aspect of prophecy, in Alfarabi's writings and those of Avicenna himself, involves the faculty of imagination. In this chapter, I examine the treatment of this faculty and the relevant spiritual exercises for its cultivation in Islamic Peripateticism. My objective is to elaborate further the practice of spiritual exercises in Islamic philosophy and the way the intellect and the imagination are integrated with each other. In this process, I contrast Islamic Peripateticism with some modern philosophical accounts of the imagination in order to summon more evidence for the narrowness of the philosophical enterprise in the latter.

4.1. Prophetic Imagination

Intimacy with the Active Intellect, as we have seen in Chapter 3, may result in prophecy. For Avicenna, prophecy involves intellectual insight along with an imaginative dispensation of the means of salvation to the layperson.[1] Alfarabi, on the other hand, allows for intellectual insight, but distinguishes it from prophecy, which is restricted to the disseminations of the insight to the multitude by means of the perfected imagination.[2] In prophecies, imagination is impregnated directly by the Active Intellect, and provides for the acquisition of intellectual truths in the prescription of laws and practices. As we have seen, the observation of these laws and the engagement of these practices provide the human being with the means of rising above the domination of animal motivations and attaining practical and then theoretical wisdom.

Starting with Alfarabi, however, the Islamic Peripatetics also identify a poetic dimension in prophecy; my focus in the rest of this chapter is to explore the significance of poetic prophecy and set out its development in the writings of Avicenna and Alfarabi. Alfarabi, as we have seen, identifies the imaginative representation (*takhyīl*) as a significant moment in the act of prophecy as performed by the philosopher-prophet-lawgiver. Imagination's prophetic function is to produce imitations of the things supplied by the Active Intellect. Greek poetics does not explicitly allow for imagination's direct imitation (*mimēsis*) of the intelligibles. Plato's Socrates curtails the production and auditions of artistic/poetic imitations in the ideal city, as they are mere imitations of imitations and thus twice removed from the reality of Forms. As such, they hinder the cultivation of the soul (*Republic*, 597e). Aristotle, on the other hand, raises the status of poetry that, for him, imitates human actions (*Poetics*, 1448a), and as such "is something more philosophic and of graver import than history, since its statements are of the nature of universals, whereas those of history are singulars" (1451b6–8).[3] By a poetic universal statement, Aristotle means "one as to what such and such a kind of man will probably or necessarily say or do" (1451b9). So, poetic statements imitate intelligibles in actions, and they differ from philosophic statement due to their imitative quality. According to Aristotle, "imitation is natural to men" (1448b5) and human beings naturally "delight in imitations" (1448b10). Poetry, then, imitates universals in action, and because it is imitative, it gives rise to pleasure in human beings. The pleasures in such imitations facilitate understanding of the good life, drawing the individual into the process of refinement and thought (1452a).[4] Plato and Aristotle, however, do not relate artistic imitation to the faculty of imagination. Gerard Watson, in "Imagination: the Greek Background," argues that such a connection is available in Hellenistic philosophy. Watson traces the imagination's representation of divine intelligibles to the third century *Life of Apollonius* attributed to Philostratus.[5] According to Watson, the view presented in the *Life of Apollonius* is the expression of a marginal Stoic position that was in circulation even earlier than the third century C.E.[6] In the Neoplatonic tradition, Plotinus allows for the direct imitation of the forms in works of art,[7] but does not recognize the role of the faculty of imagination in this. His successor, Proclus, whose *Elementatio Theologica* was available in part to Islamic philosophers as Aristotle's *Book on the Pure Good*,[8] however, advances the view that imagination transforms intellectual truths into symbols and images.[9] Despite the availability of the account of imagination's imitation of the divine intellect in certain strands of Stoic and Neoplatonic philosophical traditions, there is no evidence that the relevant texts and doctrines were known to Muslim philosophers. Richard Walzer, as we saw in Chapter 1, insists that such a text must have been available to Muslims even if we do not have access to it.[10] The lack of evidence for such a text also supports the view that Islamic philosophers in all likelihood developed the account of imagination's involvement with the divine intellect on their own. Walzer does not entertain this (more plausible) option.

In the Islamic philosophical tradition prior to Alfarabi and Avicenna, al-Kindi is notable in ascribing to the imagination of cultivated individuals the prophetic ability to receive the sensible forms of things before they happen.[11] Elsewhere, al-Kindi also attempts to explain the prophecy of messengers like Muhammad. Messengers, according to al-Kindi, have philosophical insight into the worldly and supraworldly intelligibles without the preparation that philosophers require.[12] Moreover, messengers are able to present (rhetorically) their philosophical insights more effectively.[13] Here, al-Kindi could have drawn on and enhanced his own account of prophetic imagination, but he does not. Alfarabi, however, in *Kitāb al-ḥurūf* (*Book of Letters*), advances just such a connection between philosophical prophecy, artistic imitation of intelligibles, and the faculty of imagination. He maintains the following:

> The art of [religious] lawgiving (*al-waḍʿ al-nawāmis*) consists of the ability to represent imaginatively (*takhyīl*) what is difficult for the multitude to conceive of the theoretical intelligibles. It also consists in the ability to infer each of the beneficial political actions in attaining happiness, and the ability to persuade with respect to all the theoretical and practical matters that the multitude should be taught using all persuasive methods. . . . Through religion, the multitude are taught, educated, and given all that is needed in happiness.[14]

The imagination of the multitude is gripped by animal motivations. Therefore, their cognitions and actions are bereft of intellectual guidance. In this condition, their souls rise "up to seek the thing imagined or to flee from it, and be drawn to it or dislike it, even without a conviction of truth, just as a man is disgusted with something which, when he sees it, resembles what really calls forth disgust, though he is certain that what he sees is not what calls forth disgust."[15] Artfully designed speech and poetry can affect attraction and repulsion without reference to their contents, and this feature of animal imagination can be exploited.

The Qur'an warns of the perils of demonic poetry:

> Shall I inform you, (O people!), on whom it is that the evil ones (demons, *al-shayāṭin*) descend?
>
> They descend on every lying, wicked person,
>
> (Into whose ears) they pour hearsay vanities, and most of them are liars.
>
> And the Poets (*al-shu'arā*),—It is those straying in Evil, who follow them:
>
> Seest thou not that they wander distracted in every valley?
>
> And that they say what they practise not?
>
> Except those who believe, work righteousness, engage much in the remembrance of Allah, and defend themselves only after they are unjustly attacked. And soon will the unjust assailants know what vicissitudes their affairs will take! (26: 221–27)[16]

Demonic inspiration is the mark of the lying, the wicked and those who do not practice what they preach. In fact, there is a *ḥadith*—transmitted by Muḥammad ibn Isḥāq—that Prophet Muhammad, on receiving the first of his revelations, was devastated:

> Of all God's creatures there was none more odious to me than a poet or one possessed! I couldn't bear to look at them. . . . I said, "Oh, wretched me! A poet or a man possessed? Never shall Quraysh say that about me! Let me climb to the mountain's bare peak, hurl myself, and kill myself! Then shall I surely have rest!"[17]

The angel of revelation, Gabriel, intervenes and prevents him from this rash act, assuring him that his inspirations point to the truth, as they come from God.[18] Now, Alfarabi's account of religious imaginative representations follows the Islamic paradigm closely. The prophetic lawgiver exploits the pleasure and repulsion characterizing the behavior of animal imagination. He imitates, using the prophetic (perfected) imagination, the intellectual truths—theoretical and practical—given by the philosophical adaptation of the angel Gabriel (i.e., the Active Intellect).[19] Of course, as we have seen in Chapter 3, Alfarabi's philosophy provides a more important role for the Active Intellect, beyond that described by Aristotle. Alfarabi also assigns to it the role of the bestower of intelligibility (*al-wāhib al-ṣuwar*).[20] Given this modification, for Alfarabi, imaginative (poetic) imitations are not restricted to practical intelligibles, as is the case for Aristotle; imagination can also imitate theoretical intelligibles. Such imitations (of both the theoretical and the practical intelligibles), then, appeal to the multitude's animal motivations (the appetitive and the irascible). In other words, the intellectual truths, in their imaginative camouflage, become attractive to the public. As a result, the people's imaginations become engaged intellectually (albeit in a sensory disguise) and they can be set on the path to virtue and wisdom.

In describing the effectiveness of artistic imitations in bringing about a life ruled by intellect, Alfarabi gives the following analogy: "What the poet suggests in things by his words is like what the sculptor of a man suggests in the man and he who represents the other animals of animals he represents, and like the chess player suggests of military actions."[21] In other words, the representation of man (or animal) by the sculptor and the representation of combat by a game of chess are suggestive of that which is represented. The chess player or the viewer of the sculpture experiences military action and the body of the human being (or animal) by proxy. The result of these surrogate experiences is a training and preparation of the person for the actual experience. This is precisely what the imaginative representations of the prophetic lawgiver do. They guide the person toward the condition of dialogical thinking (*mufakira*), in which the intellect engages the animal powers of the soul, leading to the attainment of practical and theoretical virtue.

For Alfarabi, poetic prophecy is a mere reflection of and preparation for the intellectual life of the person and his fulfillment in conjunction with the Active Intellect. In other words, the poetic quality of the productions of the perfected imagination is significant only insofar as it persuades the person to embark on the ultimately intellectual path of conjoining with the spiritual order. Overall, for Alfarabi, prophecy is philosophy for the multitude.[22]

As we saw in Chapter 3, Avicenna, following Alfarabi, considers imagination's symbolism of the insights of theoretical intellect as essential to prophecy. For Avicenna, the philosopher-prophet, the one whose intellect is an acquired intellect, is conjoined to the Active Intellect, and thinks like the Active Intellect, that is, has theoretical knowledge actively (the knower and the known are one). In this state, it is "not unlikely that some of the effects of the holy spirit should . . . emanate into man's imagination (*al-mutakhayyala*)."[23] Such emanations are then depicted "in perceptible and audible images."[24] A capable imagination expresses in concrete form the abstract knowledge of the acquired intellect. All things considered, it seems that Avicenna accepts the general thrust of Alfarabi's account of the role of imagination in prophecy. However, Avicenna departs slightly from Alfarabi's position in accounting for prophecy as knowledge of past, present, and future events. Whereas Alfarabi declares that this form of prophecy is also a result of imagination's transactions with the Active Intellect, Avicenna considers it to be the result of imagination's contact with the souls of the celestial spheres.[25] (I will discuss this kind of imaginative prophecy in the next chapter.) Despite this modification in Avicenna's account of the prophecies of the faculty of imagination, the similarities between Avicenna and Alfarabi on prophetic imagination abound. Dimitri Gutas, however, argues that Avicenna's account of the prophecy of imagination moves away from Alfarabi's position because, in the latter, imagination conjoins with the Active Intellect.[26] In this case, the position ascribed to Alfarabi is questionable because the imagination is a faculty of the animal soul and it would be problematic if it received knowledge from the spiritual/intellectual realm. Jean (Yaḥyā) Michot points out that this account implies the unlikely view that animals could become prophets.[27] Michot and then later Gutas argue that Avicenna moves away from this knotty position by claiming that in each case of imaginative prophecy the faculty of intellect mediates between the spiritual realm and the imagination. In the case of imagination's articulation of the emanations of the Active Intellect, the theoretical intellect receives the knowledge and passes it to the imagination. Imagination's prophecies of past, present, and future events, however, is mediated by the practical intellect's reception of the relevant knowledge from the celestial souls.[28] This view prevents Avicenna from maintaining the awkward commitment to the prophetic abilities of animals, but is itself exegetically problematic in that it goes against Avicenna's claims about direct interactions between the faculty of imagination and the spiritual world.[29] In order to dismiss the difficult textual evidence, Michot argues that Avicenna *develops* the view that in each case of prophecy by the faculty of imagination, the human intellect receives knowledge from the spiritual world and passes it down to the imagination. The passages where Avicenna talks of the imagination's direct commerce with the spiritual realm hark back, in this view, to his earlier position that still was in the grip of Alfarabi's questionable view. Gutas, on the other hand, argues that the latter passages are elliptic and problematic formulations of the former.[30]

I agree that imagination needs the mediation of the intellect for its prophecies, but I want to show that this mediation is not in the forms that Michot and Gutas advocate. In other words, I submit that for Avicenna the intellect disciplines the imagination in order that it can receive the influences of the Active Intellect and the celestial souls. Furthermore, the intellectual disciplining of the imagination is supplemented by an account in which imaginative representation is independent of intellectual representation. This view, I believe, is available in Avicenna's *Poetics,* where he sets forth a more profound account of the uniqueness of imaginative representation. To do justice to the intricacies of Avicenna's position, we must enrich the language of our analysis by appeal to more modern philosophical accounts of aesthetic experience and judgment. What I have in mind is Immanuel Kant's account of the judgments of taste, and I submit that Kant's theories of the judgment of taste, and that of the sublime, are helpful in understanding more clearly Avicenna's account of imaginative prophecy and its autonomy vis-à-vis the cultivation of the intellect.

4.2. The Beautiful and the Sublime

In the *Critique of Judgment,* Kant maintains that the judgment of taste is a reflective judgment that is aesthetic, that is, it involves the receptivity of the subject to itself and yields the feelings of pleasure or displeasure (Ak. 203–4, trans. 44).[31] This judgment does not determine the appearance given in experience according to any purpose or interest: "Taste is the ability to judge an object, or a way of presenting it, by means of a liking or disliking devoid of all interest" (Ak. 211, trans. 53). The ability to resist interest in the object is an acquired capacity and Kant does not give a fair treatment of this issue. Had he done so, his claim that the judgment of taste involves a subjective universality would have become more accessible (Ak. 214–16, trans. 57–60). Subjective universality prescribes the norm observed by all subjects who have acquired the ability to approach an object not as a means but as an end in itself. Therefore, for the cultivated subject, if the presentation of the object involves the harmony of the imagination and understanding—the *ability* that presents us with an object and that of making it a cognition (without *actually* making it a cognition)—then we feel pleasure and judge the object beautiful. In this state, the subject is free of all interests including the interest to know or the interest to assess the object morally.

The judgment of taste is the judgment of reflection that lays open the space of things themselves. It is the Kantian equivalent of Heidegger's hermeneutic unveiling of the phenomena. Heidegger's account, however, has the added advantage of accentuating the practice of freeing the person from the interference of interests. Surprisingly, Heidegger himself is aware of the phenomenological significance of Kant's account of disinterested pleasure in the beautiful. In a rare reference to Kant's aesthetics, he writes: "Precisely by means of the 'devoid of interest' the essential relation to the object itself comes into play . . . now for the first time the object comes to the fore as pure object and that such coming forward into appearance is the beautiful. The word 'beautiful' means appearing to the radiance of such coming to the fore."[32] In this light, authenticity is the cultivation of taste, i.e., the ability to suspend one's interests before the phenomenon in order to experience it as it presents itself.

In the *Critique of Judgment*, Kant distinguishes the reflective judgment of taste from that of the sublime. He writes: "In presenting the sublime in nature the mind feels agitated, while in an aesthetic judgment about the beautiful in nature it is in restful contemplation. This agitation (above all at its conception) can be compared with a vibration, i.e., with a rapid alternation of repulsion from, and attraction to, one and the same object" (Ak. 258, trans. 115). The imagination presents an object, which it cannot contain as a totality according to the conceptual repertoire of understanding; this results in a feeling of repulsion, but then reason and its idea of the supersensible engage the presentation of the imagination and a harmony is struck; a feeling of pleasure ensues. The vibration or the oscillation between repulsion and attraction determines the presented object as sublime. What is expressed in this experience is the un-presentable, the power of "pure and independent reason" (Ak. 258, trans. 116). In other words, what is presented is that which makes possible the presentation of the ordinary phenomena. Reason's purposiveness (yet done without purpose) unveils the phenomena in the judgments of taste, and in the sublime it is itself presented indirectly (Ak. 246, trans. 100).

4.3. After Kant

Kant's self-described Copernican revolution in metaphysics involves the claim that the source of knowledge is reason's productive activity: "reason has insight only into that which it produces (*hervorbringt*) after a plan of its own (Bxiii)." Apparently, for knowledge to be possible, the rational subject must have already produced the object of knowledge.[33] In the B edition of the "Transcendental Deduction," Kant refers to the productive agency of reason as the "original synthetic unity of apperception" and the "I think" (B157). This ego, as distinguished from the empirical ego that is given in perception, is not experienced. The Kantian account of knowledge is offered to take the place of knowledge as conformity to the object because it allows for the demonstration of the claims to knowledge. Claims to knowledge are justified when they conform to the formal concepts involved in their production rather than by correspondence to things in themselves. Kant takes a similar step in regard to moral judgments: Their propriety is determined by the formal constraint of practical reason, articulated as the moral law or the categorical imperative.[34]

Iris Murdoch captures the problematic feature of the Kantian revolution well. In her insightful "Sovereignty of Good over Other Concepts," she writes:

> When Kant wanted to find something clean and pure outside the mess of the selfish empirical psyche he followed a sound instinct but, in my view, he looked in the wrong place. His inquiry led him back again into the self, now pictured as angelic; and inside this angel-self his followers have tended to remain.[35]

Murdoch's point is that rather than looking into the categorical structures of the thinking ego to buttress the claims of knowledge, Kant should have engaged in what she calls "unselfing," the work of removing the falsifying veil of self-absorption in order to gain access to the way things are.[36] Instead of engaging in self-transformative spiritual exercises to get at the things themselves, Kant's anxiety over the truth of our empirical claims to knowledge draws him into the inner vaults of the human mind. Nevertheless, in his account of the judgment of taste, as we have seen, he does approximate to Murdoch's notion of unselfing when he discusses reason's purposiveness without purpose. Furthermore, in his analysis of the judgment of the sublime, the forgotten magnificence of reason is recalled, when its power and grandeur—pale reflections of its glorious past—provide solace before empirical shock.[37]

G.W.F. Hegel, Kant's successor, aims to retrieve the glories of reason by providing a history of Spirit, an account of reason's attainment of self-consciousness. In his *Aesthetics*, Hegel divides the various forms of art in a way that corresponds to the different stages of the history of Spirit, because, for Hegel, art is the sensuous expression of the Spirit's consciousness of itself[38] (*Aes* I, 103; trans. 72).[39] The different forms of art are the symbolic, the classical, and the romantic (*Aes* I, 389–92; trans. 300–2). Symbolic art is the form of art during the Oriental phase of the history of Spirit. Jewish symbolism of the sublime relegates the Spiritual essence to a realm transcendent to the natural and, as such, mediates between the Persian—which still considers the Spiritual as natural—and the classical (*Aes* I, 412–13; trans. 318). To the classical corresponds the art of the Greek and Roman worlds. The classical art gives positive expression to the Spiritual; the Spiritual becomes real (*Aes* I, 391; trans. 301). Therefore, the classical is the transition to the romantic age when the Spiritual is finally appropriated by the individual human subject, whose free agency expresses the self-consciousness of the divine reason in the world (*Aes* II, 142; trans. 530). For Hegel, the romantic is the artistic manifestation of the Christian German world. In my essay, "Hegel and the Divinity of Light in Zoroastrianism and Islamic Phenomenology," I show that the symbolism of the sublime should not be understood, *pace* Hegel, as a mere relic of a past moment in the history of humanity.[40] In fact, an unprejudiced attention to the relevant phenomena indicates that Hegel construes prophetic symbolism too narrowly and that full human realization, through intellectual spiritual exercises, may yet establish a connection with and an inspiration by the transcendent Divine. In other words, prophecy has significance beyond the Hegelian account of it as the symbolism of the sublime (*Aes* I, 412–13; trans. 318), and, in fact, presupposes the Hegelian notion of the cultivation and liberation of the human subject. It is important to point out that Hegel's historicizing of spiritual development is also problematic in that it introduces a fundamental inequality among human beings, granting an essential superiority to those who occupy the later phases of the Spirit's progress. The Islamic Peripatetic theory of prophecy is devoid of such chauvinism.

Philippe Lacoue-Labarthes, in an essay titled "Sublime Truth," identifies the Heideggerian version of the judgment of the sublime in his work on the origin of the work of art. A great work of art, according to Heidegger, unveils the unveiling of beings; it accomplishes this by defamiliarizing, alienating, deranging, shocking, transporting, and retreating.[41] And for Lacoue-Labarthes, these terms bear striking resemblance to the vocabulary of the sublime. But the similarity is more than nominal:

> But it is obviously not merely a matter of vocabulary, just as one cannot say that Heidegger is innocent in matters of

> traditional vocabulary. What this text ("The Origin of the Work of Art") describes, in its own way and at a depth doubtless unknown before it, is the experience of the sublime itself. That is, it describes precisely what Heidegger elsewhere—notably concerning anxiety or being-unto-death—ascribes to the *ek-static* comportment of *Dasein* and *ek-sistence*. The shock produced by the work, the estrangement of the being, is such an ecstasy or ravishment. "It is the precipitation beyond oneself," as Burke says, which, from Longinus to Boileau and from Fenelon to Kant, has been described as the properly sublime emotion or affect.[42]

The experience of the sublime is ecstatic, it transports us beyond the ordinary, the familiar, and presents us with that which is beyond the realm of beings. It presents the unpresentable, the transcendence that makes possible the very presentations themselves. For Heidegger, therefore, the sublime unveils Dasein's authentic possibility for being, that which reaches beyond the "they-self." Here, Hegel's developmental history of Spirit has been abandoned, but the spiritual remains restricted to the human being's potential for authenticity or freedom. Heidegger's construal of the being of the human as Being-towards-Death also reflects the neglect of the manifold spiritual experiences beyond the features of the soul that draw us to self-realization and practical perfection. In the Islamic Peripatetics' account of the spiritual exercises of the theoretical intellect and imagination, the experience of the sublime gets articulated differently. For Avicenna, as we will see, the sublime experience is that experience which brings us to *divinalia* (i.e., the spiritual entities) whose symbolic manifestations help in the further transformation of the soul and its continuing perfection.

4.4. Avicenna on the Poetic Cultivation of Imagination

For Avicenna, the faculty of imagination (*al-mutakhayyala*) is one of the internal senses (*al-ḥawāss al-baṭina*). Avicenna's account of the internal senses expands on Aristotle's depiction of imagination (*phantasia*) as the faculty that mediates between sensation and thinking.[43] The expansion is also influenced by Alfarabi's fourfold classification of internal senses.[44] Avicenna's internal senses include the common sense (*al-ḥiss al-mushtarak* or *binṭāsyā*), representation (*muṣawwira* or *khayāl*), imagination (*mutakhayyala*), estimation (*wahm*), and memory (*ḥafiẓa al-dhākira*).[45] The faculty of imagination synthesizes and analyzes the psychological representations of empirical forms and embodied universals (i.e., intentions)[46] that are obtained by the common sense and estimation and are stored in representation and memory, respectively. The cultivation of the faculty of imagination comes to the fore when we turn to the way this internal faculty comes into interaction with the intellect (*al-'aql*), which names the two rational faculties of the human soul, the practical (*'amaliyya*) and the theoretical (*'ālima* or *naẓariyya*).[47] As we saw in the previous chapter, for Avicenna, the intellect, even in its potency, is the voice that challenges the combining and the dividing of the deliverances of sensory powers. Using the primary intelligibles (i.e., truths that are easy to perceive), the intellect bids the soul to think through the combinations of forms and intentions obtained by the animal cognitive powers, in order to arrive at the knowledge of the world and the grasp of the intelligibles.[48] In Chapter 3, we also discussed the close alliance between the animal perceptive powers and the animal motivational powers (i.e., the appetitive and the irascible). For Avicenna, the uncultivated intellect, which is in the grip of animal perceptive and motive powers, perceives and acts for the sake of basic sustenance, survival, and worldly interests. In Avicenna's account of the prerequisite ethical training for philosophy, it is the intellect that imposes a regimentation in a way that the soul becomes capable of acting for the sake of relevant moral intentions in the situation, rather than for the sake of one's animal needs and desires. The culmination of this ethical training is practical wisdom (i.e., the ability to recognize the objective good and act for the sake of it). The practically wise soul then empowers the theoretical intellect in its reflection on the deliverances of animal perceptive powers. The thinking that is freed from the obfuscation of animal motivations deliberates on the abstracted forms or intentions in a way that their combinations and separations correspond to the way things are in the world rather than to the interpretation we impose on it. In this way, thinking becomes all things, and its motion becomes activity (*energeia*). As such, it resembles the Active Intellect, receives emanations (i.e., secondary intelligibles), and may ultimately conjoin with the Active Intellect.

In the Poetics of *al-Shifā'* (the *Healing*), Avicenna distinguishes between philosophy and poetry thus: "One of these [philosophy] tells us of what was and can be, the other [poetry] speaks of that which exists only in word."[49] The Avicennan philosopher, as we have seen, cultivates the soul and conjoins with the Active Intellect by acquiring knowledge of the existents, both mundane and transcendent. The poet, however, educates the soul by attending to the existents "in words." Avicenna calls the verbal existent the imaginative representation. He observes:

> The imaginative representation (*al-takhyīl*) and the true-to-life presentation (*al-taṣdīq*) are both a kind of acceptance (*idh'ān*), except that the imaginative representation is an acceptance of the astonishment (*al-ta'ajjub*) and the delight (*al-iltidhādh*) in the discourse itself, while the objective presentation is an acceptance of the object as it is said to be. Thus, the imaginative representation is created by the locution itself, while the objective presentation is created by the objectivity of the locution's content.[50]

The philosopher pursues the discipline of the intellect by looking outward to become aware of objective truths. The poet, on the other hand, turns his attention inward and disciplines his imagination by discovering the criteria for the correctness of its synthesis and analysis of forms and intentions in the feelings of astonishment and delight.[51]

An imaginative representation may produce pleasure by fitting within the network of our particular ambitions or the web of our idiosyncratic preferences. Avicenna's poet is not interested in these feelings of pleasure because they point to purposes beyond the imaginary space. The authentic pleasure of the poet is in the intrinsic purposiveness of the image. So the poet's pleasure, to use Kantian aesthetic terminology, results from a purposiveness without purpose.[52] Avicenna's concept of astonishment can also be understood in relation to the Kantian text, specifically in relation to the notion of the sublime.[53] Astonishment is felt when an image overwhelms our ability to have a purpose—either by its magnitude or power. The pain of the disruption of our purposiveness is then supplemented by the pleasure of appreciating the image as a manifestation of an immense and powerful spiritual power (the Active Intellect for Avicenna and reason for Kant) that conditions the very possibility of having images.[54]

For Kant, the judgment of the sublime, like that of taste, is an acquired talent. It presupposes not only the cultivation of taste, but also moral sensibility (Ak. 292, trans. 158).[55] The person must have cultivated his practical faculty and recognized the weight of the moral law in his actions. Only then can reason interfere in imagination's desperation and provide solace to the anguished soul.[56] This helps in the appreciation of the significance of poetic pleasure and astonishment for Avicenna. The cultured subject is able to turn away from the material world with the aid of a training in virtue and a recognition of its spiritual source (i.e, the Active Intellect). For Avicenna, both the philosopher and the poet aim to conjoin with the Active Intellect. We have seen in Chapter 3 that the philosopher's practice begins with the cultivation of virtue, that is, the process of ruling the soul by the practical intellect. The training in virtue cuts off distractions and the distortions of mundane interests, enabling the soul to attend to things as they are. This then begins the process of outwardly directed study and thinking that draws from the emanations of the Active Intellect and culminates in the conjunction with the Active Intellect. The poet also benefits from a cultivation of virtue, by submitting to the rule of the practical intellect and curtailing appetites, passions and ambitions. As a result, he frees the imagination from its mundane servitude. The liberated imagination acquires its objectivity by being attentive to the intrinsic interestingness of the images and genuine feelings of pleasure and astonishment. In an earlier work, *Provenance and Destination* (*al-Mabda' wa'l-ma'ād*),[57] Avicenna describes the inspiration that befalls the liberated imagination:

> He who has a very powerful imagination and a very powerful soul is not completely distracted or engrossed by the sensible. That part of him which misses no opportunity to come into contact with that [intellectual/spiritual] realm is abundant—it being possible for it also in the waking state—and it pulls the imagination with it and sees the truth and retains it, while the imagination does its work: it represents what it sees in images, in the form of a visible and audible object of the senses.[58]

A liberated, strong imagination—one that is no longer governed by animal distractions and motivations and has acquired disinterestedness—is drawn to the Active Intellect, receives its inspirations, symbolizes them, and is enthralled by their sublimity: "The imagination then begins to represent these intelligibles (radiated upon the soul by the Active Intellect) and depict them in the common sense at which time the senses perceive an indescribable grandeur and power that belongs to God."[59] Finally, as we saw in Chapter 3, the prophetic symbols can then be communicated to the multitude for the sake of encouraging their exegesis, which in turn trains the exegete (in conjunction with the relevant spiritual exercises administered by the practical intellect) to the point of receiving the emanations of the Active Intellect.

Avicenna's account of poetry should not be construed too narrowly so as to exclude his symbolic narratives. Although a discussion of these three narratives, *Ḥayy ibn Yaqẓān*, the *Recital of the Bird*, and *Salāmān and Absāl*, is beyond the scope of this work, I note that these texts are also poetic in the sense previously stated.[60] I agree with

Sarah Stroumsa that we must distinguish these stories from fables (*amthāl*), which, for Avicenna, communicate results of experience and are not poetic as they do not deal primarily with the imaginative representation.[61]

The properly poetic symbolization of the emanations of the Active Intellect also affect the soul through their exegesis, refining imaginative understanding through the criteria supplied by the feelings of astonishment and pleasure and promoting the conjunction with the divine intellect. In the next chapter, I supply a philosophical model of symbolic exegesis when I discuss Avicenna's interpretation of the Qur'an's *Āyat al-nūr*, as well as his account of imaginative prophecy of the unseen and the future events in the context of Ghazali's appropriation of Avicenna's philosophy of imagination. Finally, I set forth the Islamic Peripatetic alliance of prophetic imagination and reason, when I face the challenges of Ghazali's attacks on the Peripatetics and their account of the unbounded reason.

Chapter 5

The Theologian's Dream

Imagination and Intellectual Heresy

It has been my overall objective in this book to argue that Islamic Peripateticism offers, to use Muhsin Mahdi's phrase, "a genuine form of rationalism" that is free of modern philosophy's excessively narrow construal of human reason. I have done this by articulating the Islamic Peripatetic account of the pervasiveness of intellect, and the cultivation of human intellect to the point of gaining access to what modern philosophy conveniently places out of the intellect's reach. One such "inaccessible" region is that of spiritual visionary phenomena; in Chapter 4, I elaborated on the spiritual dimension of the philosophical progress by working out the interaction between the intellect and the imagination, and the cultivation of prophetic imagination. In this chapter, I confront salient aspects of Ghazali's famous attack on Islamic Peripatetics in order to make clear how Peripatetics succeeded in preserving the full range of the philosophical spiritual practices and the associated quest for perfection.

Ghazali finds the Islamic Peripatetic project of reconciling philosophical enlightenment and Islamic salvation problematic, and I show that his rejection of the success of this project involves a misunderstanding. I begin with a description of Ghazali's privileging of dreams over intellect, and I show that his account of dreams draws from Peripatetic explanations of dreams, which are, in turn, derived from their accounts of prophetic imagination. I then contrast Ghazali's interpretation of prophetic symbols, and the self-cultivation contained therein, with that of Avicenna in order to illustrate their varying prophetologies. Finally, I present Ghazali's official objections to the Peripatetics and draw from Averroes' replies to diagnose the underlying reasons for Ghazali's polemics. I contend that he interprets philosophy merely as the production of rational thought and, and as a result, misses out on the spiritual core of the Islamic philosophical project. I then show that Ghazali's misunderstanding of philosophy as mere rational discourse issues from a misapprehension of the function of the faculty of intellect, and culminates in an unnecessary restriction of the spiritual reach of the philosophical enterprise. It is a version of this restriction that replicates itself in modern philosophy and contributes to the problematic modern receptions of Islamic philosophy.

5.1. Ghazali on Dreams

Ghazali sought to restrict the faculty of intellect to its discursive function. In other words, for Ghazali, intellect is restricted to its role in deliberation, that is, dialogical thinking (*mufakira*);[1] it engages the deliverances of imagination and apprehends "things necessary, possible, impossible."[2] In his spiritual autobiography, *Al-Munqidh min al-ḍalāl* (*The Deliverer from Error*), Ghazali argues that "[b]eyond intellect, there is yet another stage. In this another eye is opened, by which he beholds the unseen, what is to be in the future, and other things which are beyond the ken of intellect in the same way as the objects of intellect are beyond the ken of" (*Munqidh*, 73; trans. 64) lower faculties. Ghazali rejects the Islamic philosophers' commitment to the intellect's perception of theoretical intelligibles as well as the spiritual realm of separate intellects. In their place, he defends a purely Islamic spiritual domain, and assigns to the power of imagination, instead of the intellect, the key to that domain:

> God most high, however, has favoured his creatures by giving them something analogous to the special faculty of prophecy, namely dreams. In the dream state, a man apprehends what is to be in the future, which is something of the unseen; he does so either explicitly or else clothed in symbolic form whose interpretation is disclosed. (ibid.)

The special faculty of prophecy is restricted to God's chosen prophets. Dreaming, however, according to Ghazali, is analogous to it and can be prophetic (*Munqidh*, 73–74; trans. 66). Ghazali's account of dreams draws from an aspect of the Peripatetic account of the prophetic imagination (i.e., prophecies involving the knowledge of past, present, and future events) in order to counter Peripatetic intellectualism. To show the full significance of Ghazali's account of imagination, it is helpful to see it in the context of the Peripatetic views on the role of the faculty of imagination in veridical dreams.

Aristotle claims that it is unlikely that veridical dreams, i.e., dreams that foretell the future, were sent by God, as the people who enjoyed such dreams were "commonplace persons and not the most intelligent" (*Parva Naturalia*, 464a20).[3] For Aristotle, these dreams were a result of the dormancy of the senses and the relinquishment of the bond of thinking (464a23). In this state, imagination gets impregnated by a demonic nature, intermediate between man and the divine, and prophesizes the future (463b13–15).[4] In the Islamic Peripatetic tradition, the demonic intermediary becomes identified as the Active Intellect and veridical dreams become God-sent, because the Active Intellect is, in turn, identified with the angel of revelation. The author of the *Treatise on Dreams* (attributed to Avicenna) maintains:

> From this it is clear that the cause of veridical dream-visions is God, may He be praised, and that He informs man, through the Intermediary of the Universal Intellect (*al-'aql al-kullī*), of what will happen in the future to himself and of what will happen to the whole world. This Universal Intellect is, as it were, an intermediary between the Creator, may He be exalted, and man's particular soul; (and) God, may He be praised, has created (in the Universal Intellect) at one and the same time (*daf'atan*) the forms of (the things) that came to pass (*al-kā'ināt*).[5]

The Universal Intellect or the Active Intellect[6] mediates between man and God, bestowing the latter's gift of guidance upon the former. The veridical dreams are then imaginative prophecy in that they are the mundane expression of emanations from the Active Intellect. The Avicennan text rejects the Aristotelian thesis that the veridical dreams do not occur to the wise man. In fact

> [t]here are two classes among the generality of people over which the providence (due to this force) watches most particularly, and the protection of which (on this force's part) is more perfect—be it in dreams by showing and warning (a man) about things which are going to happen or in other circumstances. . . . (These two classes are): 1. The just kings . . . 2. The excellent philosophers (*ḥukamā*) and men of knowledge (*'ulamā*). . . . Hence there is no doubt that the providence of him that safeguards (these) two (classes of people) is proportionate to the multiplicity of the benefits (they bestow) and their great worth.[7]

The divine favor and the prophetic insight that are conferred on the perfected souls are standard features of Islamic Peripatetic prophetology. In this prophetology, the highest station of human perfection belongs to the philosopher-prophet-king, as confirmed by the author of the Dream treatise: "If the king were to be full of knowledge, wise, just, good, he would (attain) the ultimate source of human perfection and nobility and the provisions (deriving) from the divine force would be (proportionately) most perfect and complete in relation to him."[8]

I find the discussion in this text (attributed to Avicenna) to have Aristotelian roots, but it certainly does not capture the full scope of the views of Alfarabi and Avicenna on the matter of imaginative prophecy. It is Aristotelian in that in it imaginative productions represent particular (future) events, and not the theoretical intelligibles. The account of the imagination's imitation of the intelligibles, as we have seen, is a central feature of Alfarabi's *Book of Letters* and its enrichment by Avicenna marks the peculiar feature of the Islamic Peripatetic account of the poetic quality of prophetic imagination. Moreover, Avicenna, in his authentic works, accounts for the prophecy of the future events (*al-kā'ināt*) and the unseen (*al-mughayyabāt*) in the past and the present in a different way. According to Avicenna, the prophecy of such events is a result of the transmission of images by the souls of heavenly bodies. The heavenly souls imagine the decrees of separate intelligences, and the veridical visions (in dreams and while awake) receive these images and can recognize in them the knowledge pertaining to one's concerns in this world.[9] This is due to the congeneric similarity (*al-mujānasa*) between human souls and the souls of celestial bodies, on account of the latter's knowledge of the physical world.[10] Avicenna maintains that, in order to receive the relevant influx from the souls of the heavenly bodies, the imagination must be strong;[11] this strength, as in the case of the imagination that receives from the Active Intellect, is obtained through a training in virtue.[12]

I should mention that together with intellectual prophecy and the prophecy of the imagination, Avicenna advocates a third kind of prophecy involving the motive faculty (*al-quwwa al-muḥarraka*). This is prophecy as the working of miracles, and the prophet can "cure the sick and make evil persons sick, disintegrate and integrate organisms . . . [and bring] ruins and prosperity, the sinking of the earth and plagues."[13] A discussion of this kind of prophecy is beyond the scope of this text, but I address imaginative prophecy and the symbolic expressions of the emanation of the Active Intellect in the next section of this chapter. Here, it is worth mentioning that some historians of Avicenna's philosophy have tried to underplay the dimension of prophecy emphasized in religious contexts (i.e., the prophecy of imagination and the working of miracles). Dag Hasse, for example, finding it difficult to team the plausible intellectual prophecy with the other forms, claims that it is unlikely that the three types of prophecy can ever be present in one person: "It seems improbable that a prophet could at the same time have visions through a strong imaginative faculty, produce rain through his strong will, and hit easily upon middle terms of syllogisms through his strong intellect."[14] Muhammad Afifi al-Akiti, however, rejects this conclusion and points to passages from Avicenna's *Mabda'* and *Aḥwāl*, in which Avicenna explicitly states that the properties are, at times, combined in one person.[15] Al-Akiti shows that Avicenna's prophetology is motivated by religious (Islamic) considerations, and its religious appropriations by subsequent thinkers, like Ghazali, is not against the grain of Avicenna's view. He concludes that Ghazali's "'Islamization' was only made possible by Avicenna, who successfully adapted *falsafa* to the Islamic milieu in the first place."[16]

Ghazali's debt to the Avicennan account of prophetic imagination is complex. We have seen that he rejects the intellectualism of the Peripatetics and substitutes Islamic spiritual entities in place of the separate intellects. In *Tahāfut al-falāsafa* (*The Incoherence of the Philosophers*), for instance, he affirms the Peripatetic notion of imaginative prophecy thus:

> When it [imagination] becomes dominant and strong and does not become absorbed by the senses and preoccupation [with them], it sees the Preserved Tablet, the forms of future particular events becoming imprinted on it. This happens to the prophets in their waking hours, to the rest of people in their sleep.[17]

Here, the reference to the Preserved Tablet (*al-lawḥ al-maḥfūẓ*) is meant to make sense of the prophecy of particulars in the future, as involving the Preserved Tablet which according to the Qur'an contains the destiny of the world.[18] The Preserved Tablet is the Islamicization of the images of the decrees of separate intelligences formed by the imagination of the heavenly bodies. Ghazali also emphasizes that the imagination must be strong, and in the *Deliverer from Error* he specifies that the acquisition of this strength is a feature of Sufi ascetic practices (*Munqidh*, 74; trans. 66), which, like the Peripatetic training in virtue, enable the moderation of the animal soul.

It is important to emphasize that, for Avicenna, the prophecy of the future is not the same as the prophetic insight into spiritual entities;[19] the latter insight is possible either through intellectual intuition of the acquired intellect or through the Active Intellect's direct inspiration of the perfected imagination.[20] Both possibilities are only available to individuals who have achieved conjunction with the Active Intellect (i.e., prophets or philosopher-prophets). Ghazali, as I have mentioned above, dismisses the Islamic Peripatetic account of separate heavenly intellects (and their bodies and souls), and limits intellect to its commerce with the physical world. For him, the apprehension of extra-intellectual entities is an important function of prophecy proper (*Munqidh*, 74; trans. 66). Therefore, both Ghazali and Avicenna allot a lower status to the prophecy of future events and distinguish it from the kind of prophecy that has insight into heavenly beings. For Avicenna, the intellection or the imagining of the separate intellects and the theoretical intelligibles is a principle feature of prophecy. For Ghazali, the encounter with God's angels, the substitutes for Peripatetic separate intellects, is available to prophets and trained mystics (*Munqidh*, 69; trans. 61). In regard to spiritual beings, the mystic can work with the symbols and representations given by the prophet and cultivate himself by understanding their meaning and value.

5.2. Ghazali and Avicenna on the Interpretation of Prophetic Symbols

In *Mishkāt al-anwār* (*The Niche of Lights*), Ghazali illustrates the mystic's traffic with the *divinalia* through the exegesis of the famous Qur'anic Light verse:

> God is the light
> Of the heavens and the earth.
> The parable of His Light
> Is as if there were a Niche
> And within it a Lamp:
> That lamp enclosed in a Glass:
> The glass as it were a brilliant star:
> Lit from the blessed Tree,
> An Olive, neither of the East
> Nor of the West,
> Whose oil is well-nigh
> Luminous,
> Though fire scarce touched it:
> Light upon Light!

God doth guide
Whom he will
To His Light:
God doth set forth Parables
For men; and God
Doth know all things. (24: 35)

Ghazali begins by examining the meaning of "light" (*nūr*) as that "which is seen in itself and through which other things are seen, such as the sun."[21] He then argues that this sense of "light" (i.e., the natural light) is not the primary one, because there are other luminous beings that, in addition to the qualities possessed by the natural light, "see" themselves and others. Therefore, sense perception is superior to the sun as the more primary bearer of the name "light" (because the sun does not perceive) [*Mishkāt,* 4]. Intellect, however, corrects sense perception, so it is even more primary than sense perception as that which "light" names (*Mishkāt,* 9). Ghazali does not end his analysis here; he proceeds by arguing that if there is something that "allows other things to see, while seeing itself and others, then it is [even] more worthy of the name 'light' " (*Mishkāt,* 12–13). All prophets, whose succession terminates in Prophet Muhammad, are lights in this sense.[22] They give human beings prophetic wisdom (*ḥikma*) that illuminates their minds as the sun illuminates the eyes (*Mishkāt,* 10). The laws and practices that the prophets institute provide the guidance and illumination by which human beings cultivate their souls and acquire the ability to see the divine light. Wisdom is the withdrawn source of light whose laws make absolute demands on the faithful's actions. Through the observation of the law and the path (leading to the cultivation of the character and the mind), the human subject *tastes* the transcendent divine wisdom (*Mishkāt,* 32–34). He becomes the intimate of the prophet and his divine wisdom.

However, beyond the prophets, the even more worthy bearer of the name "light," according to Ghazali, is "the holy prophetic spirit" (i.e., Gabriel, the messenger angel of revelation). He truly deserves this name in relation to earthly lights (*Mishkāt,* 13). Insofar as the heavenly lights are concerned, God, "the Lordly Presence," is, of course, the most perfect, and the angels or heavenly lights (in whose company Gabriel is included) are ranked in accordance with their proximity to the divine light (*Mishkāt,* 14). In relation to the symbols of the Qur'anic verse, Ghazali interprets the light-giving lamp as the Prophet Muhammad, and the luminous oil is understood as the holy prophetic spirit, which is lighted by the fire of the highest archangel (not Gabriel), "who has seventy thousand faces: in every face are seventy thousand tongues, through all of which he glorifies God" (*Mishkāt*, 13).

In summary, Ghazali enumerates the various luminous phenomena (natural light of the sun, perception, intellect, and prophecy) and looks for the primary sense of "light" by discovering internal criteria that distinguish a luminous phenomenon as conditioning the others. In this process, he purports to suspend all assumptions, attends to how things appear, and describes their particular intelligibility.[23] The suspension of prejudice and the ability to attend to the actual features of things are won through a training that frees the subject from error. In the *Niche of Lights*, Ghazali articulates this training for virtue in the move toward the more primary referents of the term "light." Every recognition of a more primary sense of "light" involves a transmutation in the subject. As the subject turns away from the enchantments of the empirical and the abstract, the bodily and the rational, he is drawn away from the accidental, toward the essential. This interpretive movement (*ta'wīl*) involves the subduing of the lower dimensions of the self, and brings about his intimacy with the divine source of intelligibility (*Mishkāt*, 6–10).[24]

Although unique in important respects, Ghazali's interpretation of the Light verse is indebted to the work of his predecessor, Avicenna. In *Fī ithbāt al-nubuwwāt* (*On the Proof of Prophecies*), Avicenna, after characterizing prophecy philosophically, proceeds to the interpretation of the aforementioned Qur'anic light verse. God is light, the "niche" is the material intellect (*al-'aql al-hayūlānī*)—the lowest level of human intellect, and the "lamp" is the acquired intellect (*al-'aql al-mustafād*)—the intellect of the philosopher and the prophet. The glass separating the niche from the lamp symbolizes the intermediate levels of the intellect, that is, the stages in the development of the intellect preceding the acquired intellect's conjunction with the Active Intellect. The intermediate intellects include the habitual intellect (*al-'aql bi-l-malaka*) and the actual intellect (*al-'aql bi-l-fi'l*). Active Intellect is symbolized by the fire that illuminates the fine oil of the intellectual power, endowing it with an understanding beyond what the intellect could obtain on its own resourcefulness. This fire, of course, is not God, because it is not a unity. The true God is one and gives unity to the manifoldness of the Active Intellect.[25]

Avicenna is committed to the symbolic dimension of prophetic utterances, not as a ploy to make the meaning inaccessible to the average audience. Rather, as we have seen, he believes that symbolism provides for a cultivation of the imagination based on feelings of pleasure and astonishment. The cultivation of imagination makes transparent the relation between the symbol and its referent. In the case of prophetic symbolism, the hermeneutics of the inspired symbols brings us to imaginatively entertain what the philosopher's intellectual hermeneutics aims to behold intellectually. In the above interpretation of the Light Verse, Avicenna is emphasizing the relation between what the accomplished philosopher understands intellectually and what the adept exegete of symbols beholds imaginatively.

Comparing Ghazali's interpretation of the light verse with that of Avicenna, it becomes apparent that both place the subject in a regimen (i.e., a set of spiritual exercises) to improve his soul. This regimen involves the acquisition of virtue and culminates in the conjunction with *spiritualia*. The prophet institutes the elements of this regimen, which is comprised of the laws and the practices of religion. The ideal subject learns to appreciate the various meanings of "light" that are beyond natural light, by submitting to the conditioning for wisdom in religious practice.[26] The difference is the premium that Avicenna places on intellectual training and the resulting (intellectual) access to what the prophet depicts symbolically. Ghazali denies intellectualism and accuses Avicenna and his fellow Islamic Peripatetics of heresy. In the next section, I examine the core of Ghazali's charges against Muslim Peripatetics and defend them using Averroes' replies.

5.3. Ghazali's Charge of Heresy Against Islamic Peripatetics and Averroes' Reply

It is well known that Ghazali accused the Muslim Peripatetics of being heretics on account of their adherence to three specific doctrines. To challenge this verdict, I draw from the work of the great Andalusian Muslim Peripatetic, Ibn Rushd (Averroes). In a short work titled *Kitāb faṣl al-maqāl (The Decisive Treatise)*, Averroes refutes Ghazali's case against the Islamic Peripatetics by rejecting Ghazali's understanding of philosophy as the production of rational knowledge beholden to the beliefs of its Greek founders. Averroes maintains that philosophy as appropriated by Muslims should rather be understood as a legitimate practice within the constraints of Islam.[27]

In the *Incoherence of the Philosophers*, Ghazali maintains that the Islamic Peripatetics hold twenty theses that are false, three of which he considered so grave as to constitute heresy (*kufr*).[28] Already in this account we see that Ghazali is approaching his Peripatetic rivals as heretics because of the theses they advance and defend rather than the nature of their philosophical activity. The heretical theses endorsed by Muslim Peripatetics are (1) God does not know the particulars, (2) the world is eternal, and (3) bodies are not resurrected.[29] Ghazali refutes each of the twenty theses rationally, with evidence from the Qur'an and other relevant sources. I will not relate the details of Ghazali's arguments, but rather show how Averroes, for each of the heretical theses, diminishes the force of the controversy and presents the philosophers as dealing with the Islamic revelation legitimately, albeit differently than Ghazali. To begin, Averroes argues that philosophers do not claim that God does not know the particulars; they claim rather that He does not know them the way humans do. God knows the particulars as their creator while humans know them as a privileged creation of God would know them.[30] In regard to the eternity of the world, Averroes shows that the philosophers agree with Ghazali that there is a God, that God created the existent things, and that the world (containing the existent things) extends infinitely into the future. What the dispute concerns is merely the past of the world. Philosophers argue that the world is without a beginning in time, whereas Ghazali disagrees. Averroes argues that the scope of this disagreement is insufficient to constitute heresy and he also introduces Qur'anic verses to defend the Peripatetic view (*Faṣl al-maqāl*, 16). Finally, as to the resurrection of bodies, Averroes argues that Peripatetic philosophers agree with Ghazali that the soul is immortal and that bodies are resurrected on the judgment day. The dispute rather turns on the issue whether the bodies that will be resurrected will be the same material bodies that had perished. Islamic Peripatetics argue that "existence comes back only to a likeness of what has perished" (*Faṣl al-ṃaqāl*, Appendix 46). More precisely, the resurrected body is identical in its attributes to the perished body but it is not composed of the same material. Again the point is that the difference in the position of the philosophers and that of Ghazali is insignificant and does not constitute grounds for the condemnation of the former as heretics (*Faṣl al-maqāl*, 20–21).

Averroes' engagement in the above dialectical joust with Ghazali aims at mitigating the effect of the latter's attack on the philosophers and is not the substance of his response to Ghazali. The substance concerns Ghazali's metaphilosophical assumptions. Averroes distinguishes between three methods (*ṭuruq*, sing. *ṭarīqa*), aimed at generating true presentation (*taṣdīq*): rhetorical (*khiṭābiyya*), dialectical (*jadaliyya*), and demonstrative (*burhāniyya*) (*Faṣl al-maqāl*, 24). The rhetorical method is suitable to the public preacher for the purpose of appealing to an audience's (untutored) imagination and passions.[31] The dialectical method is the preferred approach of the theologians in order to explore the truth through rational analysis and argumentation. The demonstrative method, however, is that of the philosopher, and it is a spiritual hermeneutics (*ta'wīl*) that gets at the origin (*awwal*) of things (i.e., their truth). The first two methods begin by assumptions shared by and *apparent* to the multitude and then proceed to other assumptions based on either persuasive or rational norms. Only the demonstrative method gets at the real by going beyond *appearances*:

> God has been gracious to His servants for whom there is no path by means of demonstration—either due to their innate dispositions, their habits, or their lack of facilities for education—by coining for them likenesses (*amthāl*) and similarities of these [hidden things] and calling them to assent by means of those likenesses, since it is possible for assent to those likenesses to come about by means of the indications shared by all—I mean, the dialectical and the rhetorical. This is the reason for the Law (*al-shar'*) being divided into an apparent sense and an inner sense. For the apparent sense is those likenesses coined for those meanings, and the inner sense is those meanings that reveal themselves only to those adept in demonstration. (*Faṣl al-maqāl,* 19)

The method of demonstration is the method of getting at the real things. But God has provided—by means of revelation—likenesses of the real for those disinclined to engage in the demonstrative method. The Law, which includes the Qur'an and the Sunna, contains the images of the real. Theologians and preachers work on these images without seeking the originals. Philosophers, however, pierce the image and unveil the hidden original (*awwal*) through their certain hermeneutics (*al-ta'wīl al-yaqīnī*). Averroes also refers to the demonstrative *ta'wīl* as the art of wisdom (*ṣinā'at al-ḥikma*) (*Faṣl al-maqāl,* 26), a practice which has something to do with the aptitude (*al-fiṭra*), the habit (*al-'āda*), and the education (*al-ta'allum*). The articulation of *ta'wīl*, as an art that has to be cultivated in the person, points to the practice of spiritual exercises constituting the core of philosophy. These exercises are geared toward molding the character and mind such that one shuns falsehoods and becomes intimate with the source of truth, the Active Intellect. It is here that Averroes' principal criticism of Ghazali's attack on the philosophers comes out. According to Averroes, Ghazali assesses philosophical theses as if they were theological ones that are arrived at through the employment of the dialectical method (*al-ṭarīqa al-jadaliyya*). Rather, according to Averroes, philosophical principles must be examined for their service to the practice of philosophy (*al-ṭarīqa al-burhāniyya*) and the activity of aiming at the original (*al-ta'wīl*).

Averroes' interpretation suggests that, in general, philosophy is aligned with Islam. But, more importantly, *Muslim* philosophers have the further advantage of working with the Islamic law and practices (i.e., the laws and practices given by the culminating divine revelation) and therefore possess a more direct path to the truth. In *Tahāfut al-tahāfut* (*Incoherence of the Incoherence*), a text devoted to a more detailed refutation of Ghazali's attacks on the philosophers, Averroes writes:

> [Islamic Peripatetic philosophers] are of the opinion that a human being has no life in this abode but by means of practical arts, and no life in this abode or in the final abode but by means of theoretical virtues; that neither one of these two is completed or obtained by him but by means of the practical virtues; and that the practical virtues are not firmly established but through cognizance of God (may He be exalted) and magnifying Him by means of devotions set down in the law for them in each and every religion—such as offerings, prayers, invocations, and similar speeches spoken in praise of God (may He be exalted), the angels, and the prophets.[32]

It is evident then that Averroes follows the earlier Muslim Peripatetics in understanding philosophy as a way of life aspiring to the cultivation of practical and theoretical virtues. Moreover, this cultivation is in accord with the Islamic revelation (i.e., the final revelation) as containing the truth and the practices leading to this truth in a way that entices the imagination and the intellect of the multitude. The reliance on Islamic law, practices, and beliefs as supplied by the revelations of Prophet Muhammad confirms the status of Averroes and his Peripatetic predecessors as Muslims—a point that I explored in detail in Chapter 3 in dealing with earlier Peripatetic prophetology. Perhaps it would be appropriate to end this discussion with Avicenna's quatrain, which he composed in response to those who accused him of heresy:

> It is not so easy and trifling to call me a heretic;
> No faith in religion is firmer than mine.
> I am a unique person in the whole world and if I am a heretic,
> Then there is not a single Muslim anywhere in the world.[33]

In this chapter, I examined Ghazali's influential reaction to Islamic Peripateticism, concluding that Ghazali aims to preserve Islamic spirituality from a Peripatetic fusion. Certainly, his apparent thought is that such a fusion corrupts the authentic revelation and results in heresy. As we have seen, the concern with philosophical corruption of Islam emerges from Ghazali's (perhaps intentional) misunderstanding of the nature of the philosophical enterprise. Ghazali interprets philosophy as the production of rational discourse, and as I already showed in Chapter 1, this reading of philosophy misses out on the spiritual focus of philosophy (including the Peripatetic tradition). On the reading that recognizes the focus on spiritual practice, Islamic philosophical intellectualism is understood as a practice of spiritual exercise, aiming to return the individual to the font of intelligibility (i.e., to the Divine source of truth). This is a far cry from Ghazali's construal of intellect as the faculty of rational discourse. As a result, Ghazali substitutes the faculty of imagination for the intellect, and advocates a cultivation of imagination as the preparation for intimacy with the Divine. I have shown that Ghazali's privileging of the imagination draws from the Islamic Peripatetic account of the prophecies of imagination, and that Avicenna had already reconciled the imagination and the intellect.

It is hard to understand how Ghazali, despite his keen mind and deep erudition, failed to recognize the nuances of the merger between Islam and philosophy. In an earlier work, I proposed that Ghazali's attacks on philosophy had a political source.[34] Ghazali was a protégé of the powerful Seljuq vizier, Niẓām-al-mulk.[35] The Seljuq military, powered by Turcoman tribesmen, conquered the eastern Islamic world under the banner of Sunni Islam, but it faced resistance from the Shi'i Fatimids in the west and the Isma'ili assassins in its own territories. It is also important to note that the western part of the Seljuq empire was previously governed by the Buyids, who were Duodeciman Shi'a, and these governors and leaders had, for the most part, promoted the work of Islamic philosophers.[36] The Isma'ili thinkers also had systematically incorporated philosophy into their core theology. Ghazali was, for a while, the dean of the most prominent Sunni *madrasa*,[37] the *Niẓāmiyya* of Baghdad (named after its aforementioned founder, Nizām-al-Mulk who sought to challenge the intellectual influence of Shi'i Islam).[38] Therefore, it is not surprising that his work contains assaults on Shi'i Islam and its ally, Islamic philosophy. Although Ghazali's work succeeded in weakening the mainstream reception of Islamic philosophy, Islamic philosophy survived Ghazali's assault and continued to prosper. However, it is important to note that Averroes' influence on the subsequent Islamic philosophical tradition was not significant. In the conclusion, I treat briefly the appropriation of the Islamic Peripatetic tradition by the great Sunni philosopher and Sufi, Suhrawardi. His Illuminationist philosophy preserved and expanded the central insights of Peripatetic Islamic philosophers, preparing the ground for the sixteenth-century renaissance of Islamic philosophy in the Shi'i school of Isfahan. I then examine the central features of the position of the greatest of Isfahan's philosophers and discuss the status of philosophy as a practice of spiritual exercises in the contemporary Islamic world.

Chapter 6

On Human Finitude, Conscience, and Exemplarity

A Comparison between Islamic Peripateticism and Heideggerian Phenomenology

We have already seen that the Islamic Peripatetic ideal of humanity acquires a spiritual (i.e., prophetic) status through an intellectual cultivation of his soul. The account of the being of the human (i.e., the soul) must accommodate this spirituality. In Chapter 2, we examined Corbin's critique of the limitations of the Heideggerian account of the being of the human (i.e., Dasein). More specifically, we saw that the Heidegger of *Being and Time,* who defines Dasein as a Being-towards-Death, ignores the spiritual dimension of the human individual, which becomes available when the practice of spiritual exercises continues beyond the stage of autonomous tarrying alongside entities. In the Islamic philosophical tradition, the being of the human—the human soul—gets articulated, to use Corbin's phrase, as a Being-towards-*Beyond*-Death. The Being-towards-Beyond-Death of Islamic philosophy receives its explicit treatment in the Peripatetic psychology of Avicenna, in his famous Flying Man argument, where he argues for the separate existence of the soul from the body and the soul's immortality. In this chapter, I examine the Islamic Peripatetic notion of the immortality of the soul and its constitution through the practice of spiritual exercises. I then contrast the position advanced by Islamic Peripatetic philosophers with that of Heideggerian phenomenology. I maintain that Islamic Peripateticism is in possession of a more comprehensive sense of philosophy, which is capable of better accommodating the range of human experiences and possibilities.

6.1. Being-Towards-Beyond-Death: On the Immortality of the Soul in Islamic Peripateticism

In chapter 1 of the Psychology of *al-Shifā'*, Avicenna defines the soul as "the primary entelechy (*kamāl awwal*) of a natural body organized so as to carry out the function of life" (*al-Shifā' DA* 12; trans. 559).[1] He defines "entelechy" as that by which a living being becomes an actual and functioning living being (*al-Shifā' DA* 8; trans. 557). The soul is a *primary* entelechy as distinguished from a secondary entelechy. He defines primary entelechy as "what makes things actually members of their species" (*al-Shifā' DA* 11; trans. 559). So soul is what makes living things alive. This is in contrast to a secondary entelechy, which is "some activity or disposition attendant on members of the species" (ibid.). Thus, secondary entelechies are exhibited by some members of a species, but their exhibition is not necessary for membership in that species. In the case of human beings, Avicenna mentions discrimination, vision, perception, and motion as examples of secondary entelechy (ibid.).

Avicenna reluctantly and with qualification employs the familiar Aristotelian account of the soul as the form of the body. He says that entelechy in relation to matter "may be called a form" (*al-Shifā' DA* 6; trans. 556). We do not need to appeal to this language to see the parallel between Avicenna's view of the soul and that of Aristotle. It is well known that in the *De Anima*, Aristotle defines the soul as "the entelecheia of the body" (414a26).[2] But both Avicenna and Aristotle have a more complex account of the soul.

For Aristotle, as he is commonly understood, the soul as the form of the body could not exist separately from the body as such. At least part of the soul would corrupt with the body (*De Anima*, 413a4–6). Avicenna, however, underscores that a part of the soul does not corrupt with the body, because for him the soul, properly understood, is a substance that exists independently of the body. This independence is emphasized when Avicenna defines substance as that which "exists in nothing whatever as in a substrate" (*al-Shifā' DA* 9; trans. 558). Substantiality is not relative, according to Avicenna. In other words, if something "is present in a thousand things 'otherwise than as in a substrate,' once it is found in such a manner as things are found in a substrate, then it is an accident (and not a substance)" [*al-Shifā' DA* 9–10; trans. 558].

Having introduced his account of the soul, Avicenna states the famous Flying Man argument for the existence of the soul.

> Each of us must suppose himself to have been created all at once, fully developed and perfectly formed but veiled to the sight of external objects, floating in the atmosphere or in space, not buffeted by the air in which he floats (which might allow perception) and with all his organs disjoined from one another, no contact or continuity among them. Then he should consider whether he could still affirm the existence of his self. No doubt he could—but without adding to it any of his limbs or internal organs, not his brain, or his heart, or guts—or anything external. . . . And if in such a state it were possibly for him to imagine such a thing as a hand or other organ, he would not imagine it as a part of himself or a condition of his existence. (*al-Shifā' DA* 16; trans. 561–62)[3]

So it appears that for Avicenna the soul is the separately existing subject of self-awareness. In the accounts supplied by some historians of Greek philosophy, Avicenna's view would amount to a synthesis of Platonism and Perpipateticism. Michael Frede, for instance, argues that "[a]ccording to the Platonists the soul not only is that in virtue of which body is alive, it also is the proper subject of what we might call mental functions, things like believing and desiring."[4] For Frede, the Aristotelian view is restricted to the first part of the Platonic account of the soul: "Both Aristotle and the scholastic Aristotelians believe that the soul is that in virtue of which a living body is alive."[5] We saw this view in Avicenna's account of the soul as the entelecheia of the body, but we have also seen that Avicenna supplements it with the Flying Man argument and maintains that the soul is the separately existing subject of self-consciousness. The Platonic account of the soul as the subject of mental functions is not yet Avicenna's account of the soul as the subject whose existence is established by self-awareness. To get to Avicenna's view, Fazlur Rahman argues that we need to consider the contributions of Plotinus. In a Platonic manner, Plotinus admits "a higher soul which is the subject of cognition . . . [and] a lower soul which is essentially connected with the body, which shares its affections, movements, and changes, and which is, therefore, not separable from it."[6] Plotinus, then, ascribes to the higher soul the attribute of self-consciousness and claims that it cannot be entirely objectified and that it owns the contents of consciousness.[7] Avicenna's Flying Man argument (for the existence of the soul as separate from the body) is then in alliance with Plotinus' view of the soul. Following the traditional readings, one could then saddle Avicenna with an inconsistent position that embraces, without reflection, the incompatible views of his Greek predecessors. I disagree with this uncharitable reading.

A reasonable explanation for Avicenna's combination of Platonic and Peripatetic accounts of the soul may begin with a consideration of the historical context for Avicenna's intellectual activity: the tenth-century Muslim intellectuals adhered to a Peripatetic standard. On this view, Avicenna is constrained by the pressure of that standard and couches his genuinely Neoplatonic view in a Peripatetic frame. There is reason to accept some version of this explanation. In the Prologue to the *Kitāb al-shifā'*, written some time after the work had been completed, Avicenna reports of a book called *al-Ḥikma al-mashriqiyya* (*Eastern Philosophy*).[8] He writes: "But as for the present book [*al-Shifā'*], it is more elaborate and accommodating to my Peripatetic colleagues. Whoever wants the truth (stated) without indirection, he should seek the former book [*Eastern Philosophy*]."[9] Unfortunately, only about half of the contents of *Eastern Philosophy* has survived.[10] In the introduction to that work, Avicenna distinguishes his brand of philosophy from some (other) forms of Peripateticism.

> Although we admit the wisdom of the most learned predecessor of these philosophers (that is Aristotle), and we know that in discovering what his teachers and companions did not know, in distinguishing between various sciences, in arranging the sciences in a better manner than before, in discovering the truth of many subjects . . . he was superior to those who came before him, the men who came after him should have brought to order whatever confusion had existed in his thought. . . . But those who came after him could not transcend what they had inherited from him . . . and since those who were in favor of learning were strongly in favor of the Greek Peripatetics, we did not find it appropriate to separate ourselves and speak differently from everyone else. So we took their side, and with those philosophers who were more fanatical than any of the Greek sects, we too became fanatical. . . . We overlooked their faults and provided a leader and tutor for them in matters in which no patience was possible. . . . We were forced to associate with people devoid of understanding who considered . . . the opposition to common opinion as sin.[11]

This passage, together with the earlier one—excerpted from the prologue to the *al-Shifā'*, allow us to see that Avicenna views himself as departing from the Peripatetic view. Dimitri Gutas claims that Avicenna "in his later period . . . stops referring indiscriminately to all his earlier works as compendia or summaries of Aristotle's books,"[12] and that in this same period "Avicenna expresses his ideological independence from the Peripatetics."[13] I differ from Gutas' view that Avicenna's attitude to the Peripatetic tradition evolves as he becomes an independent philosopher. Rather, I argue that although Avicenna's position departs from some forms of Peripateticism, one should not include Aristotle (and some other Aristotelians, e.g., Alfarabi) in the same group as Avicenna's Peripatetic antagonists.

Gutas identifies Avicenna's main departure from the Aristotelian tradition to be "his singular preoccupation with the subject of the survival and fate of the rational soul."[14] He gives this preoccupation the title of the Metaphysics of the Rational Soul and maintains that Avicenna classifies it as "a fourth subdivision of the Metaphysics."[15] Gutas explains, "the study of the rational soul thus involves both the theoretical sciences . . . and the practical sciences. . . . The rational soul is the meeting point of theory and praxis because when it becomes 'like a polished mirror,' there ensues an automatic practicing of the philosophical sciences. The science that engages in this study, the Metaphysics of the Rational Soul, is thus the highest stage of the philosophical sciences."[16] Gutas then relates this science to Avicenna's claim in the Introduction to *Eastern Philosophy* that he (Avicenna) "perfected what they [the Peripatetics] meant to say but fell short of saying."[17] Gutas concludes that "[h]istory bore out his claim [about perfecting Peripateticism] because after him Aristotelianism in the Islamic East became Avicennism."[18] In other words, Eastern Islamic philosophy inherited Avicenna's preoccupation with the immortality of the rational soul. I return to this claim in the conclusion of the book.[19]

Corbin arrives at the same conclusion when he examines Avicenna's references to Eastern philosophy in his comments on the *Theology of Aristotle*. As we have seen earlier, the *Theology* is in fact an Aristotelian adaptation of the arguments of the last three *Enneads* (of Plotinus) into Arabic. As Peter Adamson puts it, one way the adaptor achieves this reconciliation is by treating the Neoplatonic "brute soul [the animal soul] in a rather Aristotelian way, and emphasizes its connection to the body in contrast to the rational soul . . . the lower bodily faculties [of the soul] are destroyed with the body, but the part that is related to the intellect is eternal."[20] Corbin claims that, in his comments on the *Theology*, Avicenna mentions Eastern philosophy no less than six times, each time rejecting the view that the soul is corruptible.[21] Of course, given his strong endorsement of the separation of the soul and the body, Avicenna does not endorse the adaptor's claim that part of the soul perishes with the body, as that would imply that the soul is an accident of the body. Nevertheless, Avicenna identifies the separate existence of the soul and its immortality, a view pervading the spirit and the letter of the *Theology*, as a central article of his Eastern philosophy.[22]

It turns out that Aristotle himself is not a consistent "Aristotelian"! Despite the position ascribed to him, Aristotle lapses into what one might call a Platonism, when he claims that the body is an instrument used by the soul (*De Anima*, 415b18ff). For Aristotle, like Avicenna, the soul has two meanings. On the one hand, the soul is "the first actuality of a natural body with the potentiality of having life" (412a27–b1). This corresponds to Avicenna's account of the soul preceding his Flying Man argument. In the same passage, in which he gives the account of the soul as the form of the body with the potentiality of having life, Aristotle refers to a sense of the soul which is related to the body as the sailor is related to the ship (413a9). He worries that the soul as first actuality cannot be this sense of the soul. He then maintains that "with regard to intellect, that is, the theoretical faculty, it is not yet clear, but it seems to be a kind different from the soul, and only this is possibly separate, just in the way that the eternal is separate from the destructible" (ibid.). Intellect is then (possibly) a separate entity from the soul as the first actuality of a body, and, because of its separation from the body, incorruptible and immortal. The intellect's activity is thinking, but, as Lloyd Gerson argues, this thinking "is not, according to Aristotle, the presence of intelligible form in the intellect; it is the awareness of the presence of intelligible form in the intellect by that which is identical with that in which the intelligible form is present."[23] The soul *qua* actuality of a body thinks in the sense of having the intelligible form (i.e., being informed), but as it is in a physical composite, the informed part cannot be the part that is aware of the presence of the form. Therefore, for the aware soul and the informed soul to be one, the real subject of thinking has to be separate from the body, incorruptible, and thus immortal. This is the Neoplatonic soul, and it is available in Aristotle's position as well. There is of course a tension between the two senses of "soul,"[24] and the subsequent inheritors of Aristotle's work attempt to deal with this tension.

Some of Aristotle's successors, such as Alexander of Aphrodisias, however, in order to stabilize the apparent tension in the Aristotelian account of the soul, purge the so-called Platonic element from Aristotle's view and advance the thesis that the soul is inseparable from the body (discarding the sense of "soul" as immortal intellect).[25] Robert Wisnovsky refers to Alexander as a participant in the lesser *sumphōnia*, the tradition's project of "reconciling Aristotle with Aristotle."[26] Wisnovsky contrasts the lesser *sumphōnia* with the greater *sumphōnia*, the Neoplatonic reconciling of Plato and Aristotle.[27] The Neoplatonists, as we have seen, posited the unity of the soul in its separation from the body. Wisnovsky, however, argues that Avicenna's position is the heir to and the culmination of the Ammonian synthesis of the lesser and the greater *sumphōnia*.[28] It suffices to say that Avicenna accounts for the lesser *sumphōnia* by maintaining that the soul comes into being with the body (it is its first entelechy), but he then allows for the greater *sumphōnia* by maintaining that the soul becomes separate from the body as it becomes the intellect that is aware of the presence of the intelligible form in itself. This is the separate and therefore immortal acquired intellect (i.e., the intellect that has conjoined with the Active Intellect). Wisnovsky writes, "each human rational soul can attain the immortality which the Active Intellect possesses and which serves as the final cause *qua to hou* of the activation of the activities of the theoretical intellect and its lower faculties. Once the theoretical intellect has attained that immortality, it becomes identical in species, rather than numerically identical with the Active Intellect, thus allowing the theoretical intellect to retain its individuality."[29] By final cause *qua to hou*, Wisnovsky is drawing on Aristotle's distinction "between the type of final cause which is 'that in view of which' (*to hou*) and the type of final cause which is 'that for the benefit of which' (*to hōi*)."[30] The theoretical intellect is that faculty of the soul which is both final cause *qua to hou* and *qua to hōi*, "it both *is* an end and *has* an end:"[31] it is the perfection of the living body and aims for perfection in conjunction with the Active Intellect. Moreover, as conjoined with the Active Intellect, the theoretical intellect is aware of itself as containing the intelligible form, and therefore separate from body and immortal.

I agree with Wisnovsky that Avicenna's unique synthesis is available in both earlier and later texts; therefore, the expression of the synthesis is determined by the type of work (i.e., its Peripatetic or independent style).[32] Shlomo Pines suggests that we should understand Avicenna's "independent" style as addressed to an audience opposed to the Western Peripatetic school of Baghdad.[33] Pines is probably thinking of Peripatetics such as Abu-l-Ḥasan Mukhtar ibn Buṭlān (Ibn Butlan). A student of the Peripatetic Abu al-Faraj ibn al-Ṭayyib, Ibn Butlan argues that the soul cannot exist without the body and that they are co-dependent.[34] It is likely that some Baghdadi Peripatetics (as represented by Ibn Butlan) are the proper targets of Avicenna's attacks in his Eastern philosophy.

Elsewhere, Pines introduces evidence from Avempace's discussion of Alfarabi's lost *Commentary on the Nicomachean Ethics*, where Alfarabi apparently denies the immortality of the soul and argues that political perfection is the supreme felicity. Avempace quotes Alfarabi as saying that some of the Ancients

> [opposed] a violent negation [to the teaching concerning the separation of the soul from the body]. . . . It is an evident consequence of this doctrine that happiness [consists] in a [human] individual being a part of the city in such a way that he serves [it] in a manner appropriate to his degree so that he and the people [of the city] obtain many good things perceived by the senses, [things] that pertain to civic [life] and that procure pleasure in ways consonant with the interests of the community.[35]

Avempace does not reject Alfarabi's authorship of the alleged view, but rather maintains that "Abu Nasr has made these remarks at his first reading [of the *Ethics*]."[36] Moreover, Avempace does not even want this view ascribed to the ancients. Instead, he attributes it to the much maligned Brethren of Purity (*Ikhwān al-ṣafa*),[37] in order to dismiss it quickly. Pines, however, maintains that Alfarabi must have advanced such a reading of Aristotle, and given Alfarabi's training with the Baghdadi Peripatetics, it would not be unusual for him to have done so. In fact, Pines suggests that the aforementioned Baghdadi Peripatetic, Ibn Butlan, derived his belief on the mortality of the soul from Alfarabi's *Commentary on Ethics*.[38] I have no objection to the claim that Alfarabi has expressed the Baghdadi/lesser *sumphōnia* doctrine in some of his works. However, in his principal treatise, *On the Perfect State*, Alfarabi, in no uncertain terms, argues for the immortality of the soul. In the chapter titled "After-life," he writes that the increase in the actions that bring felicity and their repetition bring the soul to that "stage of perfection in which it can dispense with matter so that it becomes independent of it, neither perishing, when matter does, nor requiring matter in order to survive."[39] Alfarabi, then, goes on to say that the separation of the soul from matter does imply the individuality of the soul. In a move anticipating the individuation principle (that the body individuates the soul) ascribed to his successor, Avicenna,[40] he argues that

> since these souls which have now become separate were before in various matter and since it has become clear that the dispositions of the souls depend on the temperaments of the bodies, some more and some less—each soul's

> disposition having been conditioned by the temperament of the body in which it was—it follows necessarily that these dispositions differ, because the bodies in which they were differed. And since the differences of bodies cannot be determined in number, the differences of the souls are equally indeterminable in number. (*al-Madīna al-fāḍila*, 262–65)

The indeterminable bodily differences translate into differences in the dispositions of the souls individuating them. The Alfarabi/Avicenna principle is not the Platonic principle of the individuation of the soul (i.e., the pre-existence of the individual soul). Plato's principle has the advantage of avoiding the problem of the infinite number of souls by allowing for transmigration of a finite number of souls over bodies. Alfarabi, and Avicenna after him, reject transmigration,[41] thereby seeming to succumb to the existence of an actual infinity (of souls). This thesis, as Aristotle has shown, allows for a part of the actual infinity to be identified and then applied to the whole resulting in the absurdity that the part is equal to the whole (*Physics*, 204a21–29). Avicenna recognizes this and replies that souls can form an actual infinity because a soul has no position in nature.[42] This position is anticipated by Alfarabi:

> When this generation passes away as well and is released [from matter], they occupy in their turn the same ranks in felicity as those who passed away before, and each joins those who resemble him in species, quantity and quality. And since they are not bodies their associations, whatever number it were to reach, would never get them into each other's way, since they are not in space at all, and they do not meet and join in the same way as bodies do. (*al-Madīna al-fāḍila*, 264–65)

Because souls don't occupy a spatial position, the absurdity attending actual infinites does not affect them.

Averroes rejects Avicenna's (and Alfarabi's) argument that averts Aristotle's account of the problem of actual infinities. He does not give any philosophical reasons but simply claims that the argument is an invention not found in the writings of the ancients.[43] Averroes, however, accepts the existence of an intellectual soul, one that is cultivated in relation with the Active Intellect and separate from matter.

He also argues that this intellectual soul (i.e., the material intellect) is not a plurality but one.[44] Avicenna and Alfarabi, however, believe that the intellectual soul is essentially individual and remains so after death. They both allow for happiness and misery of the disembodied individual soul based on the level of perfection he attains during his mundane existence.[45]

According to Avicenna, a preparation is necessary for the human subject to recognize his incorruptible, intellectual soul. In his account of the Flying Man, Avicenna maintains that the demonstration of the existence of the intellectual soul is available to "someone who has the power of noticing (*mulāḥaẓa*) the truth himself, without the need of having to educate him, constantly prod him, and divert him from what causes sophistical errors."[46] In other words, the addressee must be equipped with a philosophical sensibility that is either innate, or acquired before his encounter with the proof. In "Avicenna's 'Flying Man' in Context," Michael Marmura suggests that the Flying Man thought experiment involves a process of alerting (*al-tanbīh*) so that the soul is made aware of the awareness of its own essence.[47] My contention is that the process of alerting is more complicated and draws from the account of philosophy as the practice of spiritual exercises. I read the above passage as saying that the one who can recognize the existence of the intellectual soul (has "the power of noticing") has received some kind of cultivation of the soul, and that Avicenna's account of this education follows the philosophical account of the training of virtue in the individual. For Avicenna, as we have seen, the acquisition of a just and balanced soul must precede intellectual thought (and education) and the subsequent possibility of recognizing the intellectual soul as the subject of his self-awareness. For Aristotle, intellectual thinking (*noiēsis*) is an activity in which the knower, the self-aware subject, and the known, the informed subject, are the same (*De Anima*, 430a10–25). As we saw in Chapter 3,[48] Aristotle characterizes a certain kind of thinking as an activity (*energeia*), that is, an act that has its end in itself. This thinking characterizes the state of the acquired intellect, the intellect that is conjoined with the Active Intellect. The soul, as it is thinking through the deliverances of the senses, is involved in a movement (*kinēsis*); it has its end (i.e., purpose) outside of itself and when it reaches it, comes to an end, that is, to a termination (*Metaphysics*, 1048b18–30). The ethical preparation requires that one convert the soul's movements to activities and in so doing, one begins the cultivation of the intellect to make it an acquired intellect, which occurs when knowing has become an activity as well.

The cultivation of the soul beyond the satisfaction of animalistic needs and desires toward intimacy and a conjunction with the Active Intellect enables a recognition of a subjectivity that is separate from the body, and therefore incorruptible and immortal. This is the sense of the being of man as Being-towards-Beyond-Death that forms the basis of Avicenna's and Alfarabi's Eastern Peripatetic philosophies and marks their divergence from Baghdadi Peripateticism of Ibn Butlan as well as that of Averroes.

6.2. Conscience and the Active Intellect

It is worth noting, at this point, that Heidegger's account of the being of man (i.e., Being-towards-Death) contains a rejection of the separateness of the Active Intellect. This is indicated by the way he reduces the awakening of the finite individual, which is mediated by the external Active Intellect in Islamic Peripateticism, to the internal call of conscience. In *Being and Time*, Heidegger writes: "*In conscience Dasein calls itself*."[49] But what does this call say?

> The call does not report events; it calls without uttering anything. The call discourses in the uncanny mode of keeping silent . . . in calling the one to whom the appeal is made, it does not call him into the public idle talk of the "they," but calls him back into the reticence of his existent potentiality-for-Being. (*SZ* 277; *BT* 322)

The silence here is not without consequence. It is a reticent discourse of the concernful solicitude, which aims to make one authentic. "This kind of solicitude pertains essentially to authentic care—that is, to the existence of the Other, not to a 'what' with which he is concerned; it helps the Other to become transparent to himself in his care and to become free for it" (*SZ* 122; *BT* 159). In the silent discourse of conscience, the individual Dasein is both the caregiver, the teacher, and the recipient of care, the disciple. This silent mode of discourse calls the inauthentic Dasein toward care for authentic existence. "As a mode of discoursing, reticence Articulates the intelligibility of Dasein in so primordial a manner that it gives rise to a potentiality-for-hearing which is genuine, and to a Being-with-one-another which is transparent" (*SZ* 165; *BT* 208). Dasein's inner solitary reticent discourse (between the authentic potential of Dasein and the Dasein as it is drowned in everydayness) raises it out of its lostness in the public space and moves it toward resoluteness and authenticity. The relentless scrutiny of the inner other frees the self from the grip of mistaken and insufficiently understood beliefs and desires available to him in conventional modes of thought and action. Such a self-assessment situates the person in truth, in the way things show themselves in their authentic intelligibility.

Although the tracing of the various influences on Heidegger's account of the call of conscience is beyond the scope of this work, one influence is particularly relevant to the discussion at hand and requires closer scrutiny. Heidegger inherits the internalization of the initiator of human awakening from Thomas Aquinas.[50] In the second book of the *Summa Contra Gentiles*, chapter 76, titled "That the Active Intellect Is Not A Separate Substance But Part of the Soul," Aquinas argues:

> [I]f the active intellect is a separate substance, it is manifest that it is above man's nature. Now an operation which man performs by the power alone of a higher substance is a supernatural operation; for instance, the working of miracles, prophesying, and other like things which men do by God's favor. Since man cannot understand except by the power of the agent intellect, understanding will not be for man a natural operation if the agent intellect is a separate substance. Nor in that case can man be defined as being *intellectual* or *rational*.[51]

In this passage, Aquinas states that the assumption that the Active Intellect is a separate substance leads to the absurdity that man cannot be defined as intellectual or rational.[52] To avoid this absurdity, Aquinas maintains that it is enough that we reject the thesis that the Active Intellect is a separate substance. This rejection, however, ignores the care with which the Islamic Peripatetics account for the intellectual labor of the rational soul toward conjunction with the Active Intellect and the attainment of immortality.[53]

More importantly, Aquinas' rejection of the notion of a separate Active Intellect undermines the spiritual dimension of the philosophical quest. Corbin expresses this implication of the Thomistic interpretation of the Active Intellect rather eloquently:

> When, for example, St. Thomas Aquinas gives each individual an active intellect, yet affirms that this intellect is not a "separate" spiritual entity, he severs the direct relationship of the individual with the divine world, a rela-

> tionship established by Avicenna's doctrine of the Active Intelligence, itself identified with the Holy Spirit or Angel of Revelation. . . . Instead of the religious norm signifying the liberty in the sense that it affirms an essentially individual initiation, it now becomes socialized; and spirit and soul rise in revolt against it. Once socialized, this norm ceased to be religious, and veered from monotheism to monism, from the idea of divine Incarnation to the idea of social Incarnation.[54]

For Aquinas, it is the church—the social incarnation—that mediates the human commerce with the *spiritualia*. In this sense, the Islamic Peripatetic account of a philosophical initiation by a spiritual being (i.e., the Active Intellect) threatens to undermine the authority of the church and its monopoly over human salvation.[55] The internalization of the Active Intellect also enables Aquinas to assert the incorruptibility and the immortality of the soul,[56] independently of its dependence on the philosophical relation between the human individual and the Active Intellect. Heidegger's approach to the being of man, Dasein, combines Thomas's rejection of the separate Active Intellect together with the Alexandrian approach to the soul. Heidegger's refusal to engage the notions of a separate Active Intellect and the immortality of the human soul stems from his efforts to resuscitate a philosophy that is free of doctrinal bondage to nonphilosophical commitments. But he goes too far; unlike his dogmatic predecessors who acted to curtail the philosophical enterprise, Heidegger misses out on the potential of philosophy (central to Islamic philosophy) by which "the philosopher would be carried away . . . to an unforeseen beyond, and certainly beyond established dogma; for an immediate and personal relationship with a spiritual being [the Active Intellect] from the Pleroma . . . [is] unlikely to predispose a philosopher to bow before the Magisterium here below."[57] In the Islamic intellectual tradition, a similar reaction to the spiritual reach of the philosophical quest is available. In Chapter 5, I spelled out Ghazali's charge of heresy against the Peripatetics and his strategy for reining in the spiritual dimension of philosophy. I showed that Ghazali attacked an impoverished account of philosophical reason and that account was not true to the spirit nor the letter of the account offered by his philosophical targets. The outcome of that attack, however, was not as devastating as its Thomistic counterpart in Western philosophy. It curtailed the influence of Islamic philosophy to some extent, but Averroes's reply and Suhrawardi's renewal preserved and expanded on the philosophy of their Peripatetic predecessors.

6.3. Paradigms of Emulation: Divine Exemplars and Existential Heroes

It is useful here to compare the Islamic Peripatetic accounts of the relation between religion and philosophy with the relevant features of Heidegger's phenomenology. The Islamic Peripatetics, as we have seen, maintain that the public space, the space of the multitude, is pervaded by religion. Religion articulates the divinely sanctioned *nomos* (i.e., the custom and the practices required for the cultivation of the self and the acquisition of virtue). Heidegger's account of the public space, however, has been denuded of this religious quality, due to his commitment to the spiritual incapacitation of the philosophy he inherited. However, Heidegger manages to retrieve, as we have seen, some important features of a genuine notion of philosophy. Here, I set out Heidegger's appropriation of the notion of the philosophical exemplar.

Heidegger's account of the pragmatic involvement relations and the unity of these relations in Dasein's self-understanding does show, as we have seen, the structure of the domain of interaction between human beings and their surroundings. An inauthentic Dasein is absorbed in the world and understands itself and other entities in terms of its interests and needs as dictated by the institutions and practices that define the involvement relations. The absorbed inauthentic Dasein has an environment (*SZ* 67; *BT* 95): it deals with the world pragmatically for the sake of the public values foisted on it in the situation that it finds itself.[58] The authentic Dasein, on the other hand, has freed the self from the lostness in the environment and dwells autonomously alongside entities within the world. But how does Dasein achieve authenticity? Heidegger, as we have seen, postpones this matter, as he argues that the hermeneutic analysis of Dasein is an *existential* concern to be distinguished from the *existentiell* choice of authenticity. The latter cannot be sorted through theoretically; it gets "straightened out . . . through existing itself" (*SZ* 12; *BT* 33). In Division Two of *Being and Time*, however, Heidegger addresses the problematic of authenticity more directly.

We have already seen that for Heidegger authenticity involves the heeding of the call of conscience. This silent call emanates from the authentic potential of Dasein and aims to raise it out of its lostness in the public space and move it toward resoluteness and authenticity. In the chapter titled, "Temporality and Historicality," Heidegger identifies the significance of the existential hero, who exemplifies the heeding of the call of conscience, and presents himself to be emulated:

> It is not necessary that in resoluteness one should *explicitly* know the origin of possibilities upon which that resoluteness projects itself. It is rather in Dasein's temporality, and there only, that there lies any possibility that the *existentiell* potentiality-for-Being upon which it projects itself can be gleaned *explicitly* from the way in which Dasein has been traditionally understood. The resoluteness which comes back to itself and hands itself down, then becomes the *repetition* of a possibility of existence. . . . The authentic repetition of a possibility of existence that has been—the possibility that Dasein may choose its hero (*Held*)—is grounded existentially in anticipatory resoluteness; for it is in resoluteness that one first chooses the choice which makes one free for the struggle of loyally following in the footsteps of that which can be repeated. (*SZ* 385; *BT* 437)

Resoluteness articulates Dasein's "authentic Being-one's-self" (*SZ* 298; *BT* 344). In resoluteness, Dasein pulls out of his surrender to the leveling and averageness of the public, the "they." " 'Resoluteness' signifies letting oneself be summoned out of, called away from, one's lostness in the 'they' " (*SZ* 299; *BT* 345). The resolute Dasein understands itself in terms of its "ownmost potentiality-for-being" (i.e., in terms of the self-chosen roles that define its identity). It is in resoluteness that Dasein can choose to emulate a hero. A hero is an embodiment of authenticity whose example makes audible the call of conscience and brings to view the prospect of authenticity. In this emulation, the apprentice is not lost in the "they," in a public paradigm, but rather he is following the example of an authentic person in the mode of concernful solicitude (*SZ* 298; *BT* 345). In the positive mode of concernful solicitude, the hero "leaps ahead" of the adept

> not in order to take away his "care" but rather to give it back to him authentically as such for the first time. This kind of solicitude pertains essentially to authentic care—that is, to the existence of the Other, not to a "what" with which he is concerned; it helps the Other to become transparent to himself in his care and to become free for it. (*SZ* 122; *BT* 159)

What this resolute emulation (i.e., the submission to the solicitude of the hero) effects is a cultivation of authenticity. The resolute Dasein, in following the example of a hero, submits to a practice of self-overcoming for the sake of autonomous dwelling.

The Islamic Peripatetics combine the Islamic and the Greek philosophical paradigms of human excellence and interpret the exemplar as the ideal philosopher-prophet-king. The apprentice in philosophy submits to the exemplary philosopher in order to train in virtue. The attainment of the practical virtue prepares the ground for theoretical virtue, and the realization of both may result in the conjunction with the Active Intellect and the commerce with the spiritual beings in what Corbin calls the Pleroma.[59] Heidegger shadows his Muslim counterparts part of the way. His obstruction of the Pleroma and the related account of human as a Being-towards-Death, whose perfection culminates in an autonomous tarrying alongside entities within the world, limit the possibilities of philosophical initiation and its relevant spiritual exercises. Islamic philosophers extend the practice of spiritual exercises beyond authenticity to the cultivation of the theoretical intellect and its advance to the spiritual domains. So, Heidegger shares with his Islamic predecessors an account of access to the world that overcomes the modern divide between the mind and the world; but he fails to overcome the other constriction of mainstream modern philosophy, the divide between the mind and the spiritual domain. It is in Islamic Peripatetic philosophy that we can find a supreme valorization of the intellect in the account that intellect penetrates everything and allows for unprecedented access by the trained philosopher.

In this chapter, we have seen (yet again) that the Islamic Peripatetics provide a comprehensive account of the philosophical quest, one in which spiritual exercises extend beyond the acquisition of practical virtue. The Western reception of this approach to philosophy, vis-à-vis Thomism, aims to constrain the spiritual wings of the philosopher by denying the transcendence of the Active Intellect and the theoretical spiritual exercises required for conjunction with it. Heidegger inherits this constriction of philosophy and does not overcome it despite his efforts to liberate philosophy from its various shackles.

Conclusion

The Importance of Islamic Peripateticism for Modern Philosophy in the West and Its Impact on Later Islamic Philosophy

In this text I have focused on developing two primary themes: (1) an exposition of a proper understanding of what constitutes the philosophical enterprise in Islamic Peripatetic philosophy, and (2) an appreciation of just how this enterprise can be applied to resolving the fissures underlying some of the key problems of modern philosophy. In this conclusion, I begin with the second theme, and through that analysis and the way the subsequent traditions of Islamic philosophy inherited and modified the conception elaborated by their Peripatetic predecessors, Alfarabi and Avicenna, I address the first theme.

1. Islamic Peripateticism and the Predicament of Modern Western Philosophy

This work has defended the importance of Islamic Perpateticism for modern philosophy. Specifically, I have argued Islamic Peripateticism is immunized to a reductionism in modern philosophy wherein the function of philosophy is viewed primarily as the production of rational discourse situated between two torrents of irrationalism. On one side, modern philosophy faces the irrationality of the physical world—a physical world understood as having causal regularities, but makes no regulative (i.e., rational) demands on us. As a result, modern naturalist philosophy constructs rational knowledge based on the apparent effects of causal regularities and purports to give accounts of reason's foundations in such brute patterns. On the other side, modern reason is confronted with spiritual irrationality; blind faith in dogma and superstition is a common appearance assumed by modern spirituality, and such faith, for some, is assigned the task of providing the foundations of reason. Between these two powerful currents, modern reason flounders precariously with vague hopes of rescue and dreams of autonomy.

In Chapter 1, I recounted how modern scholarship on Islamic philosophy is determined by this underlying presumption of modern reason—a reason that sees itself responding to social, political, and religious irrationality. When this scholarship is self-forgetful (i.e., does not recognize this presumption in its own method), it condemns Islamic philosophy for succumbing to these irrational forces. When it is self-aware, it prescribes "methodological self-consciousness" and resigns itself to its own impotence. I maintain, with Muhsin Mahdi, that this state of affairs must be remedied, and the cure lies in retrieving "a genuine form of rationalism" in premodern philosophy. By "a genuine form of rationalism," I mean a sense of philosophical reason that is unchained from irrational determination. We need to liberate modern philosophy by taking an unprejudiced look at premodern conceptions of philosophy, in this case Islamic Periepateticism.

The first step in this project of liberation is to examine the sense of philosophy for Islamic Peripatetics. In Chapter 3, I demonstrated that philosophy for these Muslim philosophers is not primarily the production of rational discourse, but rather what Pierre Hadot calls "the practice of spiritual exercises."[1] Hadot has the Greek tradition of philosophy in mind when he makes this claim, but I maintained that this is the sense of philosophy that the Muslims inherit from the Greeks.

Reason, in the context of a philosophy founded on the practice of spiritual exercises, is a human power capable of sustaining development and perfection. With more than a capacity for generating formally cohesive thought (and treatises), such a philosophy can gain access, through proper training, to the things themselves. I broached this form of rationality by comparing the project of Islamic Peripateticism with the phenomenology of Martin Heidegger—which prides itself in a critique of modern thought—and drawing the link between the two traditions in the work of Henry Corbin, a student of Heidegger's phenomenology as well as a prominent historian of Islamic philosophy. Drawing on Corbin, I showed that both of these approaches (Islamic philosophy and Heideggerian phenomenology) postulate an ethical preparation for access to the things themselves; the cultivation of practical reason unveils the world and identifies the being of the human being as that which enables this unveiling. Islamic Peripatetics, however, extend the practice of spiritual exercises beyond the ethical preparation. I argued that the cultivation of theoretical intellect, as advanced by Islamic philosophers, opens new prospects for a philosophical understanding of human experience, allowing for a philosophical spirituality.

In Chapter 4, I explored the Islamic Peripatetic account of imagination, as the site of spiritual experience, and showed its sophistication by comparing it with the relevant modern accounts. I also showed that Islamic Peripatetic accounts of imagination accommodate a notion of transcendence unavailable to their modern counterparts. A source for the modern restriction of the intellect and imagination to their mundane commerce is the reception of Islamic Peripatetic philosophy in the work of the Catholic theologian, Thomas Aquinas. I discussed this reception in Chapter 6 and argued that Aquinas' attempts to reconcile philosophy with the authority of the Church resulted in the narrowing of the reach of the intellect in the subsequent mainstream of Western philosophy.

In Chapter 5, I turned to the reception of Islamic Peripateticism in the work of the Muslim theologian Ghazali. I related the Islamic Peripatetic description of imagination to the account of dreams, which for Ghazali replace the prophetic dimension of the faculty of intellect. I argued that Ghazali underestimates the significance of spiritual practice for Peripatetic philosophy, construing it as the production of rational discourse. As a result, he claims that philosophy fails to embrace Islamic dogma and therefore commits heresy. I drew from the reply of the later Islamic Peripatetic, Averroes, to show that the formative Islamic Peripatetic philosophers are invulnerable to Ghazali's rendition of them. It should be apparent that the critiques of Islamic Peripateticsm, as advanced by Islamic or Christian theologians, obfuscate the true spiritual reach of philosophy. In turning to the work of Islamic Peripatetics, we can not only envision and reclaim reason's access to the world, but we can also recapture philosophy's spirituality and help it regain its genuine autonomy.

2. Peripateticism in Later Islamic Philosophy

The impact of Peripateticism on later Islamic philosophy was not mitigated by Ghazali's alleged refutations. As I mentioned in Chapter 6, the persistence of Peripateticism in Islamic thought, however, was not due to Averroes' famous reply to Ghazali. The spirit of Averroes' reply to Ghazali, however, is underscored by his contemporary mystic and philosopher, Suhrawardi, who, unlike his Andalusian counterpart, leaves a deep impact in the subsequent traditions of Islamic philosophy, especially in its renaissance in the sixteenth-century Safavid Iran. Corbin, in the *History of Islamic Philosophy*, points out the significance of Suhrawardi in the later tradition of Islamic philosophy:

> Al-Suhrawardi died just seven years before Averroes. At that moment, therefore, in western Islam, "Arab Peripateticism" was finding its ultimate expression in the work of Averroes, so much so that western historians, mistakenly confusing Averroes' Peripateticism with philosophy pure and simple, have overlong persisted in maintaining that philosophy in Islam culminates in Averroes. Yet at the same time in the East, and particularly in Iran, the work of al-Suhrawardi was opening up the road which so many thinkers and spiritual seekers were to follow down to our own days.[2]

Of course, Corbin is hesitant in admitting that "philosophy pure and simple" is available in Islamic Peripateticism. I have demonstrated that genuine philosophy as the practice of hermeneutic spiritual exercises is at the heart of the philosophies of Suhrawardi's Peripatetic predecessors, Alfarabi and Avicenna. Therefore, Suhrawardi's legacy lies not only in opening up a new road, but also in *retrieving* the path opened up already by Islamic Peripatetic philosophers. This retrieval is, in turn, a response to Ghazali's attacks on the Peripatetic philosophers.

In the introduction to his main work, *Ḥikmat al-ishrāq* (*Philosophy of Illumination*), Suhrawardi distinguishes two types of wisdom (*ḥikma*) in illuminative philosophy: intuitive (*fi al-ta'alluh*) and discursive (*fī al-baḥth*). Discursive wisdom is the mastery of logical reasoning, whereas intuitive wisdom is the becoming God-like (*ta'alluh*), which involves purification and cultivation of the soul through spiritual exercises, so that one is able to see reality directly and immediately (i.e., intuitively).[3] Suhrawardi argues that philosophers may have varying combinations and degrees of expertise in these two forms of wisdom, but the ideal philosopher is the master of both: "Should it happen that in some period there be a philosopher proficient in both intuitive and discursive philosophy, he will be ruler by right and the vicegerent of God."[4] This is an explicit endorsement of the Peripatetic account of intellect as both discursive and intuitive.[5] As such, Suhrawardi's position is at the same time an explicit rejection of the limitation imposed by Ghazali on the scope of the human intellect.

Suhrawardi's restoration of Islamic Peripateticism also includes the notion of an immortal intellectual soul. This is again in opposition to Ghazali, who sought to limit the reach of the faculty of intellect. Ghazali, in *Kīmīā-ye sa'ādat* (*Alchemy of Happiness*), admits to the separate existence of the soul, but denies its intellectual nature.[6] Suhrawardi, however, in *Kitāb al-talwīḥāt* (*Book of Intimations*) offers an account of a mystical encounter with Aristotle, who teaches him an account of the human being that extends beyond the practical and mundane dimensions of the soul. In the mystical encounter, which takes place "at a stage of this mystical world of Forms called the 'Jaburs,' "[7] Suhrawardi is in awe before the greatness of Aristotle. After recovering from the initial astonishment, he asks the master about the problem of knowledge to which Aristotle replies by urging him to engage in introspection.[8] Self-knowledge, according to Suhrawardi's Aristotle, is a paradigm case of knowledge, because "you are the one who is acquainted with himself by himself and not by mediation of any other agent and not by representation. . . . [T]he reality of your selfhood is thus a simple unity of self-knowledge by presence, the self-knowing subject, the self-known object" (*Talwīḥāt*, 70-1; trans. 182). For Suhrawardi, like Avicenna, the immediate knowledge of the self is attained, not by discursive proofs, but by spiritual exercises that free the self from absorption in the mundane: "Thus in proportion to being independent from matter the self knows itself" (*Talwīḥāt*, 72; trans. 184). Such a purification practice, aiming at self-perfection, makes intellectual access possible: " '[I]ntellection' (*ta'aqul*) is the 'presence of' the thing known in a non-material subject which is free from matter" (*Talwīḥāt*, 72; trans. 183). And freedom from matter is a function of one's perfection: "knowledge as such is the perfection of existence" (*Talwīḥāt*, 73; trans. 185). Finally, Suhrawardi's Aristotle affirms the immortality of the intellectual soul: "As long as you are in the material world, you are veiled and disconnected. But as soon as you leave that world, provided you are complete, you will enter into the state of identity and continuity" (*Talwīḥāt*, 73; trans. 186). The true self gets obfuscated in the material world, but the person who cultivates the soul, through relevant spiritual exercises, upon leaving this world attains an intellectual self-identity and a concomitant continuity with other souls. This is a position that affirms the views of Alfarabi and Avicenna on the survival of the individual intellectual soul.

Like his Peripatetic predecessors, Suhrawardi situates the self-knowledge that emerges from the spiritual exercises in relation to the transcendent Active Intellect, the angel of revelation.

> From one of the dominating lights, the incorporeal light that is the controlling light in the human fortresses is brought into being for the human—the most perfect—constitution.

> That dominating light is the lord of the talisman of the rational species (*al-naw' al-nāṭiq*). It is Gabriel—peace be upon him—the proximate father among the mighty lords of the Kingdom of dominance. It is *"Ravān Bakhsh,"* the Holy Spirit (*rūḥ al-qudus*), the bestower (*wāhib*) of knowledge and confirmation, the giver of life and virtue. This emanated light is the managing light, the commander of humanity, that which calls itself "I" (*al-mushīr ilā nafsihi bi-l-'anā'iyya*).[9]

In Chapter 5, we saw that both Avicenna and Ghazali, following the Qur'an's *Āyat al-nūr*, interpret the angel of revelation as a light that illuminates the human soul with prophetic insight. Ghazali, in contrast to Avicenna, does not consider the illuminations to be intellectual. Suhrawardi, however, follows Avicenna in this regard as he emphasizes that the angel is the bestower of knowledge. Moreover, Gabriel is also depicted as the commander of "that which calls itself 'I,'" and we have seen that the "I" is the human self-intellection obtained through spiritual exercises.

Suhrawardi also inherits the Avicennan account of the imagination's cultivation through a hermeneutics of symbols and extends Avicenna's account by arguing for the independent existence of the images of the perfected imagination.[10] He also considers the perfected imagination as a cognitive faculty that perceives the objects of a realm between the spiritual and the physical.[11] Suhrawardi calls the middle domain *'ālam al-mithāl*, the imaginal world.[12] Imagination, like a mirror, reflects the imaginative forms and perceives (imaginal) objects that are neither sensory nor intellectual. He writes:

> The truth is that the forms in mirrors and the imaginative forms are not imprinted. Instead, they are suspended fortresses—fortresses not in a locus at all. Though they may have loci in which they are made evident, they are not in them. The mirror is the locus in which the form in the mirror is made evident. . . . The imaginative faculty is the locus in which the forms of the imagination are made evident and suspended.[13]

Suhrawardi, therefore, allows imagination a cognitive function, that is, imagination perceives imaginative forms in the same way the senses perceive sensory forms and practical intentions. This implies that such forms, like their sensory counterparts, have their source in the emanation of the Active Intellect, and that the human imagination, through cultivation, can reflect these forms clearly. Now, Suhrawardi does not invoke the Avicennan form of the cultivation of imagination involving the refinement of imaginative judgment so that these judgments evoke pure feelings of pleasure and awe. For him, imagination's cultivation, just like the cultivation of the soul's perception of sensory forms and meanings, requires a training in unprejudiced cognition. In this, Suhrawardi follows Ghazali more closely,[14] with the exception that spiritual commerce does not become restricted to the functioning of the faculty of imgination. Intellect, as we have seen, is also involved. As a result, Suhrawardi brings to view the *'ālam al-mithāl*, the domain between the physical and the spiritual. Later Islamic philosophers, especially those of the Iranian traditions, devote considerable effort to the working out of the significance of this domain.[15] A detailed examination of these later traditions of Islamic philosophy and their contributions to the foundations laid out by Alfarabi and Avicenna is a fascinating subject and merits further study, which I hope to pursue in the future. In the remainder of these concluding remarks, however, I want to provide a brief outline of the continuing heritage of the Islamic Peripatetic philosophers to the present day. Special mention should be made of the school of Isfahan,[16] which emerged in the sixteenth century, and the school's most influential member, Ṣadr al-Dīn Muḥammad Shīrāzī (Mulla Sadra, 1571–1636 C.E.). The spiritual heritage of the early Islamic philosophers blossoms in the work of Mulla Sadra, and his work—in turn—has ensured the continuity of the impact of Islamic Peripateticism to this day in the Islamic world, especially in Iraq, Iran, India, and to a lesser extent Turkey.[17]

It is not inadvertent that the founding of the school of Isfahan coincided with the reign of the Safavids, the great Persian Shi'i dynasty that ruled from 1501 to 1722 C.E. Early in their assumption of power when their capital was in the city of Qazwin, Safavids had already attracted a number of intellectuals to the vicinity of their court. But, it was in Isfahan, during the reign of Shah 'Abbās I, that the dynasty reached its political and intellectual zenith. Many of the members of the school of Isfahan came from the city of Shiraz, including Mulla Sadra himself; already in Shiraz, after the second Mongol invasion of the Persianate Islamic world, an intellectual climate was thriving under the political stability instituted by the Īlkhanids.[18] Of course, this is not to suggest that after the early period, philosophy emerged *ex nihilo* in Shiraz and then migrated to Isfahan. In *Islamic Philosophy from Its Origin to the Present*, Seyyed Hossein Nasr refers to the school of Marāgha, in Azerbaijan, founded by Khawja Naṣīr al-Dīn Ṭūsī (1201–1274 C.E.), the Persian advisor to the first Mongolian conqueror of Persia, Hūlāgū Khān.[19] The school of Marāgha was instrumental in reviving the study of Avicenna's philosophy. Ṭūsī himself wrote commentaries on most of Avicenna's work. These commentaries, along with those of his preceding and subsequent scholars on Avicenna and Suhrawardi,[20] were an essential part of the philosophical education in Isfahan. Mulla Sadra's teachers in Isfahan included Mīr Muḥammad Bāqir Dāmād Ḥosseinī Astarābādī (Mir Damad). It was research into his work and its cultural milieu that led Henry Corbin and Seyyed Hossein Nasr to coin the term "School of Isfahan." Mir Damad is referred to as the "third teacher" (after Aristotle and Alfarabi) and his philosophical view comments upon and advances the work of Avicenna and Suhrawardi. Other prominent scholars of the school of Isfahan and teachers of Mulla Sadra include Sheikh Bahā al-Dīn Amulī (Sheikh Bahā'ī), Mīr Abu-l-Qāsim Findiriskī (Mir Findiriski), and Mullā 'Abd al-Razzāq Lahījī. The expertise of these scholars ranged over the whole spectrum of traditional sciences and beyond (e.g., Mir Findiriski was a scholar of Hindu philosophy). What was common among these thinkers and their disciples was the effort to reconcile rational discursive knowledge with spiritual training, and it was Mulla Sadra's work that represents the peak of Isfahan's contribution to philosophy. Although a fair treatment of this later tradition of Islamic philosophy is beyond the scope of this work, I draw on some salient themes that show specifically how the Islamic tradition of philosophy continued as a practice of spiritual exercises, a tradition that received its classical expression in the work of Alfarabi and Avicenna.

Mulla Sadra continues the Suhrawardian division between discursive (*baḥthī*) and intuitive (*ta'alluh*) wisdom, but changes the terminology; he uses formal knowledge (*al-'ilm al-ṣuwarī*) and the Qur'anic term, intuitive knowledge (*al-'ilm al-ladunnī* [18: 65]), instead. "The first is acquired in school with the aid of a teacher, and the second, based upon a greater degree of certainty than the first, is the science possessed by the prophets and saints and arrived at through the purification of the soul and the catharsis (*tajrīd*) of the intellect."[21] In the earlier chapters, I emphasized that the Muslim Peripatetics developed a systematic prophetology that combined Islamic revelation and practice with Greek notions of philosophy as the practice of spiritual exercise. Mulla Sadra's account of intuitive knowledge, no less than Suhrawardi's version, was influenced by this Peripatetic prophetology. However, we should not overlook the other intellectual current of Mulla Sadra's time, the theoretical Sufism of Muḥy al-Dīn Muḥammad ibn 'Arabī (1165–1240 C.E.), which had become available through the Persian writings of his disciple Ṣadr al-Dīn al-Qūnawī.[22]

Although an engagement of this rich form of Islamic spiritual thought is beyond the scope of this work, it is worth noting that it similarly emphasized the cultivation of spiritual insight and was consistent with Peripatetic and Suhrawardian philosophy. The discursive form of knowledge is, on the other hand, the heritage of the practitioners of Islamic theology, *kalām*. One could also trace this notion to the reception of Islamic Peripateticism by theologians like Ghazali, who, as we saw in Chapter 5, reduced the Peripatetic notion of intellection to discursive reasoning. What is fascinating about the philosophies of Muslim Peripatetics, as well as those of Suhrawardi and Mulla Sadra, is their shared interest in embracing both intellectual intuition and discursive reasoning. And this tendency continues to this day in the Persianate Islamic world, a factor due in part to the "rich and esoterically inclined [Persian] religious ambience."[23] However, as I have emphasized in this work, the richness of this ambience was enhanced by the influence of Islamic revelation as well as the availability of the Greek philosophical tradition.

In addition to implementing this concept of philosophy as the practice of spiritual exercises, Mulla Sadra also contributed to the Islamic Peripatetic discussion of the immortality of the soul and the significance of the power of imagination for visionary and eschatological experience. He accepted Suhrawardi's account of the intermediary imaginal realm, *'ālam al-mithāl*, and based on this assumption, argued that the faculty of imagination, as the perceptual faculty for the imaginal objects, has an existence independent from the physical body.[24] In other words, upon the death of the body, the faculty of imagination, like the Peripatetic "intellect," survives. If it is the dominant faculty, for those with an uncultivated intellect, it places the person, upon death, in the intermediary imaginal realm. For Mulla Sadra, some higher animals also inhabit this realm, by virtue of their possession of an imagination,[25] but other animals, as well as plants, minerals, and elements are united with their archetypal imaginal forms.[26] The spiritual cultivation of the imagination, therefore, can enable the person to access the imaginal world, and, more importantly, intellectual cultivation allows the person to transcend the physical and the imaginal realms and approach the highest ontological plane. According to Mulla Sadra, the traversing of realms of existence is only available to the cultivated wise men (*'urafā'*).[27]

Any treatment of Mulla Sadra's contributions to the traditions he inherited must include the doctrines of the primacy of existence (*al-aṣṣālat al-wujūd*) and the related thesis of the substantial motion (*al-ḥaraka al-jawhariyya*).[28] Due to his espousal of these doctrines, one could refer to Mulla Sadra as an Islamic existentialist, because, anticipating the existentialists, Mulla Sadra denies the precedence of essence over existence. This he also shares with the Islamic Peripatetics; but for the Peripatetics, including Alfarabi and Avicenna, the existence of each thing is in essence different from other existents,[29] except the human existence, which, as we have seen, is capable of transformation and growth through spiritual exercises. For Mulla Sadra, all being is fundamentally existent, ecstatic—outside of itself, and in constant transmutation. The so-called quiddities (i.e., abstract determinations of a being) are mere accidents of its dynamic nature. Superficially, this position is in sharp contrast with the one advocated by Suhrawardi who rebelled against his Peripatetic predecessors and considered existence as an abstract concept, lacking any objective reality.[30] But this opposition between Suhrawardi, on the one hand, and Mulla Sadra and the Peripatetics, on the other, does not get at the heart of the matter. Existence, in the dynamic sense indicated above, corresponds to the notion of light (*nūr*) in Suhrawardi. In *On the Hermeneutics of the Light Verse of the Qur'an*, a text of central importance to the continuation of the studies inaugurated in this work, Mulla Sadra writes: "In truth the reality of 'light' and existence (*al-wujūd*) is the same thing. The existence of everything is its manifestation, accordingly, the existence of corporeal bodies (*al-ajsām*) would also be the degrees of Light."[31] Mehdi Mohaghegh and Toshihiko Izutsu emphasize the centrality of this claim in the interpretations of Suhrawardi and Mulla Sadra: "Suhrawardi establishes, in place of 'existence,' as something really real the spiritual and metaphysical Light (*nūr*) which is the one and single reality having an infinite number of degrees and stages in terms of intensity and weakness, the highest degree being the light of all lights (*nūr al-anwār*) and the lowest being Darkness (*ẓulma*)."[32] In the Peripatetic tradition, as we have seen, emanations of "intellect" correspond to Suhrawardian propagation of light and Sadrian gradation of existence. This is confirmed when Mulla Sadra mentions approvingly Suhrawardi's characterization of light as "the simple and self-manifesting reality which brings other things to manifestation."[33] In Chapter 5, I compared Ghazali's and Avicenna's phenomenological interpretations of the light verse of the Qur'an, and showed that they both considered 'intellect' as a self-manifesting that brings other things to manifestation. Ghazali, as we saw, subsumed the light of intellect under that of prophecy, but the Peripatetic conception of intellection went beyond its delimitation by Ghazali. For the Peripatetics, intellect was essential to prophecy. This last point is captured and emphasized by Mulla Sadra's account of the Muhammadan light (*al-nūr al-Muḥammadiyya*): "The first one who knocked at the door of illumination by the light of God, and the first one who spoke 'There is no god but God' is the exalted servant, the First Intellect, the eminent contingent, the Muhammadan reality (*al-ḥaqīqa al-Muḥammadiyya*). He is the lamp of the light of God, the one who emanates the light of goodness and munificence."[34] Of course, Mulla Sadra is careful not to confuse the first intellect with God, which transcends all beings, including the first created being (i.e., the first [Muhammadan] intellect). This, however, is not just an accommodation of Ghazali; it also accords with Avicenna's cosmology, that situates God (i.e., the necessary being from whom all reality comes forth) beyond the first intellect.[35] I cannot engage a thorough treatment of the prophetology of the later Islamic philosophical tradition here, but this should suggest some of the fascinating turns and twists that Islamic philosophy takes in its later phases.

Due to the religious and political atmosphere in Iran toward the end of the Safavid rule, Mulla Sadra's philosophy did not immediately receive the widespread recognition it enjoys today.[36] But following the subsequent survival of religious persecution and the devastating Afghan invasion that brought down the Safavids, Mulla Sadra's work was brought to the center of philosophical research in Isfahan by Mullā 'Ali Nūrī (1731–1831).[37] Another important philosopher, Mullā Hādī Sabzawarī (1797–1872 C.E.), influential during the Qājār dynasty (1794–1925 C.E.), also helped in giving prominence to the work of Mulla Sadra.[38] Later, with the founding of the school of Tehran and the prominence of the commentaries of Nuri, Sabzawari and their disciples, Mulla Sadra's work achieved centrality in the Persian philosophical curriculum.[39] Outside of Iran, Mulla Sadra's philosophy was taught in the Shi'i centers in the Iraqi city of Najaf and in the Islamic traditional schools of India.[40] The school of Tehran, however, remained the main arena for Islamic philosophy in the nineteenth and twentieth centuries. To this day, the disciples of the Tehrani masters, and the school's offshoots in Qum, Shiraz, Isfahan, and Mashhad, continue the tradition of philosophy as prophetological spiritual exercises.[41] In current Persian philosophical circles, much effort is expended on establishing a fair dialogue between Western philosophy and Islamic philosophy, and it is to this effort that this work aims to contribute.

Notes

Introduction: Islamic Philosophy and the Crisis of Modern Rationalism

1. Edward Said, *Orientalism* (New York: Vintage, 1979), 14–15.

2. Ibid., 3.

3. Ibid., 272. Said's critique originates in French literary criticism. See, for example, Maxime Rodinson's "The Western Image and Western Studies of Islam," in *The Legacy of Islam*, ed. Joseph Schacht and C. E. Bosworth, 2nd ed. (Oxford: Clarendon Press, 1974), 9–62.

4. Muhsin Mahdi, "Orientalism and the Study of Islamic Philosophy," in *Journal of Islamic Studies* 1 (1990): 96.

5. Ibid.

6. Ibid., 97.

7. Said, *Orientalism*, 272.

8. Ibid., 326.

9. Mahdi, "Orientalism," 97.

10. Ibid.

11. Ibid. In Chapter 1, I explore and evaluate Mahdi's unique contributions to the study of Islamic Philosophy.

12. Throughout the book, I follow the transliteration guidelines of the *International Journal of Middle East Studies* (IJMES).

13. Michael E. Marmura, "The Islamic Philosophers' Conception of Islam," in *Islam's Understanding of Itself*, ed. R. G. Hovannisian and S. Vryonis, Jr. (Malibu, CA: Undena, 1983), 88.

14. R. Arnaldez, "Falsafah," in *The Encyclopedia of Islam*, Vol. II (Leiden: Brill, 1960), 71. Dimitri Gutas, in *Avicenna and the Aristotelian Tradition* (Leiden, Netherlands: E. J. Brill, 1988), 238–54, discusses Avicenna's endorsement of Alfarabi's account of metaphysics in contrast to that of al-Kindi.

15. See Pierre Hadot, *Exercices spirituels et philosophie antique* (Paris: Etudes Augustiniennes, 1987). Parts of this work are translated in *Philosophy as a Way of Life*, trans. Michael Chase (Oxford: Blackwell, 1995). Also see his *Qu'est-ce que la philosophie antique?* (Paris: Gallimard, 1995), translated as *What is Ancient Philosophy?*, trans. Michael Chase (Cambridge, MA: Harvard University Press, 2004). See also Michel Foucault, *Histoire de la sexualité* v. 1–3 (Paris:

Gallimard, 1976–84), translated as *History of Sexuality*, vol. 1–3, trans. Robert Hurley (NY: Vintage, 1978–86), and his 1980–82 lectures titled *L'herméneutique du sujet* (Paris: Gallimard, 2001), translated as *The Hermeneutics of the Subject*, trans. Graham Burchell (NY: Picador, 2006). Another work of relevance here is Alexander Nehamas's *The Art of Living: Socratic Reflections from Plato to Foucault* (Berkeley and Los Angeles: University of California Press, 1998).

16. Here I draw on John McDowell's reading of ancient ethics in his "Virtue and Reason," reprinted in *Mind, Value, and Reality* (Cambridge, MA: Harvard University Press, 1998). This is a view that he also develops in his other ethical writings, such as "Are Moral Requirements Hypothetical Imperatives?" and "Values and Secondary Qualities" (reprinted in the same volume).

17. In his Locke lectures: *Mind and World* (Cambridge, MA: Harvard University Press, 1994) and his Woodbridge lectures: "Having the World in View: Sellars, Kant, and Intentionality" [*The Journal of Philosophy* 95 (1998)], McDowell has attempted to steer a course between the Myth of the Given (e.g., the empiricist's appeal to sense-data) and the efforts to recoil from the Given into an epistemological coherentism (advocated by philosophers like Rorty and Davidson).

18. I draw from McDowell's recent debates with Hubert Dreyfus on the importance of Heidegger's phenomenology for contemporary debates in analytical philosophy. The exchange was occasioned by Hubert Dreyfus's presidential address to the American Philosophical Association, "Overcoming the Myth of the Mental: How Philosophers Can Profit from the Phenomenology of Ordinary Experience," *Proceedings and Addresses of the American Philosophical Association* 79 (2005). McDowell's reply and the rest of the exchange is available in *Inquiry* 50 (2007).

19. Hadot and Foucault also pursue the pedagogical dimension of (ancient) philosophy and a concern for the status of exemplars, such as Socrates.

20. I mean scholars such as Jean-François Lyotard, Slavoj Žižek, Jean-Luc Nancy, and Philippe Lacoue-Labarthe.

Chapter 1: Beyond Orientalism and Academic Rationalism

1. Pierre Hadot, "La philosophie comme manière de vivre," *Exercices spirituels et philosophie antique* (Paris: Etudes Augustiniennes, 1987), 296, translated as "Philosophy as a Way of Life" in *Philosophy as a Way of Life*, trans. Michael Chase and ed. Arnold I. Davidson (Oxford: Blackwell, 1995), 269.

2. "La philosophie comme manière de vivre," 293 ("Philosophy as a Way of Life," 267).

3. "La philosophie comme manière de vivre," 294 ("Philosophy as a Way of Life," 268).

4. "La philosophie comme manière de vivre," 289 ("Philosophy as a Way of Life," 264).

5. Hadot, "L'histoire de la pensée hellénistique et romaine," *Exercices spirituels et philosophie antique*, 269, translated as "Forms of Life and Forms of Discourse in Ancient Philosophy" in *Philosophy as a Way of Life*, 58.

6. "La philosophie comme manière de vivre," 293–94 ("Philosophy as a Way of Life," 267–68).

7. Refer to my "The Sublime Visions of Philosophy: Fundamental Ontology and the Imaginal World" *Microcosm and Macrocosm*, ed. Anna-Teresa Tymieniecka (Dordrecht, Netherlands: Springer, 2006).

8. Hadot, "Exercices spirituels," *Exercices spirituels et philosophie antique*, 71, translated as "Spiritual Exercises," *Philosophy as a Way of Life*, 107.

9. I take the distinction between agent-centered and act-centered from Julia Annas's "Ancient Ethics and Modern Morality," in *Philosophical Perspectives* 2 (1992): 119–136.

10. Kurt Baier, "Radical Virtue Ethics," in *Midwest Studies in Philosophy* 13 (1988): 126.

11. Charles Butterworth, "Medieval Islamic Philosophy and the Virtue of Ethics," *Arabica* 34 (1987): 222.

12. Ibid.

13. Ibid., 248.

14. For an interesting and insightful defense of virtue ethics (in this regard), refer to John McDowell's "Virtue and Reason," reprinted in *Mind, Value, and Reality* (Cambridge, MA: Harvard University Press, 1998), 50–73. I will develop this position in more detail in the next chapter.

15. "La philosophie comme manière de vivre," 295 ("Philosophy as a Way of Life," 269).

16. By Foucault's later work, I mean his *Histoire de la sexualité* vol. 1–3 (Paris: Gallimard, 1976–84), translated as *History of Sexuality*, vol. 1–3, trans. Robert Hurley (New York: Vintage, 1978–86), and his 1980–82 lectures titled *L'herméneutique du sujet* (Paris: Gallimard, 2001), translated as *The Hermeneutics of the Subject*, trans. Graham Burchell (New York: Picador, 2006).

17. Arnold Davidson, "Introduction: Pierre Hadot and the Spiritual Phenomenon of Ancient Philosophy," in Hadot's *Philosophy as a Way of Life*, 25.

18. Hadot, "Réflexions sur la notion de 'culture de soi,' " *Exercices spirituels et philosophie antique*, 331, translated as "Reflections on the Idea of the 'Cultivation of the Self,' " *Philosophy as a Way of Life*, 211.

19. "Réflexions," 326–27 ("Reflection," 208).

20. Davidson, "Introduction: Pierre Hadot and the Spiritual Phenomenon of Ancient Philosophy," in Pierre Hadot's *Philosophy as a Way of Life*, 24.

21. Hadot, "Réflexions," 330 ("Reflection," 211).

22. Hadot, "Le sage et le monde," *Exercices spirituels et philosophie antique*, 343–60, translated as "Sage and the World," *Philosophy as a Way of Life*, 251–63.

23. "Postscript: An Interview with Pierre Hadot," in *Philosophy as a Way of Life*, 280.

24. Richard Walzer, "Alfarabi's Theory of Prophecy and Divination," *Greek into Arabic* (Cambridge, MA: Harvard University Press, 1962), 213.

25. Edward Said, *Orientalism* (New York: Vintage Books, 1979), 3.

26. This reading dominated the approach to Islamic philosophy in the West until the 1950s. For example, Bertrand Russell, in *A History of Western Philosophy*, maintains that "Arabic philosophy is not important as original thought. Men like Avicenna and Averroes are essentially

commentators. . . . Muhammedan civilization in its great days was admirable in the arts and in many technical ways, but it showed no capacity for independent speculation in theoretical matters" (New York: Simon and Schuster, 1965), 427.

27. Another scholar of Islamic philosophy committed to this form of Orientalism is T. J. DeBoer. See his *The History of Philosophy in Islam*, trans. Edward R. Jones (New York: Dover, 1967), 28–30.

28. See Mahdi's review of Walzer's translation and commentary in "Alfarabi's Imperfect State," *Journal of the American Oriental Society* 110 (1990): 691–726. Mahdi does not use the term "orientalism" explicitly here but his objections to Walzer amount to what Said has labeled Orientalism.

29. Muhsin Mahdi, *Alfarabi and the Foundations of Islamic Political Philosophy* (Chicago, IL: The University of Chicago Press, 2001), 123.

30. Ibid., 58.

31. Plato, *Republic*, trans. Paul Shorey, in *The Collected Dialogues of Plato*, eds. Edith Hamilton and Huntington Cairns (Princeton, NJ: Princeton University Press, 1962).

32. Muhsin Mahdi, *Alfarabi and the Foundations of Islamic Political Philosophy*, 58–59.

33. Leaman, "Orientalism and Islamic Philosophy," in *History of Islamic Philosophy*, Part II, ed. Seyyed Hossein Nasr and Oliver Leaman (London: Routledge, 1996), 1145. For a discussion of Strauss and Mahdi's Straussianism, see Dimitri Gutas, "The Study of Arabic Philosophy in the Twentieth Century," in *British Journal of Middle Eastern Studies* 29 (2002): 19–25.

34. Leo Strauss, *Persecution and the Art of Writing* (Chicago, IL: University of Chicago Press, 1980), 19.

35. Oliver Leaman, "Orientalism and Islamic Philosophy," 1145.

36. Strauss, *Persecution and the Art of Writing*, 19.

37. Hadot, "Exercices spirituels," 71–2 ("Spiritual Exercises," 107–8).

38. Joel Kraemer, "The Jihād of the Falāsifa," *Jerusalem Studies in Arabic and Islam* 10 (1987): 291.

39. Sarah Stroumsa, "Philosopher-King or Philosopher-Courtier? Theory and Reality in the *Falāsifa*'s Place in Islamic Society," *Identidades Marginales* (Madrid: Consejo Superior de Investigaciones Cientificas, 2003), 434.

40. Muhammed 'Abed al-Jabri, *Arab-Islamic Philosophy*, trans. Aziz Abbassi (Austin: The Center for Middle Eastern Studies, The University of Texas at Austin, 1999), 48.

41. Ibid., 49.

42. See Henry Corbin's *Histoire de la philosophie islamique* (Paris: Gallimard, 1964), 437–96. Translated as *History of Islamic Philosophy*, trans. Liadain Sherrard (London: Kegan Paul, 1993), 319–63.

43. Oliver Leaman, *An Introduction to Classical Islamic Philosophy* (Cambridge, UK: Cambridge University Press, 1985), 16.

44. Leaman, "Orientalism and Islamic Philosophy," 1145.

45. This interpretation echoes the approach that some Indian and Pakistani scholars of Islamic philosophy have adopted. They refer to their

subject matter as Muslim philosophy because they claim it is cultivated by Muslims and is not Islamic, that is, it is not derived from Islamic sources. An example is M. M. Sharif's *A History of Muslim Philosophy* (Wiesbaden: Harrassowitz, 1963–66).

46. Oliver Leaman, "Concept of Philosophy in Islam," in *Routledge Encyclopedia of Philosophy*, Vol. 5 (London; Routledge, 1998), 6.

47. See, for instance, Dimitri Gutas's defense of "Arabic philosophy" (as opposed to "Islamic Philosophy") as the proper rendition of *falsafa* ("The Study of Arabic Philosophy in the Twentieth Century," 18–19). Gutas's view has attracted a following among some prominent historians of philosophy (see, for instance, *The Cambridge Companion to Arabic Philosophy*, ed. Peter Adamson and Richard C. Taylor [Cambridge, UK: Cambridge University Press, 2005], xiii–xv). Gutas's account assumes an understanding of philosophy as rational discourse meant to explain the various aspects of reality systematically, so he is alarmed when someone like Corbin finds an "overpowering religious dimension" in *falsafa* ("The Study of Arabic Philosophy in the Twentieth Century," 18). In this work, I defend Corbin's reading by questioning the account of philosophy as a mere rational treatment of a range of different topics. We can begin to recognize the central role of religion in *falsafa* once we understand that "Islamic philosophers" understood philosophy as the practice of spiritual exercises for the attainment of wisdom.

A further problem with the rendition of *falsafa* as "Arabic philosophy" lies in its exclusion of *falsafa* texts in Persian. Gutas responds that in these "late" texts, "the terminology was still completely Arabic as was the way of thinking that underlay the expression" (ibid.). As the Persian texts drew on the Arabic translations of Greek sources, their use of Arabic terminology is understandable. Seyyed Hossein Nasr, moreover, shows that Persian philosophical sources constitute an important corpus, and that along with figures such as Avicenna and Ghazali, who wrote both in Arabic and Persian, there are others in "earlier and later centuries of Islamic history who wrote mostly or completely in Persian, such as Nāṣir-i Khusraw and Afḍāl al-Dīn Kāshānī, and who are usually left out of consideration in most of the general histories of Islamic philosophy precisely because of the language in which they expressed their ideas" ("The Significance of Persian Philosophical Works in the Tradition of Islamic Philosophy," in *Essays on Islamic Philosophy and Science*, ed. G. F. Hourani [New York: SUNY Press, 1975], 67). Some scholars, for example Henry Corbin, have also challenged the dubious claim that Persian philosophical texts express the Arabic "way of thinking!" Gutas's curious (and problematic) phrase overlooks at least some continuity between Islamic and pre-Islamic Persian thought (see, e.g., Corbin's *L'Iran et la philosophie* (Paris: Fayard, 1990), 44–66, translated as *The Voyage and the Messenger: Iran and Philosophy*, trans. Joseph Rowe [Berkeley, CA: North Atlantic Books, 1998], 37–60; see also Corbin's *Terre céleste et corps de résurrection de l'Iran mazdéen à l'Iran shî'ite* (Paris: Buchet/Chastel, 1960), 23–174, translated as *Spiritual Body and Celestial Earth: From Mazdean Iran to Shī'ite Iran*, trans. Nancy Pearson [Princeton, NJ: Princeton University Press, 1977], 3–105). Finally, Gutas's view misses out on conceptions of philosophy that do not consider philosophical activity as a mere expression of certain historical cultural configurations. This is part of the reason for Gutas's dismissal of Nasr's approach to *falsafa* as a "confessional esotericism" ("The Study of Arabic Philosophy in the Twentieth Century," 18). I, on the other hand, read Nasr as a pioneer in challenging the metaphilosophical assumption of scholars like Gutas; Nasr interprets *falsafa* as a practice of spiritual exercises rather than an academic exercise manufacturing rational discourse (see the discussion of Nasr's approach in section six of this chapter). Gutas, however, is blind to this possibility and rushes (in what is at best an *ad hominem*) to judge Nasr's reading of the *falsafa* tradition as a promotion of his "ethnic or religious chauvinism" (ibid.).

48. See M. M. Sharif's *A History* of *Muslim Philosophy* (Wiesbaden: Harrassowitz, 1963–66).

49. Ibid., 7.

50. Seyyed Hossein Nasr, "The Meaning and Concept of Philosophy in Islam," in *History of Islamic Philosophy,* Part I, ed. Seyyed Hossein Nasr and Oliver Leaman (London: Routledge, 1996), 24–25.

51. Ibid., 23.

52. Ibid.

53. Ibid., 22. Nasr admits that before Avicenna the Isma'ili philosophers had gone beyond the Peripatetics in combining philosophical theory and the practice of a virtuous life; see "The Meaning and Concept of Philosophy in Islam," 23.

54. Quoted by Mehdi Aminrazavi, "The Logic of Orientals: Whose Logic and Which Orient?" in the *Beacon of Knowledge*, ed. Mohammad H. Faghfoory (Louisville, KY: Fons Vitae, 2003), 48.

55. Dimitri Gutas's *Avicenna and the Aristotelian Tradition* (Leiden, Netherlands: E. J. Brill, 1988), 286–96, is perhaps a good antidote to Nasr's postulation of a radical divide between Avicenna the Peripatetic and Avicenna the Oriental.

56. Hadot writes that "'theoretical' is not opposed to 'practical.' In other words, theoretical can be applied to a philosophy which is practiced, lived, and active, and which brings happiness," *Qu'est-ce que la philosophie antique?* (Paris: Gallimard, 1995), 129, translated as *What is Ancient Philosophy?*, trans. Michael Chase (Cambridge, MA: Harvard University Press, 2004), 81. Claudia Baracchi, in *Aristotle's Ethics as First Philosophy*, affirms this reading of Aristotle. She maintains that "[q]ua *bios*, the *bios theōrētikos* is a matter of action, of praxis. In other words, *theōrein* is a manner of life, neither outside nor above life, hence always involved in life even as it tries to examine it. *Theōrein* will, in this sense, never have meant separation from life" (Cambridge, UK: Cambridge University Press, 2007), 90.

57. See for instance his alignment of ethics with the act-centered divine-command principles of the *sharīʿa* in "Islamic Philosophy—Reorientation or Re-understanding," in *Islamic Life and Thought* (Albany: State University of New York Press, 1981), 155.

58. Prophetology assumes a central place in the modern discussion of Islamic philosophy through the efforts of Henry Corbin (see *Histoire de la phi-*

losophie islamique, 49–154 [*History of Islamic Philosophy*, 23–104]; see also Nasr's "The Qur'ān and *Ḥadith* as Source and Inspiration of Islamic Philosophy," in *History of Islamic Philosophy*, Part I, 28 & 38, fn. 3).

Chapter 2: To the Things Themselves

1. See Chapter 1, §1.2.

2. "De Heidegger à Sohravardî: Entretien avec Philippe Nemo," *Cahiers de l'Herne: Henry Corbin*, ed., Christian Jambet (Paris: L'Herne, 1981), 23. The interview was recorded for *Radio France-Culture*, on Wednesday, June 2, 1976.

3. Seyyed Hossein Nasr, "Henry Corbin: The Life and Works of the Occidental Exile in Quest of the Orient of Light," in *Traditional Islam in the Modern World* (New York: KPI, 1987), 276.

4. Ibid.

5. Steven M. Wasserstrom, *Religion after Religion* (Princeton, NJ: Princeton University Press, 1999), 146.

6. Henry Corbin, *Philosophie iranienne et philosophie comparée* (Paris: Buchet/Chastel, 1985), 23. Translated as *The Concept of Comparative Philosophy*, trans. Peter Russell (Ipswich: Golgonooza Press, 1981), 5.

7. "De Heidegger à Sohravardî," 26. I draw from (and modify where necessary) the English translation, "From Heidegger to Suhrawardi: An Interview with Phillipe Nemo," trans. Kathleen Raine, *Temenos Academy Review* 6 (2003): 123.

8. "De Heidegger à Sohravardî," 25 ("From Heidegger to Suhrawardi," 123).

9. Martin Heidegger, *Sein und Zeit*, in *Martin Heidegger: Gesamtausgabe* 2 (Frankfurt am Main: Vittorio Klostermann, 1977), 45–50; hereinafter page numbers will be cited in the text after "*SZ*." Translated by John Macquarrie and Edward Robinson as *Being and Time* (New York: Harper & Row, 1962), 71–75; hereinafter page numbers will be cited in the text after "*BT*" and after the reference to the German original.

10. I agree with Robert Brandom's claim in "Heidegger's Categories in *Being and Time*" that the objective entities (the present-at-hand) of positive sciences, which at first may appear to be different from equipment, are not an entirely different category of entities.

> The crucial point to understand here is that the move from equipment ready-to-hand, fraught with socially instituted significance, to objective things present-at-hand, is not one of decontextualization, but of *re*contextualization. Asserting and the practices of giving and asking for reasons which make it possible are themselves a special sort of practical activity. (*Monist* 66 [1983]: 403)

The scientific present-at-hand entities do not exist independently of human social practices, but rather they appear as the equipment of the social practices of giving and asking for reasons. Positive sciences are social practices of giving and asking for reasons that involve the confirmation of a logically organized body of assertions. In *Being and Time,* Heidegger advances the claim that "[t] heoretical research is not without a *praxis* of its own" (*SZ* 358; *BT* 409).

11. Heidegger identifies the unity of the various structures of the various ways of the being of Dasein (as being-in-the-world) in the structure of Care (*SZ* 193; *BT* 237–38). Care as being-ahead-of-itself and as always not-yet is comprehended in its totality in the phenomenon of temporality (*SZ* 234; *BT* 277). Temporality as completing Care "has the unity of a future which makes present in the process of having been" (*SZ* 326; *BT* 374). Temporality, according to Heidegger, is the completion of the being of Dasein and the condition for the possibility of the understanding of being.

12. In *Being and Time,* Heidegger maintains that "inauthenticity is based on the possibility of authenticity" (*SZ* 259; *BT* 303).

13. Husserl also adopts an ascetic approach to cultivating the self in his phenomenological investigations. In the *Paris Lectures,* he writes: "To be a meditating philosopher who, through these meditations, has himself become a transcendental ego, and who constantly reflects upon himself, means to enter upon often endless transcendental experience. . . . It means to see all that which is to be seen, to explain and penetrate it, to encompass it descriptively by concepts and judgments. But these latter must only be terms which have been derived without alteration from their perceptual source . . . I am detached inasmuch as I 'suspend' all worldly interests (which I nonetheless possess)" (trans. Peter Koestenbaum [The Hague: Martinus Nijhoff, 1975], 12–14).

14. Wilfrid Sellars, "Empiricism and the Philosophy of Mind," in *Minnesota Studies in the Philosophy of Science,* Vol. 1, eds. Herbert Feigl & Michael Scriven (Minneapolis: University of Minnesota Press, 1956), 255.

15. Ibid., 298–99.

16. Ibid., 253–55.

17. John McDowell, *Mind and World* (Cambridge, MA: Harvard University Press, 1994), 51.

18. Ibid., 9.

19. In "Wittgenstein on Following a Rule," McDowell writes:

> When we say " 'Diamonds are hard' is true if and only if diamonds are hard," we are just as much involved on the right-hand side as the reflections on rule-following tell us we are. There is a standing temptation to miss the obvious truth, and to suppose that the right-hand side somehow presents us with a possible fact, pictured as an unconceptualized configuration of things in themselves. But we can find the connection between meaning and truth illuminating without succumbing to that temptation. [*Mind, Value and Reality* (Cambridge, MA: Harvard University Press, 1998), 255]

20. Hubert Dreyfus, "Overcoming the Myth of the Mental: How Philosophers Can Profit from the Phenomenology of Ordinary Experience." *Proceedings and Addresses of the American Philosophical Association* 79 (2005): 3–4.

21. Ibid., 4–5.

22. John McDowell, "What Myth?" *Inquiry* 50 (2007): 342.

23. Ibid., 342.

24. "Virtue and Reason," in *Mind, Value and Reality*, 51

25. McDowell's *Mind and World*, in contrast to his ethical writings, does not emphasize the complexity of the *Bildung* required to access the things themselves clearly. McDowell simply maintains that the initiation into a language provides the rational animal with the appropriate access to things themselves. This leaves out the fine points of the struggle that the knower must experience to win an unclouded access. It is perhaps with that problem in mind that McDowell revises his position in a recent essay titled "Avoiding the Myth of the Given," where he rejects his *Mind and World* thesis that experience has propositional content (*Having the World in View* [Cambridge, MA: Harvard University press, 2009], 258–59). In the revised position, McDowell distinguishes between intuitional experiential content and the discursive content of assertions and judgments. Discursive content is articulated (and propositional), and intuitional content is not (ibid., 262). Nevertheless, McDowell claims that both are conceptual (ibid.), so he preserves the earlier relevant thesis that the conceptual is unbounded. Therefore, we have access to things in principle, but this access is not fixed so that the world must express itself each time in the same way that our judgment expresses its content. I read his revision as motivated, at least in part, by the failure of *Mind and World* to provide for a more developmental account of the quality of the person's access to the things themselves. Since the content of experience does not have the same structure as the content of thoughts about experience, our access to things themselves can become more precise and accurate without sacrificing the access itself. In the new view, it is easier to speak of an access to the things themselves (i.e., having the world in view), while maintaining that this access can become more precise and accurate through a training in virtue. Virtue frees us from interests that cloud our understanding of things as they show themselves. As I show in relation to Heidegger's account of phenomenology, we cannot simply assume (*pace* earlier McDowell) that learning a language is an adequate training to allow our *perspicuous* access to things themselves.

26. See Victor Farias, *Heidegger and Nazism*, trans. Paul Burrell (Philadelphia: Temple University Press, 1991).

27. Nasr, "Henry Corbin: The Life and Works," 280.

28. *Philosophie iranienne et philosophie comparée*, 33 (*The Concept of Comparative Philosophy*, 14–15).

29. In Islamic thought, *kashf al-maḥjūb* is a term that has wide usage. It means the unveiling the veiled, the shy, or rather the one that conceals himself. Along with its usage in philosophical texts, there are two mystical treatises that bear it as their title: (1) Abū Ya'qūb Sijistānī's *"Kashf al-Mahjub,"* trans. Hermann Landolt, in *An Anthology of Philosophy in Persia*, Vol II, eds. S. H. Nasr & M. Aminrazavi (London: Oxford University Press, 2001). (2) 'Alī ibn 'Uthmān al-Ḥujwirī, *The Kashf al-Mahjub, The Oldest Persian Treatise on Sufism*, trans. R. A. Nicholson (London: Luzac, 1959).

30. On the relation between the Islamic Peripatetic account of the soul (*al-nafs*) and Heidegger's Dasein, see Nader El-Bizri's *The Phenomenological Quest: Between Avicenna and Heidegger* (Binghamton, NY: Global Publications, 2000), 13–14. El-Bizri confirms my reading that *al-nafs* and Dasein are alike in that they constitute themselves.

31. "De Heidegger à Sohravardî," 31 ("From Heidegger to Suhrawardi," 133)

32. Ibid.

33. "De Heidegger à Sohravardî," 32 ("From Heidegger to Suhrawardi," 135)

34. El-Bizri, in *The Phenomenological Quest: Between Avicenna and Heidegger*, argues that for Heidegger Dasein is not in time but temporality (64), but then he defines temporality as finite, terminating in death (ibid., 64–65). This is a peculiar notion of *not* being in time. I believe that El-Bizri's analysis is not sufficiently critical of Heidegger's account of the being of Dasein.

35. "De Heidegger à Sohravardî," 25 ("From Heidegger to Suhrawardi," 123).

36. "De Heidegger à Sohravardî," 25 ("From Heidegger to Suhrawardi," 122).

37. Henry Corbin, *L'homme de lumière dans le soufisme iranien* (Paris: Éditions Présence, 1971), 106. Translated as *The Man of Light in Iranian Sufism*, trans. Nancy Pearson (New Lebanon, NY: Omega Publications, 1978), 68.

38. The *locus classicus* of the hermeneutic principle is Socrates' remark in Plato's *Theaetetus*: "evils . . . can never be done away with, for the good must always have its contrary; nor have they any place in the divine world, but they must haunt this region of our mortal nature. That is why we should make all speed to take flight from this world to the other, and that means becoming like the divine so far as we can, and that again is to become righteous [just] with the help of wisdom" [176b. I use the F. M. Cornford translation in *The Collected Dialogues of Plato*, ed. Edith Hamilton and Huntington Cairns (Princeton, NJ: Princeton University Press, 1962)]. In "The Political Interpretation of the Maxim: The Purpose of Philosophy is the Imitation of God," Lawrence Berman quotes an interesting passage from Ibn Ṭayyib's *Introduction to Isagoge*. This passage helps us to see the prevalence of the so-called principle of hermeneutic phenomenology in Islamic philosophy: "The fifth definition is from the remote end. Understand it of practical and theoretical philosophy. It says that philosophy is likeness to God, may he be exalted, according to man's capacity, through the knowledge of truth and the doing of good" [*Studia Islamica* 15 (1961): 55].

39. Corbin, in "Nāṣir-i Khusrau and Iranian Ismā'īlism," identifies this cultivation of the soul in Nasir Khusraw's Isma'ili (*baṭinī*) hermeneutics as a "spiritual birth (*wilādat rūḥānīya*)," but Corbin does not see its philosophical significance: "[this birth] is an inner event quite different from mere philosophical redemption" [*The Cambridge History of Iran*, vol. 4, ed. R. N. Frye (Cambridge, UK: Cambridge University Press, 1975), 540].

Chapter 3: From the Things Themselves to Prophecy

1. David C. Reisman, "Al-Fārābi and the Philosophical Curriculum," in *The Cambridge Companion to Arabic Philosophy*, ed. Peter Adamson and Richard C. Taylor (Cambridge, UK: Cambridge University Press, 2005), 54.

2. William Chittick, in *The Heart of Islamic Philosophy* (London: Oxford University Press, 2001), 73, draws from al-Kindi's "On the Definition and Description of Things" and elaborates on his sixth definition of "philosophy": "They also defined it in respect of its act, and they said, 'Philosophy is becoming similar to God's acts to the extent of human capacity.' They meant that the human should be perfect in virtue" [*Fī ḥudūd al ashyā' wa rusūmihā* in *Rasā'il al-Kindī al-falsafiyya*, ed. M. 'A. Abū Rīda (Cairo: Dār al-fikr al-'Arabī, 1950), 172]. Also see al-Kindi's "On the Means of Dispelling Sorrows" in John McGinnis and David C. Reisman's *Classical Arabic Philosophy: An Anthology of Sources* (Indianapolis: Hackett, 2007), 23–35. For a discussion of the importance of spiritual practices in this work of al-Kindi, see Peter Groff, "Al-Kindī and Nietzsche on the Stoic Art of Banishing Sorrow," *Journal of Nietzsche Studies* 28 (2004): 139–73.

3. See Rāzī's "On the Philosopher's Way of Life," in McGinnis and Reisman's *Classical Arabic Philosophy: An Anthology of Sources*, 49–53. See also *The Spiritual Physick of Rhazes*, trans. Arthur J. Arberry (London: J. Murray, 1950).

4. Fārābī, *Taḥṣīl al-sa'āda*, ed. 'Alī Bū Mulḥim (Beirut: Dār wa maktabat al-hilāl, 1995), 95–96; hereinafter page numbers will be cited in the text after "*Taḥṣīl al-sa'āda*." I draw from Muhsin Mahdi's translation of this book as *The Attainment of Happiness*, in *Philosophy of Plato and Aristotle* (Ithaca, NY: Cornell University Press, 1962), 48. The page numbers for the translation follow the Arabic text's page number.

5. Paul Moraux, *Der Aristotelismus bei den Griechen*, I (Berlin: W. De Gruyter, 1973), 79. In "The Starting Point of Philosophical Studies in Alexandrian and Arabic Aristotelianism," Dimitri Gutas discusses a passage from Alfarabi's *Prolegomena to the Study of Aristotle's Philosophy* in which "Theophrastus allegedly maintained that the starting point of philosophical studies is ethics or the improvement of one's character" [in *Theophrastus of Eresus: On His Life and Work*, ed. W.W. Fortenbaugh (New Brunswick, NJ: Transaction Publishers, 1985), 115]. In this connection, Gutas mentions Moraux's account of prephilosophical morality in the Aristotelian tradition and proceeds to shed more light on the Peripatetic debates concerning the priority of logic or ethics as the starting point of philosophy (debates that eventually led to Alfarabi's ascription of the aforementioned claim to Theophrastus), but he is careful to point out that among the Aristotelians, even when logic is considered the starting point, an ethical training is presupposed, where this ethical training is distinguished from philosophical ethics, that is, the formal inquiry into the good life ("The Starting Point of Philosophical Studies," 116–17). Moreover, he does admit that the *general* concern with the prephilosophical training goes "at least as far back as Aristotle himself . . . and was engaged in, in addition

to the Peripatetics, by the representatives of all major schools of philosophy, Epicureans, Stoics, and Sceptics" (ibid., 122, fn. 4). I agree and add that the discussion in *The Attainment of Happiness* is in line with this general sense of the "prephilosophical" cultivation of the self in the preceding Greek philosophy.

6. Seyyed Hossein Nasr, *Islam: Religion, History, Civilization* (New York: HarperCollins, 2003), 76.

7. Fazlur Rahman, "Some Key Ethical Concepts of the Qur'an," *Journal of Religious Ethics* 11 (1983): 170.

8. Ibid., 182.

9. Ibid., 178.

10. Toshihiko Izutsu, *Ethico-Religious Concepts in the Qur'an* (Montreal: McGill-Queen's University Press, 2002), 189.

11. Ibid., 190.

12. Ibid., 196.

13. Fazlur Rahman, "Some Key Ethical Concepts of the Qur'an," 176.

14. Ibid.

15. Nasr, in *Islam: Religion, History, Civilization,* places *iḥsān* at the culmination of the triadic process, 87–90.

16. *The Heart of Islamic Philosophy,* 30.

17. Ibid.

18. Chittick's account privileges Sufism over philosophy (ibid., 31). My reading reverses that order.

19. Fazlur Rahman identifies a Stoic precedent in this account of religion: According to the Stoic "tripartite theology," "the 'civil' theology or religion, as opposed to the philosophic religion, is the lot of the masses who can not only not understand philosophy but must not understand it for it would harm their religion. This doctrine was formulated by the Stoic Panätius as a defense of the popular religion against the onslaught of Hellenic enlightenment. The pagan Roman pontiff, Scaevola, gave it clerical authority"[*Prophecy in Islam* (London: George Allen and Unwin, 1958), 62]. Rahman does not offer evidence on the availability of this Stoic doctrine to Muslim Peripatetics. Plato's *Statesman,* however, offers a version of the thesis that religious law is an imperfect copy of the philosophical truths (300c), and a version of it was available to the Muslims. On the form and content of the Platonic material available to the Muslims, see Franz Rosenthal's "On the Knowledge of Plato's Philosophy in the Islamic World," in *Islamic Culture* 14 (1940): 387–422.

20. Alfarabi, according to Seyyed Hossein Nasr, Islamicizes the Platonic/ Pythagorean *nomos,* identifying it with the *sharī'a* ["The Concept and Reality of Freedom in Islam and Islamic Civilization," in *The Philosophy of Human Rights,* ed., Alan Rosenbaum (Westport, CT: Greenwood Press, 1980), 98]. The use of *al-nawāmis* (sing. *al-nāmūs*) in this text and context supports Nasr's claim.

21. Abū Naṣr Fārābī, *On the Perfect State (Mabādī ārā' ahl al-madīna al-fāḍila),* trans. & comm. Richard Walzer (Oxford: Oxford University Press, 1985), 244–47; hereinafter page numbers will be cited in the text after *"al-Madīna al-fāḍila."* The page numbers for the translation follow the Arabic text's page number.

22. Henry Corbin's *Histoire de la philosophie islamique* (Paris: Gallimard, 1964), 76. Translated as *History of Islamic Philosophy*, trans. Liadain Sherrard (London: Kegan Paul, 1993), 44.

23. *Histoire de la philosophie islamique*, 225–35 (*History of Islamic Philosophy*, 158–65).

24. Mohammad Ali Amir-Moezzi, *The Divine Guide in Early Shiism*, trans. David Streight (Albany: SUNY Press, 1994), 29.

25. Henry Corbin, in "The Imams and the Imamate," writes: "The Imams are at once the eyes through which God watches the world and the eyes through which men contemplate the divine Attributes, since the divine Essence is inaccessible to them" [in *Shi'ism: Doctrines, Thought, and Spirituality*, eds. Seyyed Hossein Nasr, Seyyed Vali Reza Nasr, and Hamid Dabashi (Albany, NY: SUNY press, 1988), 184].

26. Refer to Reisman, "Al-Fārābi and the Philosophical Curriculum," for a categorization of *On the Perfect State* in relation to the other writings of Alfarabi (55).

27. The Greek word *prophētēs* means literally one who speaks for another.

28. Plato maintains the overflowing goodness of the Good in the *Timaeus*, 29e–30c. See Dominic O'Meara's "Neoplatonist Conceptions of the Philosopher-King," in *Plato and Platonism: Studies in Philosophy and the History of Philosophy*, vol. 33, ed. Johannes M. Van Ophuijsen (Washington, DC: Catholic University American Press, 1999), esp. 282–83, for a discussion of the self-diffusiveness of the Good in Platonism and Neoplatonism. On 288–91, O'Meara discusses the philanthropic character of the Neoplatonic ideal person in relation to the latter's imitation of divine Goodness. Also see Lawrence Berman's "The Political Interpretation of the Maxim: The Purpose of Philosophy is the Imitation of God," in *Studia Islamica* 15 (1961): 53–61, for a development of the theme of becoming diffusive of goodness like God in Islamic and Jewish philosophy. See also William Chittick's discussion of *ta'alluh*, becoming like God, in his account of the goals of the practice of Islamic philosophy (*The Heart of Islamic Philosophy* [Oxford: Oxford University Press, 2001], 73).

29. Quotations from Aristotle's *On the Soul* follow the translation of W. D. Ross in *The Complete Works of Aristotle*, ed. Jonathan Barnes (Princeton, NJ: Princeton University Press, 1984).

30. Herbert Davidson, *Alfarabi, Avicenna, and Averroes, on Intellect* (Oxford: Oxford University Press, 1992), 13–14.

31. Alexander Altmann, "Ibn Bājja on Man's Ultimate Felicity," in *Studies in Religious Philosophy and Mysticism* (London: Routledge and Kegan Paul, 1969), 74.

32. For a discussion of this modification of the role of the Active Intellect in the Islamic Peripatetics, see Davidson's *Alfarabi, Avicenna, and Averroes, on Intellect*, 29–30.

33. See also Abū Naṣr Fārābī, *Kitāb al-jam' bayna ra'yay al-ḥakīmayn*, ed. 'Alī Bū Mulḥim (Beirut: Dār wa maktabat al-hilāl, 1996), 65–72; hereinafter page numbers will be cited in the text after "*Ḥakīmayn*." I draw from the translation of Fauzi Najjar and Charles Butterworth: *Harmonization of the Two*

Opinions of the Two Sages, in *Alfarabi: The Political Writings* (Ithaca, NY: Cornell University Press, 2001), 160–65. The page numbers for the translation follow the Arabic text's page number.

34. "In the wording of one of the Arabic paraphrases of Plotinus: 'The intellectual sciences, which are the true sciences, come only from Intellect to the rational soul.' And the paraphrase known as the *Theology of Aristotle* brings the matter-form dichotomy to bear, maintaining: Soul has 'the status of matter,' it 'receives the form of' Intellect, and 'reason occurs in soul only thanks to Intellect.' The original Greek text of the passage again had the cosmic Soul, and not the individual human soul, in view. But Avicenna's comment on the passage as it appears in the *Theology of Aristotle*, shows that he took *soul* in the sense of the human soul, and *intellect* in the sense of 'active intelligences'" (Davidson, *Alfarabi, Avicenna, and Averroes, on Intellect*, 24–25).

35. Herbert Davidson maintains: "One work of Alfarabi's, Avicenna generally, and the early works of Averroes not only recognized a transcendent cause that leads human intellects to actuality; they represented the transcendent cause of human thought, the active intellect, as the cause of the existence of part or all of the sublunar world" (ibid., 29).

36. "Many times it has happened: lifted out of the body into myself; becoming external to all other things and self-encentred; beholding a marvelous beauty; then, more than ever, assured of community with the loftiest order; enacting the noblest life, acquiring identity with the divine; stationing within It by having attained that activity; poised above whatsoever within the Intellectual is less than supreme: yet, there comes the moment of descent from intellection to reasoning, and after that sojourn in the divine, I ask myself how it happened that I can now be descending and how did the Soul ever enter into my body, the Soul which, even within the body, is the high thing it has shown itself to be" (Plotinus, *The Enneads*, trans. Stephen MacKenna [New York: Pantheon, 1962], 357).

37. Corbin, *Histoire de la philosophie islamique*, 43 (*History of Islamic Philosophy*, 18).

38. See Dominic O'Meara's "Neoplatonist Conceptions of the Philosopher-King," for a discussion of the Neoplatonic reception of the Platonic notion of prophecy.

39. Al-Kindi's work also includes attempts to achieve such a synthesis. For instance, in *Fī kammiyat kutub Arisṭū* (*On the Quantity of Aristotle's Books*), al-Kindi maintains that the prophet, through the gift of prophecy and without the arduous preparation required for the philosopher, communicates philosophical wisdom in a way that is accessible to the common person (*Rasā'il al-Kindī al-falsafiyya*, edited by M. 'A. Abū Rīda [Cairo: Dār al-fikr al-'Arabī, 1950], 372–74). Al-Kindi's account does not achieve the continuity that Alfarabi and Avicenna maintain between prophecy and philosophy. I say more about al-Kindi's account of prophecy in Chapter 4, in the context of the discussion of the relation between prophecy and the faculty of imagination.

40. In *Kitāb al-milla*, Alfarabi defines religion as "opinions and action, determined and restricted with stipulations and prescribed for a community

by their first ruler, who seeks to obtain through their practicing it a specific purpose with respect to them and by means of them" [*Kitāb al-milla wa nuṣūṣ ukharā*, ed. Muhsin Mahdi (Beirut: Dār al-Mashriq, 1968), 43]; translation by Charles Butterworth as *Book of Religion*, in *Alfarabi: The Political Writings* (Ithaca, NY: Cornell University Press, 2001), 93.

41. Muhsin Mahdi, *Alfarabi and the Foundations of Islamic Political Philosophy* (Chicago, IL: The University of Chicago Press, 2001), 123.

42. In *Kitāb al-jam' bayna ra'yay al-ḥakīmayn* (*The Harmonization of the Two Opinions of the Two Sages*), Alfarabi manifests his synthesis of political Platonism and Aristotelianism by ascribing the difference in the positions of his predecessors to their personal powers and limitations. He writes that Plato

> was of the opinion that making the soul upright is the most worthwhile thing for a human being to begin with and that only after having mastered making it just and upright is one to go on to making others upright. But when he did not find the power in himself to accomplish that, he dedicated his days to his most important obligations, resolving that once he accomplished the most important and worthwhile he would then turn his attention to the closer and nearer, just as he recommended in his treatises in his politics and ethics. Aristotle proceeded in a manner similar to Plato in his political statements and epistles. But when he turned to the issue of his own soul, he sensed that he possessed the power, liberality, persistence, broad moral character, and perfection to enable him to make it upright and still have the leisure to cooperate [with others] and enjoy many political relations. (*Ḥakīmayn*, 34; trans. 129–30)

43. For a comparison of the ethico-political views of some prominent Islamic philosophers (including Alfarabi), refer to my "Interpreting Political Violence in Islamic Philosophy," *Polylog: Forum for Intercultural Philosophy* 5 (2004): <http://them.polylog.org/5/fam-en.htm>.

44. On dating Avicenna's work, see Dimitri Gutas, *Avicenna and the Aristotelian Tradition* (Leiden: Brill, 1988), pp. 79–145. See also Michael Marmura, "Plotting the Course of Avicenna's Thought," *Journal of the American Oriental Society* 111 (1991): 334–36.

45. Avicenna, *The Metaphysics of* the Healing (*Kitāb al-shifā': al-Ilāhiyyāt*), trans. Michael Marmura (Provo, UT: Brigham Young University Press, 2005), 378.

46. *Avicenna's De Anima*, ed. Fazlur Rahman (London: Oxford University Press, 1959), 46–47; hereinafter page numbers will be cited in the text after "*al-Shifā' DA*." Translation available in McGinnis and Reisman's *Classical Arabic Philosophy: An Anthology of Sources*, 183. The page numbers for the translation follow the Arabic text's page number.

47. See Peter Adamson's "Non-Discursive Thought in Avicenna's Commentary on the *Theology of Aristotle*," in *Interpreting Avicenna: Science and*

Philosophy in Medieval Islam, ed. John McGinnis (Leiden: Brill, 2004), 87–111, for a discussion of the notions of composition and division in relation to intellection in Avicenna.

48. Martin Heidegger, *Sein und Zeit*, in *Martin Heidegger: Gesamtausgabe* 2 (Frankfurt am Main: Vittorio Klostermann, 1977), 59; hereinafter page numbers will be cited in the text after "*SZ*." Translated by John Macquarrie and Edward Robinson as *Being and Time* (New York: Harper & Row, 1962), 85; hereinafter page numbers will be cited in the text after "*BT*" and after the reference to the German original.

49. See Nader El-Bizri's *The Phenomenological Quest: Between Avicenna and Heidegger* (Binghamton, NY: Global Publications, 2000), 13–14.

50. See also *The Metaphysics of* the Healing, 378.

51. Hasse's main target is Herbert Davidson. See Hasse's *Avicenna's De Anima in the Latin West* (Turin: The Warburg Institute, 2000), 183–85. See also "Abstraction in Avicenna," in *Aspects of Avicenna*, ed. Robert Wisnovsky (Princeton, NJ: Markus Wiener, 2001), 39. I believe that Davidson follows a reading of Avicenna that has been in circulation at least as early as Thomas Aquinas. See Chapter 6, §6.2, for Aquinas' version of the same reading.

52 *Avicenna's De Anima in the Latin West*, p. 185.

53. I want to guard against the suggestion that the Psychology of *Kitāb al-najāt* is a distilled version of the one in *Kitāb al-shifā'*. See Gutas's *Avicenna and the Aristotelian Tradition*, 99–100.

54. *Kitāb al-najāt*, ed. Mājid Fakhry (Beirut: Dār al-'ifāq al-jadīda, 1982), 220–21; hereinafter page numbers will be cited in the text after "*al-Najāt*." Translation available in Fazlur Rahman's *Avicenna's Psychology* (London: Oxford University Press, 1952), 55. The translation's page numbers follow the Arabic text's page number.

55. *Binṭāsyā* is the Arabization of the Greek *phantasia*. For a discussion of common sense and the other internal sense faculties, see *Kitāb al-najāt*, 200–02 (translated in *Avicenna's Psychology*, 30–31). See also *Avicenna's De Anima*, 43–45 (translated in *Classical Arabic Philosophy*, 181–82), and Wolfson's "The Internal Senses in Latin, Arabic, and Hebrew Philosophical Texts," *Harvard Theological Review* 28 (1935): 100.

56. See also Black's "Imagination and Estimation: Arabic Paradigms and Western Transformations," *Topoi* 19 (2000): 60.

57. See Gutas, *Avicenna and the Aristotelian Tradition*, 130.

58. Adamson, "Non-Discursive Thought," 91.

59. In book II, chapter 3, 414b18, of *De Anima*, Aristotle mentions that *dianoētikē* is a function of intellect (*nous*). In book III, chapter 9, 432b26, he says *nous* is synonymous with *logistikon*. See also Wolfson, "The Internal Senses in Latin, Arabic, and Hebrew Philosophical Texts," 83.

60. I use F. M. Cornford's translation in *The Collected Dialogues of Plato*, ed. Edith Hamilton and Huntington Cairns (Princeton, NJ: Princeton University Press, 1962).

61. Henry Corbin, *Avicenne et le récit visionnaire* (Teheran: Département d'iranologie de l'Institut franco-iranien, 1954), 24. Translated by Willard

Trask as *Avicenna and the Visionary Recital* (London: Routledge and Kegan Paul, 1960), 21.

62. *Avicenne et le récit visionnaire*, 77 (*Avicenna and the Visionary Recital*, 67).

63. Henry Corbin, *L'homme de lumière dans le soufisme iranien* (Paris: Éditions Présence, 1971), 37. Translated by Nancy Pearson in *The Man of Light in Iranian Sufism* (New Lebanon, NY: Omega Publications, 1978), 19.

64. In the later *What is Called Thinking?*, Heidegger explicitly relates the call of conscience to thinking [trans. J. Glenn Gray (New York: Harper and Row, 1968), 161]. Hannah Arendt, inspired by Heidegger, describes the inner dialogue by tracing it to its Socratic roots:

> For nothing can be itself and at the same time for itself but the two-in-one that Socrates discovered as the essence of thought and Plato translated into conceptual language as the soundless dialogue *eme emautō*—between me and myself. But again, it is not the thinking activity that constitutes the unity, unifies the two-in-one; on the contrary, the two-in-one become One again when the outside world intrudes upon the thinker and cuts short the thinking process. Then, when he is called by his name back into the world of appearances, where he is always One, it is as though the two into which the thinking process had split him clapped together again. [*The Life of the Mind, Volume I: Thinking* (New York: Harcourt Brace Jovanovich, 1985), 185]

65. Adamson, "Non-Discursive Thought," 91 and fn. 10.

66. Gutas argues that the later Avicenna sets up "two parallel processes of thinking, one in the rational soul and the other in the animal. The function of the former is to combine universal propositions or terms to form syllogisms and reach conclusions—only that it takes place necessarily in the intellect because of the immaterial nature of the concepts involved, the intelligible. The function of the second process in the animal soul, that of the Cogitative faculty, is to combine conceptual images of particulars in imitation (*muḥākāt*) of the process in the intellect for the purpose of aiding it" ("Intuition and Thinking: The Evolving Structure of Avicenna's Epistemology," *Aspects of Avicenna*, ed. Robert Wisnovsky [Princeton, NJ: Markus Wiener Publishers, 2001], 22). I agree but I believe that Avicenna has this distinction in his earlier *Kitāb al-najāt*.

67. *The Metaphysics of* the Healing, 378.

68. See also *Avicenna's De Anima*, 50 (*Classical Arabic Philosophy*, 185).

69. "Intuition and Thinking," 3.

70. Ibid., 3.

71. Ibid., 4.

72. Ibid., 26.

73. Avicenna, *Fī ithbāt al-nubuwwāt*, Philosophical Texts and Studies 2, ed. Michael Marmura (Beirut: Dār al-nahār, 1968), 46. Translated by Michael Marmura as *On the Proof of Prophecies*, in *Medieval Political Philosophy: A*

Sourcebook, ed. Ralph Lerner and Muhsin Mahdi (Ithaca, NY: Cornell University Press, 1961), 115.

74. Michael Marmura, in his analysis of *On the Proof of Prophecies*, confirms this reading: "The prophet, on the other hand, differs from the rest of men capable of abstraction in that he receives the secondary intelligibles directly, without the intervening preparatory activities of the soul and the learning processes associated with them" ["Avicenna's Psychological Proof of Prophecy," *Journal of Near Eastern Studies* 22 (1963): 51].

75. My account of the pedagogical aspect of prophecy is consistent with Gutas's observation, drawing from the Physics of *Dānishnāme-ye 'Alā'ī*, that for Avicenna "the middle term can be acquired in two ways, through instruction or intuition (*ḥads*), which is the movement of the Mind in its efforts to hit spontaneously upon the middle term. Instruction is ultimately reducible to intuition insofar as the theoretical first teacher, who had no one to instruct him, necessarily discovered the middle terms through his intuition" ("Intuition and Thinking," p. 3). I add that intuition must be cultivated, beginning with the acquisition of moral virtues. I will discuss Avicenna's account of the prophecy of imagination and its various forms further in chapters four and five.

76. *Fī ithbāt al-nubuwwāt*, 48 (*On the Proof of Prophecies*, 116)

77. Ibid.

78. *The Metaphysics of* the Healing, 367–70.

Chapter 4: Disciplining the Imagination

1. Avicenna, *Fī ithbāt al-nubuwwāt*, Philosophical Texts and Studies 2, ed. Michael Marmura (Beirut: Dār al-nahār, 1968), 46–48. Translated by Michael Marmura as *On the Proof of Prophecies*, in *Medieval Political Philosophy: A Sourcebook*, ed. Ralph Lerner and Muhsin Mahdi (Ithaca, NY: Cornell University Press, 1961), 115–16.

2. Abū Naṣr Fārābī, *On the Perfect State (Mabādī ārā' ahl al-madīna al-fāḍila)*, trans. & comm. Richard Walzer (Oxford: Oxford University Press, 1985), 224–25 & 244–45.

3. Quotations from Aristotle's *Poetics* follow the translation of James Hutton in *Poetics* (New York: W. W. Norton, 1982).

4. Also refer to Martha Nussbaum's exploration of this theme in "Interlude 2: Luck and the Tragic Emotions," in *The Fragility of Goodness* (Cambridge, UK: Cambridge University Press, 2001), 379–94; see especially 388–91.

5. Gerard Watson, "Imagination: The Greek Background," *The Irish Theological Quarterly* 52 (1986): 57–58.

6. Watson's later work, *Phantasia in Classical Thought* (Galway: Galway University Press, 1988), chapter 4, details this tradition (which he considers to be a mixture of Platonism and Stoicism), but does not succeed in explaining away the obscurity of the sources that he cites for this tradition.

7. Plotinus rejects Plato's account of the work of art in the *Republic* and maintains that the work of art can improve upon nature; *Enneads*, trans, Stephen McKeon (New Tork: Pantheon, 1962), 58.

8. Henry Corbin's *Histoire de la philosophie islamique* (Paris: Gallimard, 1964), 43. Translated as *History of Islamic Philosophy*, trans. Liadain Sherrard (London: Kegan Paul, 1993), 18.

9. Fazlur Rahman, *Prophecy in Islam* (London: George Allen and Unwin, 1958), 71 fn. 22.

10. "Alfarabi's Theory of Prophecy and Divination," *Greek into Arabic* (Cambridge, MA: Harvard University Press, 1962), 213.

11. *Fī mahīyyat al-nawm wa-l-ru'ya* in *Rasā'il al-Kindī al-falsafiyya*, ed. M. 'A. Abū Rīda (Cairo: Dār al-fikr al-'Arabī, 1950), 303.

12. "Fī kammiyat kutub Arisṭū" in *Rasā'il al-Kindī al-falsafiyya*, 372–73.

13. Ibid., 373.

14. Abū Naṣr Fārābī, *Kitāb al-ḥurūf*, ed. Muḥsin Mahdī (Beirut: Dār al-Mashriq, 1970), 152 (§144). I use Muhammad Ali Khalidi's translation in *The Book of Letters, Medieval Islamic Philosophical Writings*, ed. M. A. Khalidi (Cambridge, UK: Cambridge University Press, 2005), 19.

15. *Fuṣūl al-madanī: Aphorisms of the Statesman*, ed. & trans. D. M. Dunlop (Cambridge, UK: Cambridge University Press, 1961), 49. Compare with Avicenna's example of the imaginative representation of honey as vomited bile. He argues that this makes us lose our appetite even if we are convinced of the falsity of the metaphor [*al-Ishārāt wa-l-tanbīhāt, al-Manṭiq*, ed. S. Dunyā (Cairo: Dār al-ma'ārif, 1960), 413].

16. Quotations from the Qur'an follow the translation of Abdullah Yusuf Ali in *Qur'ān* (New York: Tarikhe Tarsile Qur'an, 2001).

17. Michael Zwettler, "A Mantic Manifesto: The Sūra of 'The Poets' and the Qur'ānic Foundations of Prophetic Authority," in *Poetry and Prophecy*, ed. James L. Kugel (Ithaca, NY: Cornell University Press, 1991), 81.

18. Ibid.

19. *On the Perfect State*, 222–23.

20. See Chapter 3, §3.5.

21. D. M. Dunlop, "Al-Fārābī's Introductory *Risālah* on Logic" *Islamic Quarterly* 3 (1956–57): 231.

22. Fārābī, *Taḥṣīl al-sa'āda*, ed. 'Alī Bū Mulḥim (Beirut: Dār wa maktabat al-hilāl, 1995), 88–89. I draw from Muhsin Mahdi's translation of this book as *The Attainment of Happiness*, in *Philosophy of Plato and Aristotle* (Ithaca, NY: Cornell University Press, 1962), 44.

23. *Avicenna's De Anima*, ed. Fazlur Rahman (London: Oxford University Press, 1959), 248–49.

24. Ibid., 249.

25. Ibid., 173.

26. Dimitri Gutas, "Imagination and Transcendental Knowledge in Avicenna," in *Arabic Theology, Arabic Philosophy: From the Many to the One*, ed. J. E. Montgomery (Dudley, MA: Peeters, 2006), 341, fn. 12.

27. Jean Michot, *La destinée de l'homme selon Avicenne: Le retour à Dieu (ma'ād) et l'imagination* (Louvain: Aedibus Peeters, 1986), 122–23. See also Dagg Nikolaus Hasse, *Avicenna's De Anima in the Latin West* (Turin: The Warburg Institute, 2000), 159.

28. Michot, *La destinée de l'homme selon Avicenne*, 123. Gutas, "Imagination and Transcendental Knowledge," 342.

29. Aside from the passage from the Psychology of the *Healing* cited above (fns. 37–39), see also passages from *Provenance and Destination*, translated by Gutas in "Imagination and Transcendental Knowledge," 339.

30. Gutas argues that the Psychology of *Shifā'* and that of *Najāt* are both drawn from an earlier text, *The State of the Human Soul* [*Ḥāl al-nafs al-insāniyya*] (*Avicenna and the Aristotelian Tradition* [Leiden, Netherlands: E. J. Brill, 1988], 99–100). Michot, on the other hand, reverses the order and maintains that because of its patchwork nature *The State of the Human Soul* is posterior to the other texts ["Prophétie et divination selon Avicenna. Présentation, essai de traduction critique et index de l'Épître de l'âme de la sphère,' " in *Revue philosophique de Louvain* 83 (1985): 507–35. Gutas replies that *Shifā'* and *Najāt* are also patchwork texts and adheres to his earlier proposal for dating *The State of the Human Soul* ["Imagination and Transcendental Knowledge in Avicenna," 342, fn. 15].

31. The references to Kant's works, except the *Critique of Pure Reason*, are to the *Akademie* edition (indicated by "Ak." and followed by the page number): *Kants gesammelte Schriften* (Berlin: Königlich Preussische Akademie der Wissenschaften, 1908–13). I use Werner S. Pluhar's translation of *Kritik der Urteilskraft: Critique of Judgment* (Indianapolis: Hackett, 1987). All references will be cited in the text; the page numbers for the translation follow the *Akademie* edition's page number.

32. Martin Heidegger, *Nietzsche* I (Pfullingen: Verlag Gunther Neske, 1961), 130. I use David Farrel Krell's translation, *Nietzsche: The Will to Power as Art* (New York: Harper & Row, 1979), 110.

33. In the *Critique of Pure Reason*, Kant writes: "Intuitions (sensory impressions) and concepts (spontaneous productions of understanding) constitute, therefore, the elements of all our knowledge. . . . Thoughts without content are empty, intuitions without concepts are blind" (A50–1=B74–5).

34. In *Grundlegung zur Metaphysik der Sitten* (*Groundwork for the Metaphysics of Morals*), Kant writes: "Thus morality consists in the relation of all action to the making of laws. . . . This making of laws must be found in every rational being himself and must be able to spring from his will. The principle of his will is therefore never to perform an action except on a maxim such as can be a universal law" Ak. 434 [*Groundwork for the Metaphysics of Morals*, trans. H. J. Paton (New York: Harper & Row, 1964), 101]. The principle of the will of the rational being is the moral law or the categorical imperative. This passage shows how Kant recoils from the world into the self to find confirmation for moral judgments.

35. Iris Murdoch, *Sovereignty of Good* (New York: Routledge, 1970), 83.

36. Ibid., 84.

37. Murdoch writes: "We experience the [Kantian] Sublime when we confront the awful contingency of nature or of human fate and return into ourselves with a proud shudder of rational power" (Ibid., 81–2).

38. See Charles Taylor's *Hegel* (Cambridge, UK: Cambridge University Press, 1975), 465–66.

39. G.W.F. Hegel, *Vorlesungen über die Aesthetik* I–II, in *Werke in zwanzig Bänden,* vols. 13–14 (Frankfurt am Main: Suhrkamp, 1979). Translated by T. M. Knox as *Aesthetics*, Vol. 1 (Oxford: Clarendon Press, 1975); all references to these lectures will be in the text, with "*Aes,*" the volume number, and page number(s) of the German text first and the translated text second.

40. "Hegel and the Divinity of Light in Zoroastrianism and Islamic Phenomenology." *The Classical Bulletin* 83 (2007).

41. Philippe Lacoue-Labarthe, "Sublime Truth," in *Sublime: Presence in Question,* trans. Jeffrey S. Librett (Albany, NY: SUNY Press, 1993) 94.

42. Ibid., 95.

43. For Avicenna's remark on his Aristotelian debt in this regard, see Deborah Black's "Estimation (*Wahm*) in Avicenna: The Logical and the Psychological Dimensions," *Dialogue* 32 (1993): 245, fn. 2.

44. Harry A. Wolfson, in "The Internal Senses in Latin, Arabic, and Hebrew Philosophical Texts," *Harvard Theological Review* 28 (1935), enumerates the following four: (1) *al-mutakhayyila,* (2) *al-wahm,* (3) *al-ḍakira,* (4) *al-mufakira* (94, fn. 26).

45. *Avicenna's De Anima,* 43–45. Translation available in John McGinnis, and David C. Reisman's *Classical Arabic Philosophy: An Anthology of Sources* (Indianapolis: Hackett, 2007), 181–82. See also Wolfson, "The Internal Senses in Latin, Arabic, and Hebrew Philosophical Texts," 100; and Gutas, "The Intellect Without Limits: The Absence of Mysticism in Avicenna," *Intellect and Imagination in Medieval Philosophy,* ed. C. Pacheco & J. F. Meirinhos (Turnhout: Brepols, 2006), 356–57.

46. *Avicenna's De Anima,* 43–45 (*Classical Arabic Philosophy,* 181–82). See also Black's "Imagination and Estimation: Arabic Paradigms and Western Transformations," *Topoi* 19 (2000), 60.

47. *Avicenna's De Anima,* 45 (*Classical Arabic Philosophy,* 182–83).

48. *Kitāb al-najāt,* ed. Mājid Fakhry (Beirut: Dār al-'ifāq al-jadīda, 1982), 204. Translation available in Fazlur Rahman's *Avicenna's Psychology* (London: Oxford University Press, 1952), 34.

49. Abū 'Alī Hussain ibn Sīnā, *al-Shifā': al-manṭiq* 9: *al-shi'r,* ed. A. badawī (Cairo: Dār al-miṣriyya li-l-ta'līf wa-l-tarjuma, 1966), 54. I draw my translation from Ismail M. Dahiyat, *Avicenna's Commentary on the* Poetics *of Aristotle* (Leiden: E. J. Brill, 1974) 100.

50. Ibn Sīnā, *al-Shifā': al-Manṭiq* 9: *al-Shi'r,* 24–5. Here, I draw from the translation in Vicente Cantarino, *Arabic Poetics in the Golden Age* (Leiden: E. J. Brill, 1975), 133.

51. It is in developing an account of the objectivity of imaginative representations based on criteria having to do with feelings of pleasure and astonishment that Avicenna's position differs from that of his predecessor

Alfarabi and breaks new ground. Refer to Salim Kemal, *The Poetics of Alfarabi and Avicenna*, 135–38.

52. In the *Critique of Judgment*, Kant writes: "Therefore, the liking that, without a concept, we judge to be universally communicable and hence to be the basis that determines a judgment of taste, can be nothing but the subjective purposiveness in the presentation of an object, without any purpose (whether objective or subjective), and hence the mere form of purposiveness, insofar as we are conscious of it, in the presentation by which an object is *given* us" (Ak. 221, trans. 66).

53. In the *Critique of Judgment*, Kant distinguishes the reflective judgment of taste from that of the sublime. He writes: "In presenting the sublime in nature the mind feels agitated, while in an aesthetic judgment about the beautiful in nature it is in restful contemplation. This agitation (above all at its conception) can be compared with a vibration, that is, with a rapid alternation of repulsion from, and attraction to, one and the same object" (Ak. 258, trans. 115). The imagination presents an object, which it cannot contain as a totality according to the conceptual repertoire of understanding; this results in a feeling of repulsion, but then reason and its idea of the supersensible engage the presentation of the imagination and a harmony is struck; a feeling of pleasure ensues. The vibration or the oscillation between repulsion and attraction determines the presented object as sublime. What is expressed in this experience is the un-presentable, the power of "pure and independent reason" (Ak. 258, trans. 116). In other words, what is presented is that which makes possible the presentation of the ordinary phenomena. Reason's purposiveness (without purpose) unveils the phenomena in the judgments of taste and in the sublime it is itself presented indirectly (Ak. 246, trans. 100).

54. A comparison of Kant and Avicenna on this point is beyond the reach of this essay; it suffices to say that for Avicenna, the Active Intellect is external to human intellect, whereas Kant's reason is not. A further difference is that Avicenna allows for intellectual intuition (i.e., perception), whereas Kant denies intellectual receptivity and limits intuition to sensibility.

55. Also see Jean-Francois Lyotard, *Lessons on the Analytic of the Sublime*, trans., Elizabeth Rottenberg (Palo Alto, CA: Stanford University Press, 1994), 228.

56. Ibid., 236–38.

57. For a dating of the manuscript and its place in the Avicennan corpus, refer to Gutas's *Avicenna and the Aristotelian Tradition*, 98–99.

58. *Al-Mabda' wa'l-ma'ād*, in Wisdom of Persia Series 36, ed. A. Nūrānī (Tehran: Institute of Islamic Studies, McGill University-Tehran University, 1984), 119. I have drawn from Gutas's translation in "The Intellect Without Limits," 365–66; I have omitted his insertions which transform the meaning of the text.

59. Ibid.

60. For a translation and an excellent treatment of Avicenna's narratives, refer to Henry Corbin's *Avicenne et le récit visionnaire* (Tehran: Département d'iranologie de l'Institut franco-iranien, 1954). Translated as *Avicenna and the*

Visionary Recital, trans. Willard R. Trask (London: Routledge and Kegan Paul, 1960). Also see Peter Heath's more recent *Allegory and Philosophy in Avicenna* (Philadelphia: University of Pennsylvania Press, 1992).

61. Sarah Stroumsa, "Avicenna's Philosophical Stories: Aristotle's Poetics Reinterpreted," *Arabica* 39 (1992): 200–4. Avicenna says that "[p]oetry, therefore, has come to be more akin to philosophy than the other kind of speech (fables—*amthāl*), because it has a greater grasp of the existent and a more precise execution of universal judgment," [Ibn Sīnā, *al-Shifā': al-Manṭiq* 9: *al-Shi'r*, 54 (Dahiyat, *Avicenna's Commentary on the* Poetics *of Aristotle*, 100)]. I take it to mean that poetry, contrary to fables and like philosophy, is capable of expressing emanations of the Active Intellect which are universal.

Chapter 5: The Theologian's Dream

1. See Thérèse-Ann Druart's "Imagination and the Soul-Body Problem in Arabic Philosophy," *Analecta Husserliana*, Vol. XVI, ed. A-T. Tymieniecka (Boston: Reidel Publishing, 1983), 338.

2. Ghazālī, *Al-Munqidh min al-ḍalāl*, ed., Maḥmūd Bījū (Damascus: Dār al-taqwā, 1992), 73; hereinafter page numbers will be cited in the text after "*Munqidh*." A translation is available in *The Faith and Practice of al-Ghazālī*, trans. W. Montgomery Watt (London: George Allen and Unwin Ltd., 1967), 64. The page numbers for the translation follow the Arabic text's page number.

3. I use W. D. Ross's translation in *The Complete Works of Aristotle*, ed. Jonathan Barnes (Princeton, NJ: Princeton University Press, 1984).

4. See also Alexander Altmann, "Maimonides and Thomas Aquinas: Natural or Divine Prophecy," *AJS Review* 3 (1978): 2.

5. Shlomo Pines, "The Arabic Recension of *Parva Naturalia* and the Philosophical Doctrine Concerning Veridical Dreams According to *al-Risāla al-Manāmīyya* and Other Sources," in *Israel Oriental Studies* 4 (1974): 121. The Arabic text of this passage is available in "A Unique Treatise on the Interpretation of Dreams" ed. Moh'd. 'Abdul Mu'id Khan, in *Avicenna Commemoration Volume* (Calcutta: Iran Society, 1975), 295. The editor's translation of this text is available in "Kitabu ta'bir-ir-ruya of Abu 'Ali B. Sina" in *Indo-Iranica* 9 (1956): 49. Here and below I use Pines's translation, as I find it more literal.

6. The title of the chapter in which this passage appears reads: "The philosopher Aristotle designates in speaking in the book *De Sensu et Sensato*, about dream visions, this force as Active Intellect (*al-'aql al-fa'āl*)." Then in the body the "force" is referred to as the Universal Intellect (*al-'aql al-kullī*) [Pines, "The Arabic Recension of *Parva Naturalia*," 120–21].

7. Ibid., 118.

8. Ibid., 119–20.

9. *Avicenna's De Anima*, ed. Fazlur Rahman (London: Oxford University Press, 1959), 178–80. See also *Al-Mabda' wa-l-ma'ād*, in Wisdom of Persia Series 36, ed. A. Nūrānī (Tehran: Institute of Islamic Studies, McGill University-Tehran University, 1984), 117.

10. See Gutas's discussion of this point in "The Intellect Without Limits: The Absence of Mysticism in Avicenna," 360–61. In "Imagination and Transcendental Knowledge in Avicenna," Gutas mentions two other ways Avicenna accounts for the transmission of prophecy from celestial spheres: (1) a connection between the souls of the spheres and the souls of human beings, (2) engraving [in *Arabic Theology, Arabic Philosophy: From the Many to the One*, edited by J. E. Montgomery (Dudley, MA: Peeters, 2006), 353].

11. *Avicenna's De Anima*, 173.

12. Avicenna, *Aḥwāl al-nafs*, ed. A. F. al-Ahwānī (Cairo: Dār al-iḥyā' al-kutub al-'Arabiyya, 1952), 117.

13. *Avicenna's De Anima*, 200–01. In *Prophecy in Islam*, Fazlur Rahman, drawing from *al-Isharāt* III and the Psychology of *al-Shifā'*, gives an account of Avicenna's theory of miracles: "In the case of ordinary human beings, then, the direct influence of the soul is restricted to its own body, while the exceptional souls and prophets and saints [possessing "strong moral virtue"—see Rahman 84, fn. 73], by becoming 'World Souls, as it were,' become operative throughout Nature. They can 'cure the sick and make evil persons sick, disintegrate and integrate organisms . . . and by their will ruins and prosperity, the sinking of the earth and plagues occur' " (London: George Allen and Unwin, 1958), 50–51.

14. *Avicenna's De Anima in the Latin West* (Turin: The Warburg Institute, 2000), 157.

15. "The Three Properties of Prophethood in Certain Works of Avicenna and al-Ghazālī," in *Interpreting Avicenna: Science and Philosophy in Medieval Islam* (Leiden: Brill, 2004), 192.

16. Ibid., 200.

17. Ghazālī, *The Incoherence of the Philosophers* (*Tahāfut al-falāsafa*), trans. Michael E. Marmura (Provo, UT: Brigham Young University, 1997), 167.

18. "No misfortune can happen/On earth or in your souls/But is recorded in/A decree before We bring/It into existence:/That is truly easy for God," Qur'an 57:22. See also 54:53: "Every matter, small and great,/Is on record."

19. In reply to Ghazali's objections to the account of veridical dreams as receptivity to the imagination of the heavenly bodies, Averroes claims that this theory of philosophy is peculiarly Avicennan (and therefore the problems with it are not blemishes on the Aristotelian account) [Fazlur Rahman, *Prophecy in Islam* (London: George Allen and Unwin, 1958), 75–6, fn. 34]. For Averroes, "there was no difference between veridical dreams and prophecy or for that matter between the two technical forms of divination. . . . The only difference was one of degree" [Altmann, "Maimonides and Thomas Aquinas: Natural or Divine Prophecy," 5].

20. See *Avicenna's De Anima*, 239–50. For the prophecy of imagination, see 248–49. Also see *Kitāb al-najāt*, ed. Mājid Fakhry (Beirut: Dār al-'ifāq al-jadīda, 1982), 205–6, and prophetic imagination is mentioned there as well. An English translation of the corresponding passages of *Kitāb al-najāt* is available in *Avicenna's Psychology*, trans. Fazlur Rahman (London: Oxford University Press, 1952), 35–37.

21. Ghazālī, *The Niche of Lights (Mishkāt al-anwār)*, trans. David Buchman (Provo, UT: Brigham Young University Press, 1998), 4; hereinafter page numbers will be cited in the text after *"Mishkāt."*

22. For a good discussion of the Muhammadan light in the Islamic tradition, refer to U. Rubin's "Pre-existence and Light: Aspects of the Concept of Nūr Muhammad," *Israel Oriental Studies* 5 (1975): 62–119.

23. For a more thorough discussion of the phenomenological approach to Ghazali's project, see my "Unveiling the Hidden: On the Meditations of Descartes and Ghazzali," *Passions of the Soul in the Metamorphosis of Becoming*, ed. Anna Teresa Tymieniecka (Dordrecht, Netherlands: Kluwer, 2003), 219–40.

24. See also *Al-Munqidh min al-ḍalāl*, 33–7; trans. 22–26.

25. Avicenna, *Fī ithbāt al-nubuwwāt*, Philosophical Texts and Studies 2, ed. Michael Marmura (Beirut: Dār al-nahār, 1968), 49–51. Translated by Michael Marmura as *On the Proof of Prophecies*, in *Medieval Political Philosophy: A Sourcebook*, ed. Ralph Lerner and Muhsin Mahdi (Ithaca, NY: Cornell University Press, 1961), 116–17.

26. See the excerpts from Avicenna's *The Metaphysics of* the Healing (*Kitāb al-shifā': al-ilāhiyyāt*), trans. Michael Marmura (Provo, UT: Brigham Young University Press, 2005), 367–78, where Avicenna lays out the importance of religious law and practice for the cultivation of the soul to the point of divine intimacy.

27. In my "Is 'Islamic' Philosophy Islamic?," *Voices of Islam*, vol. 5, ed. Vincent J. Cornell (Westport, CT: Praeger, 2007), 23–41, I challenge the thesis of the incompatibility of philosophy and Islam in a focused and condensed form. That argument has been expanded and improved in this work.

28. Ghazali, *Incoherence of Philosophers*, 10–11.

29. Ibid., 230.

30. Averroes, *The Decisive Treatise* (*Kitāb faṣl al-maqāl*), trans. and ed. Charles E. Butterworth (Provo, UT: Brigham Young University Press, 2001), 13; hereinafter page numbers will be cited in the text after *"Faṣl al-maqāl."*

31. In this context, Averroes does not engage the Avicennan account of poetry (*shi'r*) and the poetic imagination. His concern is with fables and stories (*amthāl*).

32. The translation is a slightly modified version of the one in Averroes, *Tahāfut al-tahāfut*, trans. and ed. Simon Van Den Bergh (Oxford: Oxford University Press, 1954), 359.

33. Trans. S. H. Barani, "Ibn Sina and Alberuni," in *Avicenna Commemoration Volume* (Calcutta, Iran Society, 1956), 8 (with certain modifications by S. H. Nasr; refer to his "The Qur'an and *Hadith* as Source and Inspiration of Islamic Philosophy," 38 fn. 2). Mehdi Aminrazavi, in "The Logic of Orientals: Whose Logic and Which Orient?," argues against the significance of spiritual exercises in Avicenna's personal life, given the philosopher's predilection for wine and women [in the *Beacon of Knowledge*, ed. Mohammad H. Faghfoory (Louisville, KY: Fons Vitae, 2003), 48–49]. In reply, one could maintain that philosophical asceticism does not involve the foreswearing of bodily pleasures altogether. However, in this case, Avicenna's habit of consuming

alcoholic drinks [Dimitri Gutas, *Avicenna and the Aristotelian Tradition* (Leiden, Netherlands: E. J. Brill, 1988), 184–87] may seem to challenge my thesis that Avicenna's spiritual practice has an Islamic dimension. For a rebuttal, refer to Gutas's discussion of Avicenna's Hanafism and the more liberal approach of this school of Islamic law to the consumption of alcoholic beverages [Ibid., 187. See also Gutas's "Avicenna's *Maḏhab* with an appendix on the Question of His Date of Birth," in *Quaderni di studi Arabi* 5–6 (1987–88): 331].

34. Mohammad Azadpur, "Unveiling the Hidden: On the Meditations of Descartes and Ghazzali," 219–40.

35. Refer to W. Montgomery Watt's "Ghazzali and Later Ash'arites," in *Islamic Philosophy and Theology* (Edinburgh: Edinburgh University Press, 1985), 86.

36. The Buyid court's support for Avicenna is rather undisputed. It should also be noted that Alfarabi enjoyed the protection of the Hamdanid Shi'i dynasty in Aleppo [refer to Corbin's *Histoire de la philosophie islamique* (Paris: Gallimard, 1964), 226. Translated as *History of Islamic Philosophy*, trans. Liadain Sherrard (London: Kegan Paul, 1993), 158].

37. Refer to Bayard Dodge's *Muslim Education in Medieval Times* (Washington, DC: The Middle East Institute, 1962), 20–22.

38. Refer to Carla S. Klausner's *The Seljuk Vezirate* (Cambridge, MA: Harvard University Press, 1973), 58–59.

Chapter 6: On Human Finitude, Conscience, and Exemplarity

1. *Avicenna's De Anima*, ed. Fazlur Rahman (London: Oxford University Press, 1959), 12; hereinafter page numbers will be cited in the text after "*al-Shifā' DA*." Translation available in "On the Soul," *Philosophical Forum* 1 (1969): 559.

2. Quotations from Aristotle's *De Anima* follow the translation of W. D. Ross in *The Complete Works of Aristotle*, ed. Jonathan Barnes (Princeton, NJ: Princeton University Press, 1984).

3. In "Avicenna's 'Flying Man' in Context," Michael Marmura identifies three different occurrences of the Flying Man argument in Avicenna's work: two in the *De Anima* and one in *Ishārāt wa-l-tanbihāt* (*Monist* 69 [July 1986]: 383–95). The version I am discussing is the lengthiest one.

4. Michael Frede, "On Aristotle's Conception of the Soul," in *Essays on Aristotle's* De Anima, ed. Martha Nussbaum and Amelie Okseberg Rorty (Oxford: Clarendon Press, 1992), 94.

5. Ibid. See also R. Heinaman, "Aristotle and the Mind–Body Problem." *Phronesis* 35 (1990): 92–99.

6. From Fazlur Rahman's introduction to *Avicenna's Psychology*, trans. Fazlur Rahman (London: Oxford University Press, 1952), 6–7.

7. Ibid., 16–17.

8. I follow Dimitri Gutas in using this title for Avicenna's work ("Avicenna's Eastern ('Oriental') Philosophy: Nature, Contents, Transmission," in *Arabic Science and Philosophy* 10 [2000]: 166–67). I also agree with him that we

should avoid the culturally loaded rendition of *mashriqiyya* as "Oriental," and translate the title of the text as *Eastern Philosophy* (ibid., 159 fn. 1).

9. Dimitri Gutas, *Avicenna and the Aristotelian Tradition* (Leiden, Netherlands: E. J. Brill, 1988), 52–53.

10. For an inventory of the contents of *Eastern Philosophy* and a list of the surviving sections, see Gutas's "Avicenna's Eastern ('Oriental') Philosophy," 168–69.

11. Seyyed Hossein Nasr, *An Introduction to Islamic Cosmological Doctrines* (Albany, NY: SUNY Press, 1993), 269. See also his "Ibn Sina's 'Oriental Philosophy,' " in *History of Islamic Philosophy*, eds. Seyyed Hossein Nasr and Oliver Leaman (New York: Routledge, 1996), 248–49.

12. Gutas, *Avicenna and the Aristotelian Tradition*, 294.

13. Ibid., 295.

14. Ibid., 254.

15. Ibid., 255.

16. Ibid., 256.

17. Ibid., 261.

18. Ibid.

19. The so-called Metaphysics of the Rational Soul inspired the Ishrâqî philosopher, Shihāb al-Dīn Suhrawardī, and climaxed in the work of the sixteenth-century Shi'i philosopher, Mullâ Ṣadrâ Shîrâzî. This tradition is still thriving today, mainly in Shi'i centers of Iran and Iraq. For a philosophical account of that tradition, see Henry Corbin's *Histoire de la philosophie islamique* (Paris: Gallimard, 1964), 437–96, translated as *History of Islamic Philosophy*, trans. Liadain Sherrard (London: Kegan Paul, 1993), 319–63. I give a brief treatment of the Avicennan aspect of the work of these later thinkers in the concluding chapter.

20. Peter Adamson, "Aristotelianism and the Soul in the Arabic Plotinus," *Journal of the History of Ideas* 62 (2001): 229.

21. Henry Corbin, *Avicenne et le récit visionnaire* (Teheran: Département d'iranologie de l'Institut franco-iranien, 1954), 44. Translated as *Avicenna and the Visionary Recital*, trans. Willard R. Trask (London: Routledge & Kegan Paul, 1961), 39.

22. *Avicenne et le récit visionnaire*, 87–89 (*Avicenna and the Visionary Recital*, 75–77).

23. Lloyd Gerson, "The Unity of Intellect in Aristotle's *De Anima*," *Phronesis* 49 (2004): 356.

24. For a contemporary effort to resolve this tension in Aristotle's texts, see Lloyd Gerson's "The Unity of Intellect in Aristotle's *De Anima*." For a careful discussion of intellect and intellection in Aristotle, refer to Paolo C. Biondi's "*Nous* as Human Intuition" and "The Causality of the Act of *Noēsis*" in his *Aristotle: Posterior Analytics II.19* (Canada: Les Presses de l'Université Laval, 2004).

25. Fazlur Rahman, *Avicenna's Psychology*, 5.

26. Wisnovsky, *Avicenna's Metaphysics in Context* (Ithaca, NY: Cornell University Press, 2003), 126.

27. Ibid.

28. Ibid.,15–16.

29. Ibid., 136. For a general discussion of the role of the Active Intellect in Islamic Peripatetic philosophy, see Chapter 3, section 4.

30. Ibid., 133.

31. Ibid., 135.

32. Ibid., 124.

33. S. Pines, "La Philosophie 'Orientale' d'Avicenne et sa Polemique contre les Bagdadiens," *Archives d'Hitoire Doctrinale et Littéraire du Moyen Age* 27 (1952): 5–37. See also R. Macuch, "Greek and Oriental Sources of Avicenna's and Suhrawardi's Theosophies," *Graeco-Arabia* 2 (1983): 9–22.

34. Mehdi Aminrazavi, "The Logic of Orientals: Whose Logic and Which Orient?" in the *Beacon of Knowledge*, ed. Mohammad H. Faghfoory (Louisville, KY: Fons Vitae, 2003), 44.

35. Shlomo Pines, "The Limitations of Human Knowledge According to Al-Farabi, Ibn Bajja, and Maimonides," in *Studies in Medieval Jewish History and Literature*, ed. Isadore Twersky (Cambridge, MA: Harvard University Press, 1979), 83.

36. Ibid., 82–83.

37. *Ikhwān al-ṣafā wa khillān al-wafā* were an anonymous group of tenth-century Muslim Neoplatonist philosophers whose work was appropriated by subsequent Isma'ili thinkers. As a result of the intellectual assault on Isma'ilism by Sunni theologians (including Ghazali, see chapter 6), they became, in some circles, the paradigm of philosophical heresy. See Ian Richard Netton's *Muslim Neoplatonists: An Introduction to the Thought of the Brethren of Purity* (Edinburgh: Edinburgh University Press, 1991).

38. Pines, "The limitations of Human Knowledge," 85.

39. Abū Naṣr Fārābī, *On the Perfect State (Mabādī ārā' ahl al-madīna al-fāḍila)*, trans. & comm. Richard Walzer (Oxford: Oxford University Press, 1985), 262–63; hereinafter page numbers will be cited in the text after "*al-Madīna al-fāḍila.*"

40. For Avicenna's account of this principle refer to *Avicenna's De Anima*, 223–27. See also Avicenna's *Risāla aḍḥawiyya fī amr al ma'ād*, ed. S. Dunya (Cairo: Dār al-fikr al-'Arabī, 1949), 90. The ascription of this principle to Avicenna is common; see, for example, Michael E. Marmura, "Avicenna and the Problem of the Infinite Number of Souls," *Mediaeval Studies* 22 (1960): 228.

41. See Marmura's "Avicenna and the Problem of the Infinite Number of Souls," 234, for a summary of Avicenna's *reductio ad absurdum* against the pre-existence of the soul and transmigration. In his treatment of the afterlife, Alfarabi does not even consider the possibility of the pre-existence of the soul.

42. *Kitāb al-najāt*, ed. Mājid Fakhry (Beirut: Dār al-'ifāq al-jadīda, 1982), 161–64.

43. Averroes, *Tahāfut al-tahāfut*, ed. M. Bouyges (Beirut: Imprimerie Catholique, 1927), 27. For an English translation see *Incoherence of the Incoherence*, trans. and ed., Simon Van Den Bergh (Oxford: Oxford University Press, 1954), 14.

44. See Richard Taylor's "Averroes on Psychology and the Principles of Metaphysics," *Journal of the History of Philosophy* 36 (1998): 516, for a discussion of Averroes's argument for the unity of the intellectual soul.

45. Avicenna allows for heavenly bliss for the soul that has perfected itself by cultivating an independence from the body. The uncultivated soul suffers eternal anguish: "The individual thus remains longing for the soul's natural activity of acquiring things by which it realizes its essence, at a time when none of the instruments for such an acquisition exists. What greater calamity can there be, particularly that the soul continues eternally in this state" (Avicenna, *Fī ithbāt al-nubuwwāt*, Philosophical Texts and Studies 2, ed. Michael Marmura (Beirut: Dār al-nahār, 1968), 57. Translated by Michael Marmura as *On the Proof of Prophecies*, in *Medieval Political Philosophy: A Sourcebook*, ed. Ralph Lerner and Muhsin Mahdi (Ithaca, NY: Cornell University Press, 1961), 119. Alfarabi also has a felicitous after-life planned for the soul that is perfect and independent of matter. The fate of the imperfect soul is oblivion: "These are men who perish and proceed into nothingness, in the same way as cattle, beasts of prey and vipers" (*al-Madīna al-fāḍila*, 272–73). Yahya Michot points out that Avicenna comes to allow for a felicity for people who heed the prescriptions of the philosophical religion without attaining intellectual perfection. This happiness or its counterpart, eternal misery, is a function of the faculty of imagination which comes to experience heavenly delights or the anguish of hell based on its performance (ethical cultivation) during its earthly existence [*La destinée de l'homme selon Avicenne: Le retour à Dieu (ma'ād) et l'imagination* (Louvain, Aedibus Peeters, 1986), 18–19 and 23–30].

46. *Avicenna's De Anima*, 16. I am using Marmura's translation in "Avicenna's 'Flying Man' in Context," 386.

47. "Avicenna's 'Flying Man' in Context," 386–93. Deborah Black also affirms this in her "Estimation (*Wahm*) in Avicenna: The Logical and Psychological Dimensions," *Dialogue* 32 (1993): 238.

48. See the discussion in Chapter 3, §3.4.

49. Martin Heidegger, *Sein und Zeit*, in *Martin Heidegger: Gesamtausgabe* 2 (Frankfurt am Main: Vittorio Klostermann, 1977), 275; hereinafter page numbers will be cited in the text after "*SZ*." Translated by John Macquarrie and Edward Robinson as *Being and Time* (New York: Harper & Row, 1962), 320; hereinafter page numbers will be cited in the text after "*BT*" and after the reference to the German original.

50. In regard to the Western reception of the Thomistic view of the Active Intellect, Herbert Davidson writes:

> Thomas Aquinas (1225–1274) accepted the argument for the existence of an active intellect that leads the potential intellect to actuality, but he rejected the transcendent construction of the active intellect and located the active intellect exclusively within the human soul. After the thirteenth century, the theory of an incorporeal active intellect transcending the human soul was kept alive [in Europe] only among the adherents of Averroes. [*Alfarabi,*

Avicenna, and Averroes, on Intellect (Oxford: Oxford University Press, 1992), 217]

51. Thomas Aquinas, *The Summa Contra Gentiles*, trans. James F. Anderson (Notre Dame, IN: Notre Dame University Press, 1975), 244.

52. For Thomas, the Active Intellect is charged with the task of abstracting "universal forms from their particular conditions; which is to make them actually intelligible" (*Summa Theologica* 1.79.4, trans. and ed. Anton Pegis [New York: Modern Library, 1945], 752).

53. I discuss this matter in Chapter 3, §3.6. In a rather elegant passage, Dimitri Gutas sums up the reply to the Thomistic criticism thus: "For Avicenna just as certainly also subscribed to the reality, and indeed, necessity, of cognitive processes: they range from Thinking in terms of images in the animal soul, through abstraction, through Thinking in terms of universals in the rational soul, and culminate with hitting upon the middle terms, with Intuition and Acumen. All these are real and necessary processes, given our corporeal existence, and indeed the only available processes for thinking. All these cognitive processes are real in Avicenna for at least two reasons. First, without them we would have been unable to acquire the intelligibles at all, emanation or no emanation; our corporeality makes it impossible to acquire intelligibles unaided by thinking. . . . Also, emanation, precisely because it is an ontological principle and not a psychological or epistemological one, is inert; it must be 'activated' by thinking" ("Intuition and Thinking: The Evolving Structure of Avicenna's Epistemology," *Aspects of Avicenna*, ed. Robert Wisnovsky [Princeton, NJ: Markus Wiener Publishers, 2001], 30).

54. Corbin, *Histoire de la philosophie islamique*, 344 (*History of Islamic Philosophy*, 249).

55. Corbin, *Histoire de la philosophie islamique*, 245–46 (*History of Islamic Philosophy*, 173–74).

56. See Herbert McCabe, "The Immortality of the Soul: the Traditional Argument," in *Aquinas: A Collection of Critical Essays*, ed. Anthony Kenny (Notre Dame, IN: University of Notre Dame Press, 1969), 297–306. Linda Farmer, in "Straining the Limits of Philosophy: Aquinas on the Immortality of the Soul," in *Faith and Philosophy* 20 (2003): 208–17, challenges the inference from the incorruptibility of the soul to the immortality of the soul. She argues that for Aquinas the immortality of the soul can only be established theologically (not philosophically).

57. Corbin, *Histoire de la philosophie islamique*, 245–46 (*History of Islamic Philosophy*, 173–74).

58. Hans Georg Gadamer appropriates the distinction here to mark the difference between the animal mode of life in an environment and the human life in the world, *Truth and Method*, trans. Joel Weinsheimer and Donald Marshall (New York: Crossroads, 1992), 438–56.

59. *Histoire de la philosophie islamique*, 129–32 (*History of Islamic Philosophy*, 85–88).

Conclusion: The Importance of Islamic Peripateticism for Modern Philosophy in the West and Its Impact on Later Islamic Philosophy

1 Pierre Hadot, "Exercices spirituels," *Exercices spirituels et philosophie antique* (Paris: Etudes Augustiniennes, 1987), 71, translated as "Spiritual Exercises" in *Philosophy as a Way of Life*, trans. Michael Chase and ed. Arnold I. Davidson (Oxford: Blackwell, 1995), 107.

2. Henry Corbin, *Histoire de la philosophie islamique* (Paris: Gallimard, 1964), 285. Translated as *History of Islamic Philosophy*, trans. Liadain Sherrard (London: Kegan Paul, 1993), 205.

3. See William Chittick's discussion of *ta'alluh*, becoming like God, in his consideration of the goals of the practice of Islamic philosophy (*The Heart of Islamic Philosophy* [Oxford: Oxford University Press, 2001], 73).

4. Shihāb al-Dīn Yaḥyâ Suhrawardî, *The Philosophy of Illumination* (*Ḥikmat al-ishrāq*), trans. John Walbridge and Hossein Ziai (Provo, UT: Brigham Young University Press, 1999), 2–3.

5. Mehdi Aminrazavi, in *Suhrawardi and the School of Illumination* (Richmond, UK: Curzon Press, 1997), 90–117, & 122–23, recognizes the epistemological significance of spiritual practices in Suhrawardi's philosophy, but like his predecessors, Nasr and Corbin, he does not admit the source of this approach in the Peripateticisms of Alfarabi and Avicenna. See also Mehdi Ha'iri Yazdi's *The Principles of Epistemology in Islamic Philosophy: Knowledge by Presence* (Albany, NY: SUNY Press, 1992).

6. Thérèse-Ann Druart, "Imagination and the Soul-Body Problem in Arabic Philosophy," *Analecta Husserliana*, Vol. XVI, ed. A-T. Tymieniecka (Boston: Reidel Publishing, 1983), 339.

7. M. Y. Hairi's "Suhrawardî's *An Episode and a Trance*: A Philosophical Dialogue in a Mystical Stage," in *Islamic Philosophy and Mysticism*, ed. Parviz Morewedge (New York: Caravan Books, 1980), 177.

8. Shihâb al-Dîn Yaḥyâ Suhrawardî, *Kitāb al-talwīḥāt al-lawḥiyya wa-l-'arshiyya*, in *Opera Metaphysica et Mystica* I, ed. Henry Corbin (Istanbul: Maarif Matbaasi, 1945), 70; hereinafter page numbers will be cited in the text after "*talwīḥāt*." Translated into English as *An Episode and a Trance*, in M. Y. Hairi's "Suhrawardî's *An Episode and a Trance*: A Philosophical Dialogue in a Mystical Stage," in *Islamic Philosophy and Mysticism*, ed. Parviz Morewedge (New York: Caravan Books, 1980), 180. I should mention that John Walbridge translates this exchange in *The Leaven of the Ancients: Suhrawardi and the Heritage of the Greeks* (Albany, NY: SUNY Press, 2000), 225–29. I use Hairi's translation.

9. Suhrawardi, *The Philosophy of Illumination*, 131–32.

10. Michot, in *La destinée de l'homme selon Avicenne: Le retour à Dieu (ma'ād) et l'imagination*, attributes this view to Avicenna and argues that, for Avicenna, imagination comes to acquire knowledge of the spiritual world; he calls Avicenna's faculty of imagination *La faculté prophétique* [(Louvain, Aedibus Peeters, 1986), 118–33]. This is hard to reconcile with Avicenna's

claims that imagination is a corporeal faculty that passes away with the death of the body. I can accept the claim that for Avicenna the *cultivated* imagination comes to possess immortality. As I understand it, Avicenna's successors embrace this claim fully.

11. Fazlur Rahman, "Dreams, Imagination, and *'Ālam al-Mithāl*," in *Islamic Studies* 3 (1964): 169.

12. Corbin chooses the word *imaginal* in contrast to the *imaginary*. He writes, "[D]espite all our efforts, we cannot prevent that, in current and non-premeditated usage, the term *imaginary* is equated with the *unreal*, with something that is outside the framework of being and existing, in brief, with something utopian . . . this is undoubtedly symptomatic of something that contrasts with an order of reality, which I call *mundus imaginalis*, and which the theosophers of Islam designate as the 'eighth clime' " [*Mundus Imaginalis or the Imaginary and the Imaginal*, trans. R. Horine (Ipswich, England: Golgonooza Press, 1976), 3–4].

13. *The Philosophy of Illumination*, 137–38.

14. Fazlur Rahman, "Dreams, Imagination, and *'Ālam al-Mithāl*," 169.

15. See Henry Corbin's *Terre céleste et corps de résurrection de l'Iran mazdéen à l'Iran shî'ite* (Paris: Buchet/Chastel, 1960), translated as *Spiritual Body and Celestial Earth: From Mazdean Iran to Shī'ite Iran*, trans. Nancy Pearson (Princeton, NJ: Princeton University Press, 1977), for a selection of relevant texts on the imaginal world by later Islamic philosophers. Corbin also attaches his own introductory yet profound study of these texts to this work.

16. The term, "School of Isfahan," was first used by Henry Corbin in "Confessions extatiques de Mīr Dāmād," in *Mélanges Louis Massignon* (Damasins: Institut français de Damas, 1956), 331–78. This essay constitutes the beginning of book five of Corbin's *En Islam iranien* (Paris: Gallimard, 1972), V, 8ff.

17. Seyyed Hossein Nasr, "The Place of the School of Isfahan in Islamic Philosophy and Sufism," in *The Heritage of Sufism* III: *Late Classical Persian Sufism, 1501–1750*, edited by Leonard Lewisohn (Oxford: Oneworld, 1999), 13–14.

18. Ibid., 5.

19. *Seyyed Hossein Nasr, Islamic Philosophy from Its Origin to the Present: Philosophy in the Land of Prophecy* (Albany, NY: SUNY Press, 2006), 186–93.

20. Aminrazavi, *Suhrawardi and the School of Illumination*, 122–24.

21. See also Mulla Sadra's *Wisdom of the Throne*, where in laying out the philosophical method, he maintains that "you must completely free the Heart (from any attachments to the body) and totally purify the innermost self. You must be rigorously detached from created being, and (devote yourself to) repeated intimate communion with the Truly Real, in spiritual retreat," trans. James Winston Morris (Princeton, NJ: Princeton University Press, 1981), 254. Seyyed Hossein Nasr, in "The Meaning and Concept of Philosophy in Islam," refers to Mulla Sadra's definition of philosophy in *Al-Asfār al-arba'a*: "*falsafah* is the perfecting of the human soul to the extent of human ability through the knowledge of the essential reality of things as they are in themselves and through judgment concerning their existence established upon demonstra-

tion and not derived from opinion or through imitation" in *History of Islamic Philosophy*, Part I, eds. Seyyed Hossein Nasr and Oliver Leaman (New York: Routledge, 1996), 24.

22. Aminrazavi, *Suhrawardi and the School of Illumination*, 124.

23. Ibid,, 122.

24. Seyyed Hossein Nasr, "Ṣadr al-Dīn Muḥammad Shīrāzī (Mullā Ṣadrā)" in *The Islamic Intellectual Tradition in Persia*, ed. Mehdi Aminrazavi (Richmond, UK: Curzon Press 1996), 289.

25. Ibid.

26. Ibid., 291. See also Fazlur Rahman, "Dreams, Imagination, and *'Ālam al-Mithāl*," 176.

27. Nasr, "Ṣadr al-Dīn Muḥammad Shīrāzī (Mullā Ṣadrā)," 290.

28. Henry Corbin's *Histoire de la philosophie islamique* (Paris: Gallimard, 1964), 468–69. Translated as *History of Islamic Philosophy*, trans. Liadain Sherrard (London: Kegan Paul, 1993), 342–43.

29. Nasr, "Ṣadr al-Dīn Muḥammad Shīrāzī (Mullā Ṣadrā)," 279

30. Ibid., 279.

31. Ṣadr al-Dīn Muḥammad Shīrāzī, *Tafsīr al-Qur'ān al-karīm*, vol. iv, ed. Moḥammad Khājavī (Qum: Bīdār, 1988), 353. Translated as *On the Hermeneutics of the Light Verse of the Qur'an*, trans. Latimah-Parvin Peerwani (London: ICAS Press, 2004), 43.

32. Mohaghegh and Izutsu, *The Metaphysics of Sabzavari* (Tehran: Iran University Press, 1983), 5.

33. Mulla Sadra, *Tafsīr al-Qur'ān al-karīm*, 348 (*On the Hermeneutics of the Light Verse*, 36).

34. *Tafsīr al-Qur'ān al-karīm*, 365 (*On the Hermeneutics of the Light Verse*, 62).

35. Seyyed Hossein Nasr, *An Introduction to Islamic Cosmological Doctrines* (Albany, NY: SUNY Press, 1993), 197–212.

36. Nasr, *Islamic Philosophy from Its Origin to the Present*, 235. See also Hamid Dabashi's "Mīr Dāmād and the Founding of the 'School of Isfahan,' " in Nasr's *History of Islamic Philosophy*, Part I, 597–634, for a more detailed account of the precarious status of philosophy under Safavids.

37. Nasr, *Islamic Philosophy from Its Origin to the Present*, 236.

38. Ibid., 131. See also Nasr, *Islamic Philosophy from Its Origin to the Present*, 238.

39. Nasr, *Islamic Philosophy from Its Origin to the Present*, 237–38.

40. Ibid., 255. For the influence on Indian thought, also see Aminrazavi's *Suhrawardi and the School of Illumination*, 139, and Rahimuddin and Salim Kemal's "Shah Walīullāh," in *History of Islamic Philosophy*, Part I, 663–70.

41. Ibid., 251–56.

Bibliography

Adamson, Peter. "Non-Discursive Thought in Avicenna's Commentary on the Theology of Aristotle." In *Interpreting Avicenna: Science and Philosophy in Medieval Islam*, edited by John McGinnis, 87–111. Leiden: Brill, 2004.

———. "Aristotelianism and the Soul in the Arabic Plotinus," *Journal of the History of Ideas* 62 (2001): 211–32.

Al-Akiti, M. Afifi. "The Three Properties of Prophethood in Certain Works of Avicenna and al-Ghazālī." In *Interpreting Avicenna: Science and Philosophy in Medieval Islam*, edited by John McGinnis, 189–212. Leiden: Brill, 2004.

Alfarabi (Abū Naṣr Fārābī). *The Book of Letters*. In *Medieval Islamic Philosophical Writings*, edited and translated by Muhammad Ali Khalidi, 1–26. Cambridge, UK: Cambridge University Press, 2005.

———. *Book of Religion*. In *Alfarabi: The Political Writings*, edited and translated by Charles Butterworth, 85–113. Ithaca, NY: Cornell University Press, 2001.

———. "Harmonization of the Two Opinions of the Two Sages: Plato the Divine and Aristotle." In *Alfarabi: The Political Writings*, translated by Fauzi Najjar & Charles Butterworth, 116–67. Ithaca, NY: Cornell University Press, 2001.

———. *Kitāb al-jam' bayna ra'yay al-hakīmayn*. Edited by 'Alī Bū Mulḥim. Beirut: Dār wa maktabat al-hilāl, 1996.

———. *Taḥṣīl al-sa'āda*. Edited by 'Alī Bū Mulḥim. Beirut: Dār wa maktabat al-hilāl, 1995.

———. *On the Perfect State* (*Mabādī ārā' ahl al-madīna al-fāḍila*). Edited and Translated by Richard Walzer. Oxford: Oxford University Press, 1985.

———. *Kitāb al-ḥurūf*. Edited by Muḥsin Mahdī. Beirut: Dār al-Mashriq, 1970.

———. *Kitāb al-milla wa nuṣūṣ ukharā*. Edited by Muhsin Mahdi. Beirut: Dār al-Mashriq, 1968.

———. *The Attainment of Happiness*. In *Philosophy of Plato and Aristotle*. Translated by Muhsin Mahdi, 13–52. Ithaca, NY: Cornell University Press, 1962.

———. *Fuṣūl al-madanī: Aphorisms of the Statesman*. Edited and translated by D. M. Dunlop. Cambridge, UK: Cambridge University Press, 1961.

Altmann, Alexander. "Maimonides and Thomas Aquinas: Natural or Divine Prophecy." *AJS Review* 3 (1978): 1–19.

———. "Ibn Bājja on Man's Ultimate Felicity." In *Studies in Religious Philosophy and Mysticism*. Edited by Alexander Altmann, 73–107. London: Routledge and Kegan Paul, 1969.

Aminrazavi, Mehdi. *Suhrawardi and the School of Illumination*. Richmond, UK: Curzon Press, 1997.

———. "The Logic of Orientals: Whose Logic and Which Orient?" In the *Beacon of Knowledge*. Edited by Mohammad H. Faghfoory, 41–49. Louisville, KY: Fons Vitae, 2003.

Amir-Moezzi, Mohammad Ali. *The Divine Guide in Early Shiism*. Translated by David Streight. Albany, NY: SUNY Press, 1994.

Annas, Julia. "Ancient Ethics and Modern Morality," In *Philosophical Perspectives* 2 (1992): 119–136.

Aquinas, Thomas. *Summa Theologica*. Translated and edited by Anton Pegis. New York: Modern Library, 1945.

———. *The Summa Contra Gentiles*. Translated by James F. Anderson. Notre Dame, IN: Notre Dame University Press, 1975.

Arendt, Hannah. *The Life of the Mind*. New York: Harcourt Brace Jovanovich, 1981.

Aristotle. *The Complete Works of Aristotle*. Edited by Jonathan Barnes and translated by W. D. Ross. Princeton, NJ: Princeton University Press, 1984.

———. *Poetics*. Translated by James Hutton. New York: W. W. Norton, 1982.

Arnaldez, Roger. "Falsafah," in *The Encyclopedia of Islam*, 2nd ed., vol. II. Leiden: Brill, 1960.

Averroes (Abū al-Walīd ibn Rushd). *The Decisive Treatise* (*Kitāb faṣl al-maqāl*). Translated and edited by Charles E. Butterworth. Provo, UT: Brigham Young University Press, 2001.

———. *The Incoherence of the Incoherence*. Translated and edited by Simon Van Den Bergh. Oxford: Oxford University Press, 1954.

———. *Tahāfut al-tahāfut*. Edited by M. Bouyges. Beirut: Imprimerie Catholique, 1927.

Avicenna (Abū 'Alī Ḥussain ibn Sīnā). *The Metaphysics of* the Healing (*Kitāb al-shifā': al-Ilāhiyyāt*). Translated by Michael Marmura. Provo, UT: Brigham Young University Press, 2005.

———. *Al-Mabda' wa-l-ma'ād*. In Wisdom of Persia Series 36. Edited by A. Nūrānī. Tehran: Institute of Islamic Studies, McGill University-Tehran University, 1984.

———. *Kitāb al-najāt*. Edited by Mājid Fakhry. Beirut: Dār al-'ifāq al-jadīda, 1982.

———. "A Unique Treatise on the Interpretation of Dreams." Edited by Moh'd. Abdul Muid Khan. In *Avicenna Commemoration Volume*, edited by V. Courtois, 255–307. Calcutta, Iran Society, 1956.

———. "On the Soul." Translated by Lenn E. Goodman. In *Philosophical Forum* 1 (1969): 555–62.

———. *Fī ithbāt al-nubuwwāt*. In Philosophical Texts and Studies 2, 41–61. Edited by Michael Marmura. Beirut: Dār Al-Nahār, 1968.

———. *Al-Shifā': al-Manṭiq* 9: *al-Shi'r*. Edited by A. Badawī. Cairo: Dār al-miṣriyya li-l-ta'līf wa-l-tarjuma, 1966.

———. "On the Proof of Prophecies." In *Medieval Political Philosophy: A Sourcebook*, edited by Ralph Lerner and Muhsin Mahdi, 112–121. Ithaca, NY: Cornell University Press, 1961.

———. *Al-Ishārāt wa-l-tanbīhāt: al-Manṭiq*. Edited by S. Dunyā. Cairo: Dār al-ma'ārif, 1960.

———. *Avicenna's De Anima*. Edited by Fazlur Rahman. London: Oxford University Press, 1959.

———. *Avicenna's Psychology*. Translated by Fazlur Rahman. London: Oxford University Press, 1952.

———. *Aḥwāl al-nafs*. Edited by A.F. al-Ahwānī. Cairo: Dār al-iḥyā' al-kutub al-'Arabiyya, 1952.

———. *Risāla aḍḥawiyya fī amr al ma'ād,*. Edited by S. *Dunyā*. Cairo: Dār al-fikr al-'Arabī, 1949.

Azadpur, Mohammad. "Hegel and the Divinity of Light in Zoroastrianism and Islamic Phenomenology." *The Classical Bulletin* 83 (2008): 227–46.

———. "Is 'Islamic' Philosophy Islamic?" In *Voices of Islam*, vol. 5, edited by Vincent Cornell, 23–41. Westport, CT: Praeger, 2007.

———. "The Sublime Visions of Philosophy: Fundamental Ontology and the Imaginal World." In *Microcosm and Macrocosm*, edited by Anna-Teresa Tymieniecka, 183–201. Dordrecht, Netherlands: Springer, 2006.

———. "Interpreting Political Violence in Islamic Philosophy." In *Polylog: Forum for Intercultural Philosophy* 5 (2004): <http://them.polylog.org/5/fam-en.htm>.

———. "Unveiling the Hidden: On the Meditations of Descartes and Ghazzali." In *Passions of the Soul in the Metamorphosis of Becoming*, edited by Anna Teresa Tymieniecka, 219–40. Dordrecht, Netherlands: Kluwer, 2003.

Barani, S. H. "Ibn Sina and Alberuni." In *Avicenna Commemoration Volume*, edited by V. Courtois, 3–14. Calcutta, Iran Society, 1956.

Baier, Kurt. "Radical Virtue Ethics." In *Midwest Studies in Philosophy* 13 (1988): 126–35.

Baracchi, Claudia. *Aristotle's Ethics as First Philosophy*. Cambridge, UK: Cambridge University Press, 2007.

Biondi, Paolo C. *Aristotle: Posterior Analytics II.19*. Canada: Les Presses de l'Université Laval, 2004.

Black, Deborah. "Estimation (*Wahm*) in Avicenna: The Logical and the Psychological Dimensions." In *Dialogue* 32 (1993): 219–58.

———. "Imagination and Estimation: Arabic Paradigms and Western Transformations." In *Topoi* 19 (2000): 59–75.

Berman, Lawrence. "The Political Interpretation of the Maxim: The Purpose of Philosophy is the Imitation of God." In *Studia Islamica* 15 (1961): 53–61.

Brandom, Robert. "Heidegger's Categories in *Being and Time*." In *Monist* 66 (1983): 387–409.

Butterworth, Charles. "Medieval Islamic Philosophy and the Virtue of Ethics." In *Arabica* 34 (1987): 221–50.

Cantarino, Vicente. *Arabic Poetics in the Golden Age*. Leiden: E. J. Brill, 1975.

Chittick, William. *The Heart of Islamic Philosophy*. London: Oxford University Press, 2001.

Corbin, Henry. "From Heidegger to Suhrawardi: An Interview with Phillipe Nemo," Translated by Kathleen Raine. *Temenos Academy Review* 6 (2003): 119–43.

———. *The Voyage and the Messenger: Iran and Philosophy*. Translated by Joseph Rowe. Berkeley, CA: North Atlantic Books, 1998.

———. *History of Islamic Philosophy*. Translated by Liadain Sherrard. London: Kegan Paul, 1993.

———. *L'Iran et la philosophie*. Paris: Fayard, 1990.

——— and 'Alammah Tabataba'i. "The Imams and the Imamate," In *Shi'ism: Doctrines, Thought, and Spirituality*, edited by Seyyed Hossein Nasr, Seyyed Vali Reza Nasr, and Hamid Dabashi, 155–188. Albany, NY: SUNY Press, 1988.

———. *The Concept of Comparative Philosophy*. Translated by Peter Russell. Ipswich: Golgonooza Press, 1981.

———. "De Heidegger à Sohravardî: Entretien avec Philippe Nemo." In *Cahiers de l'Herne: Henry Corbin*, edited by Christian Jambet, 23–37. Paris: L'Herne, 1981.

———. *The Man of Light in Iranian Sufism*. Translated by Nancy Pearson. New Lebanon, NY: Omega Publications, 1978.

———. *Spiritual Body and Celestial Earth: From Mazdean Iran to Shī'ite Iran*. Translated by Nancy Pearson. Princeton, NJ: Princeton University Press, 1977.

———. *Mundus Imaginalis or the Imaginary and the Imaginal*. Ipswich, England: Golgonooza Press, 1976.

———. "Nāṣir-i Khusrau and Iranian Ismā'īlism." In *The Cambridge History of Iran*, vol. 4, edited by R. N. Frye, 520–42. Cambridge, UK: Cambridge University Press, 1975.

———. *L'homme de lumière dans le soufisme iranien*. Paris: Éditions Présence, 1971.

———. *Creative Imagination in the Sufism of Ibn Arabi*. Translated by Ralph Manheim. Princeton, NJ: Princeton University Press, 1969.

———. *Histoire de la philosophie islamique*. Paris: Gallimard, 1964.

———. *Avicenna and the Visionary Recital*. Translated by Willard R. Trask. London: Routledge and Kegan Paul, 1960.

———. *Terre céleste et corps de résurrection de l'Iran mazdéen á l'Iran shî'ite*. Paris: Buchet/Chastel, 1960.

———. "Confessions extatiques de Mīr Dāmād." In *Mélanges Louis Massignon*. Damasins: Institut français de Damas, 1956.

———. *Avicenne et le récit visionnaire*. Teheran: Département d'iranologie de l'Institut franco-iranien, 1954.

Dabashi, Hamid. "Mīr Dmād and the Founding of the 'School of Isfahan.' " In *History of Islamic Philosophy*, Part I, edited by Seyyed Hossein Nasr and Oliver Leaman, 597–634, London: Routledge, 1996.

Davidson, Herbert. *Alfarabi, Avicenna, and Averroes, on Intellect*. Oxford: Oxford University Press, 1992.

Dahiyat, Ismail M. *Avicenna's Commentary on the Poetics of Aristotle*. Leiden: E. J. Brill, 1974.

DeBoer, T. J. *The History of Philosophy in Islam*. Translated by Edward R. Jones. New York: Dover, 1967.

Dodge, Bayard. *Muslim Education in Medieval Times*. Washington, DC: The Middle East Institute, 1962.

Dreyfus, Hubert. "Overcoming the Myth of the Mental: How Philosophers Can Profit from the Phenomenology of Ordinary Experience." *Proceedings and Addresses of the American Philosophical Association* 79 (2005): 47–65.

Druart, Thérèse-Ann. "Imagination and the Soul-Body Problem in Arabic Philosophy." In *Analecta Husserliana*, xvi, edited by A-T. Tymieniecka, 327–42. Boston: Reidel Publishing, 1983.

Dunlop, D. M. "Al-Fārābī's Introductory *Risālah* on Logic." In *Islamic Quarterly* 3 (1956–57): 224–35.

El-Bizri, Nader. *The Phenomenological Quest: Between Avicenna and Heidegger*. Binghamton, NY: Global Publications, 2000.

Farias, Victor. *Heidegger and Nazism*. Translated by Paul Burrell. Philadelphia: Temple University Press, 1991.

Farmer, Linda. "Straining the Limits of Philosophy: Aquinas on the Immortality of the Soul." In *Faith and Philosophy* 20 (2003): 208–17.

Foucault, Michel. *The Hermeneutics of the Subject*. Translated by Graham Burchell. New York: Picador, 2006.

———. *L'herméneutique du sujet*. Paris: Gallimard, 2001.

———. *History of Sexuality*, vol. 1–3. Translated by Robert Hurley. New York: Vintage, 1978–86.

———. *Histoire de la sexualité*, v. 1-3. Paris: Gallimard, 1976–84.

Frede, Michael. "On Aristotle's Conception of the Soul." In *Essays on Aristotle's* De Anima, edited by Martha Nussbaum and Amelie Oksenberg Rorty, 93–109. Oxford: Clarendon Press, 1992.

Gadamer, Hans Georg. *Truth and Method*. Translated by Joel Weinsheimer and Donald Marshall. New York: Crossroads, 1992.

Gerson, Lloyd. "The Unity of Intellect in Aristotle's *De Anima*." In *Phronesis* 49 (2004): 348–73.

Ghazali (Abû Ḥāmid Muḥammad Ghazzālī). *The Niche of Lights*. Translated by David Buchman. Provo, UT: Brigham Young University Press, 1998.

———. *The Incoherence of the Philosophers* (*Tahāfut al-falāsafa*). Translated by Michael E. Marmura. Provo, UT: Brigham Young University, 1997.

———. *Al-Munqidh min al-ḍalāl*. Edited by Maḥmūd Bījū. Damascus: Dār al-taqwā, 1992.

———. "Deliverance from Error." In *The Faith and Practice of al-Ghazali*, translated by W. Montgomery Watt, 16–85. London: George Allen and Unwin, 1953.

Groff, Peter. "Al-Kindī and Nietzsche on the Stoic Art of Banishing Sorrow." In *Journal of Nietzsche Studies* 28 (2004): 139–73.

Gutas, Dimitri. "Imagination and Transcendental Knowledge in Avicenna." In *Arabic Theology, Arabic Philosophy: From the Many to the One*, edited by J. E. Montgomery, 337–54. Dudley, MA: Peeters, 2006.

———. "The Intellect Without Limits: The Absence of Mysticism in Avicenna." In *Intellect and Imagination in Medieval Philosophy*, edited by C. Pacheco & J. F. Meirinhos, 351–72. Turnhout: Brepols, 2006.

———. "The Study of Arabic Philosophy in the Twentieth Century." In *British Journal of Middle Eastern Studies* 29 (2002): 5–25.

———. "Intuition and Thinking: The Evolving Structure of Avicenna's Epistemology." In *Aspects of Avicenna*, edited by Robert Wisnovsky, 1–38. Princeton, NJ: Markus Wiener Publishers, 2001.

———. "Avicenna's Eastern ('Oriental') Philosophy: Nature, Contents, Transmission." In *Arabic Science and Philosophy* 10 (2000): 159–180.

———. *Avicenna and the Aristotelian Tradition*. Leiden, Netherlands: E. J. Brill, 1988.

———. "Avicenna's *Maḏhab* with an Appendix on the Question of His Date of Birth." In *Quaderni di studi Arabi* 5–6 (1987–88): 323–36.

———. "The Starting Point of Philosophical Studies in Alexandrian and Arabic Aristotelianism." In *Theophrastus of Eresus: On His Life and Work*, edited by W. W. Fortenbaugh, 115–23. New Brunswick, NJ: Transaction Publishers, 1985.

Hadot, Pierre. *What is Ancient Philosophy?* Translated by Michael Chase. Cambridge, MA: Harvard University Press, 2004.

———. *Philosophy as a Way of Life*. Translated by Michael Chase and edited by Arnold I. Davidson. Oxford: Blackwell, 1995.

———. *Qu'est-ce que la philosophie antique?* Paris: Gallimard, 1995.

———. *Exercices spirituels et philosophie antique*. Paris: Etudes Augustiniennes, 1987.

Hairi, M. Y. "Suhrawardī's *An Episode and a Trance*: A Philosophical Dialogue in a Mystical Stage." In *Islamic Philosophy and Mysticism*, edited by Parviz Morewedge, 177–89. New York: Caravan Books, 1980.

Ha'iri Yazdi, Mehdi. *The Principles of Epistemology in Islamic Philosophy: Knowledge by Presence*. Albany, NY: SUNY Press, 1992.

Haldane, John. "Aquinas and the Active Intellect." In *Philosophy* 67 (1992): 199–210.

Hasse, Dag Nikolaus. "Avicenna on Abstraction." In *Aspects of Avicenna*, edited by Robert Wisnovsky, 39–72. Princeton, NJ: Markus Wiener, 2001.

———. *Avicenna's De Anima in the Latin West*. Turin: The Warburg Institute, 2000.

Heath, Peter. *Allegory and Philosophy in Avicenna*. Philadelphia: University of Pennsylvania Press, 1992.

Hegel, G. W. F. *Aesthetics*, vol. 1. Translated by T. M. Knox. Oxford: Clarendon Press, 1975.

———. *Vorlesungen über die Aesthetik* I–II. In *Werke in zwanzig Bänden*, vols. 13-4. Frankfurt am Main: Suhrkamp, 1979.

Heidegger, Martin. *Nietzsche: The Will to Power as Art.* Translated by David Farrel Krell. New York: Harper & Row, 1979.
———. *Sein und Zeit.* In *Martin Heidegger: Gesamtausgabe* 2. Frankfurt am Main: Vittorio Klostermann, 1977.
———. *What is Called Thinking?* Translated by J. Glenn Gray. New York: Harper & Row, 1968.
———. *Being and Time.* Translated by John Macquarrie and Edward Robinson. New York: Harper & Row, 1962.
———. *Nietzsche I.* Pfullingen: Verlag Gunther Neske, 1961.
Heinaman, R. "Aristotle and the Mind-Body Problem." *Phronesis* 35 (1990): 92–99.
Al-Ḥujwirī, 'Alī ibn 'Uthmān. *The Kashf al-Maḥjūb, The Oldest Persian Treatise on Sufism.* Translated by R. A. Nicholson. London: Luzac, 1959.
Husserl, Edmund. *Paris Lectures.* Translated by Peter Koestenbaum. The Hague: Martinus Nijhoff, 1975.
Izutsu, Toshihiko. *Ethico-Religious Concepts in the Qur'an.* Montreal: McGill-Queen's University Press, 2002.
——— and Mehdi Mohaghgeh. *The Metaphysics of Sabzavari.* Tehran: Iran University Press, 1983.
Al-Jabri, Muhammed 'Abed. *Arab-Islamic Philosophy.* Translated by Aziz Abbassi. Austin: The Center for Middle Eastern Studies, The University of Texas at Austin, 1999.
Kemal, Salim. *The Poetics of Alfarabi and Avicenna.* Leiden: Brill, 1991.
——— and Rahimuddin Kemal. "Shah Walīullāh." *In History of Islamic Philosophy*, Part I, edited by Seyyed Hossein Nasr and Oliver Leaman, 663–670. London: Routledge, 1996.
Al-Kindī, Abū Yūsuf Ya'qūb ibn Isḥāq. *Rasā'il al-Kindī al-falsafiyya.* Edited by M. 'A. Abū Rīda. Cairo: Dār al-fikr al-'Arabī, 1950.
Kant, Immanuel. *Critique of Judgment.* Translated by Werner S. Pluhar. Indianapolis: Hackett, 1987.
———. *Critique of Pure Reason.* Translated by Norman Kemp Smith. New York: St. Martin's Press, 1965.
———. *Groundwork for the Metaphysics of Morals.* Translated by H. J. Paton. New York: Harper & Row, 1964.
———. *Kants gesammelte Schriften.* Berlin: Königlich Preussische Akademie der Wissenschaften, 1908–13.
Klausner, Carla S. *The Seljuk Vezirate.* Cambridge, MA: Harvard University Press, 1973.
Kraemer, Joel. "The Jihād of the Falāsifa." In *Jerusalem Studies in Arabic and Islam* 10 (1987): 372–90.
Lacoue-Labarthe, Philippe. "Sublime Truth." In *Sublime: Presence in Question,* translated by Jeffrey S. Librett, 71–108. Albany, NY: SUNY Press, 1993.
Leaman, Oliver. "Concept of Philosophy in Islam." In *Routledge Encyclopedia of Philosophy,* vol. 5, ed. Edward Craig, 5–9. London: Routledge, 1998.

———. "Orientalism and Islamic Philosophy." In *History of Islamic Philosophy*, Part II, edited by Seyyed Hossein Nasr and Oliver Leaman, 1143–48. London: Routledge, 1996.

———. *An Introduction to Classical Islamic Philosophy*. Cambridge, UK: Cambridge University Press, 1985.

Lyotard, Jean-Francois. *Lessons on the Analytic of the Sublime*. Translated by Elizabeth Rottenberg. Palo Alto, CA: Stanford University Press, 1994.

Macuch, R. "Greek and Oriental Sources of Avicenna's and Suhrawardi's Theosophies." In *Graeco-Arabia* 2 (1983): 9–22.

Mahdi, Muhsin. *Alfarabi and the Foundations of Islamic Political Philosophy*. Chicago, IL: The University of Chicago Press, 2001.

———. "Alfarabi's Imperfect State." In *Journal of the American Oriental Society* 110 (1990): 691–726.

———. "Orientalism and the Study of Islamic Philosophy." In *Journal of Islamic Studies* 1 (1990): 73–98.

Marmura, Michael E. "Plotting the Course of Avicenna's Thought." In *Journal of the American Oriental Society* 111 (1991): 333–42.

———. "Avicenna's 'Flying Man' in Context." In *Monist* 69 (1986): 383–95.

———. "The Islamic Philosophers' Conception of Islam." In *Islam's Understanding of Itself*, edited by R. G. Hovannisian and S. Vryonis, Jr., 87–102. Malibu, CA: Undena, 1983.

———. "Avicenna's Psychological Proof of Prophecy." In *Journal of Near Eastern Studies* 22 (1963): 49–56.

———. "Avicenna and the Problem of the Infinite Number of Souls." In *Mediaeval Studies* 22 (1960): 232–39.

McCabe, Herbert. "The Immortality of the Soul: the Traditional Argument." In *Aquinas: A Collection of Critical Essays*, edited by Anthony Kenny, 297–306. Notre Dame, IN: University of Notre Dame Press, 1969.

McDowell, John. "Avoiding the Myth of the Given." In *Having the World in View*, 256–72. Cambridge, MA: Harvard University Press, 2009.

———. "What Myth?" In *Inquiry* 50 (2007): 338–50.

———. "Having the World in View: Sellars, Kant, and Intentionality." In *The Journal of Philosophy* 95 (1998): 431–92.

———. *Mind, Value, and Reality*. Cambridge, MA: Harvard University Press, 1998.

———. *Mind and World*. Cambridge, MA: Harvard University Press, 1994.

McGinnis, John and David C. Reisman, eds. *Classical Arabic Philosophy: An Anthology of Sources*. Indianapolis: Hackett, 2007.

Michot, Jean R. *La destinée de l'homme selon Avicenne: Le retour à Dieu (ma'ād) et l'imagination*. Louvain, Aedibus Peeters, 1986.

———. "Prophétie et divination selon Avicenna. Présentation, essai de traduction critique et index de l'Épître de l'âme de la sphère.' " In *Revue philosophique de Louvain* 83 (1985): 507–35.

Moraux, Paul. *Der Aristotelismus bei den Griechen*, I. Berlin, W. De Gruyter, 1973.

Morewedge, Parviz. "The Logic of Emanationism and Sufism in the Philosophy of Ibn Sina (Avicenna)." In *Journal of the American Oriental Society* 92 (1972): 1–18.

Mulla Sadra (Ṣadr al-Dīn Muḥammad Shīrāzī). *On the Hermeneutics of the Light Verse of the Qur'an*, trans. Latimah-Parvin Peerwani (London: ICAS Press, 2004).

———. *Tafsīr al-Qur'ān al-karīm*. Edited by Moḥammad Khājavī. Qum: Bīdār, 1988.

———. *Wisdom of the Throne*. Translated by James Winston Morris. Princeton, NJ: Princeton University Press, 1981.

Murdoch, Iris. *Sovereignty of Good*. New York: Routlege, 1970.

Nasr, Seyyed Hossein. *Islamic Philosophy from Its Origin to the Present: Philosophy in the Land of Prophecy*. Albany, NY: SUNY Press, 2006.

———. *Islam: Religion, History, Civilization*. New York: HarperCollins, 2003.

———. "The Place of the School of Isfahan in Islamic Philosophy and Sufism." In *The Heritage of Sufism* III: *Late Classical Persian Sufism, 1501–1750*, edited by Leonard Lewisohn, 3–15. Oxford: Oneworld, 1999.

———. "Ibn Sina's 'Oriental Philosophy.' " In *History of Islamic Philosophy*, Part I, edited by Seyyed Hossein Nasr and Oliver Leaman, 247–51. New York: Routledge, 1996.

———. "Ṣadr al-Dīn Muḥammad Shīrāzī (Mullā Ṣadrā)." In *The Islamic Intellectual Tradition in Persia*, edited by Mehdi Aminrazavi, 271–303. Richmond, UK: Curzon Press 1996.

———. "The Meaning and Concept of Philosophy in Islam." In *History of Islamic Philosophy*, Part I, edited by Seyyed Hossein Nasr and Oliver Leaman, 21–26. London: Routledge, 1996.

———. "The Qur'ān and *Ḥadith* as Source and Inspiration of Islamic Philosophy." In *History of Islamic Philosophy*, Part I, edited by Seyyed Hossein Nasr and Oliver Leaman, 27–39. London: Routledge, 1996.

———. *An Introduction to Islamic Cosmological Doctrines*. Albany, NY: SUNY Press, 1993.

———. "Henry Corbin: The Life and Works of the Occidental Exile in Quest of the Orient of Light." In *Traditional Islam in the Modern World*, edited by Seyyed Hossein Nasr, 273–90. New York: KPI, 1987.

———. "Islamic Philosophy—Reorientation or Re-understanding." In *Islamic Life and Thought*, edited by Seyyed Hossein Nasr, 153–57. Albany, NY: SUNY Press, 1981.

———. "The Concept and Reality of Freedom in Islam and Islamic Civilization." In *The Philosophy of Human Rights*, edited by Alan Rosenbaum, 103–12. Westport, CT: Greenwood Press, 1980.

———. "The Significance of Persian Philosophical Works in the Tradition of Islamic Philosophy." In *Essays on Islamic Philosophy and Science*, edited by G. F. Hourani, 67–75. Albany, NY: SUNY Press, 1975.

Nehamas, Alexander. *The Art of Living: Socratic Reflections from Plato to Foucault*. Los Angeles: University of California Press, 1998.

Netton, Ian Richard. *Muslim Neoplatonists: An Introduction to the Thought of the Brethren of Purity*. Edinburgh, Edinburgh University Press, 1991.

Nussbaum, Martha. *The Fragility of Goodness*. Cambridge, UK: Cambridge University Press, 2001.

O'Meara, Dominic. "Neoplatonist Conceptions of the Philosopher-King." In *Plato and Platonism: Studies in Philosophy and the History of Philosophy*, vol. 33, ed. Johannes M. Van Ophuijsen, 278–91. Washington, DC: Catholic University American Press, 1999.

Plato. *The Collected Dialogues of Plato*. Edited by Edith Hamilton and Huntington Cairns. Princeton, NJ: Princeton University Press, 1962.

Plotinus. *The Enneads*. Translated by Stephen MacKenna. New York: Pantheon, 1962.

Pines, Shlomo. "The limitations of Human Knowledge According to Al-Farabi, Ibn Bajja, and Maimonides." In *Studies in Medieval Jewish History and Literature*, edited by Isadore Twersky, 82–109. Cambridge, MA: Harvard University Press, 1979.

———. "The Arabic Recension of *Parva Naturalia* and the Philosophical Doctrine Concerning Veridical Dreams According to *al-Risāla al-Manāmiyya* and Other Sources." In *Israel Oriental Studies* 4 (1974): 104–53.

———. "La Philosophie 'Orientale' d'Avicenne et sa Polemique contre les Bagdadiens." In *Archives d'Histoire Doctrinale et Littéraire du Moyen Age* 27 (1952): 5–37.

Rahman, Fazlur. "Some Key Ethical Concepts of the Qur'an." In *Journal of Religious Ethics* 11 (1983): 170–85.

———. "Dreams, Imagination, and *'Ālam al-Mithāl*." In *Islamic Studies* 3 (1964): 167–80.

———. *Prophecy in Islam*. London: George Allen and Unwin, 1958.

Reisman, David C. "Al-Fārābi and the Philosophical Curriculum." In *The Cambridge Companion to Arabic Philosophy*, edited by Peter Adamson and Richard C. Taylor, 52–71. Cambridge, UK: Cambridge University Press, 2005.

Rodinson, Maxime. "The Western Image and Western Studies of Islam." In *The Legacy of Islam*, 2nd edition, edited by Joseph Schacht and C. E. Bosworth, 9–62. Oxford: Clarendon Press, 1974.

Rosenthal, Franz. "On the Knowledge of Plato's Philosophy in the Islamic World." In *Islamic Culture* 14 (1940): 387–422.

Rubin, U. "Pre-existence and Light: Aspects of the Concept of Nūr Muhammad." In *Israel Oriental Studies* 5 (1975): 62–119.

Russell, Bertrand. *A History of Western Philosophy*. New York: Simon & Schuster, 1965.

Said, Edward. *Orientalism*. New York: Vintage Books, 1979.

Sellars, Wilfrid. "Empiricism and the Philosophy of Mind." In *Minnesota Studies in the Philosophy of Science*, vol. 1, edited by Herbert Feigl & Michael Scriven, 253–328. Minneapolis: University of Minnesota Press, 1956.

Sharif, M. M. *A History of Muslim Philosophy*. Wiesbaden: Harrassowitz, 1963–66.

Suhrawardî, Shihāb al-Dīn Yaḥyâ. *The Philosophy of Illumination (Ḥikmat al-ishrāq)*. Translated by John Walbridge and Hossein Ziai. Provo, UT: Brigham Young University Press, 1999.

———. *Kitāb al-talwīḥāt al-lawḥiyya wa-l-'arshiyya*. In *Opera Metaphysica et Mystica* I, edited by Henry Corbin. Istanbul: Maarif Matbaasi, 1945.

Strauss, Leo. *Persecution and the Art of Writing*. Chicago, IL: University of Chicago Press, 1980.

Stroumsa, Sarah. "Philosopher-King or Philosopher-Courtier? Theory and Reality in the *Falāsifa*'s Place in Islamic Society." In *Identidades Marginales*, edited by Cristina de la Puente, 433–59. Madrid: Consejo Superior de Investigaciones Cientificas, 2003.

———. "Avicenna's Philosophical Stories: Aristotle's Poetics Reinterpreted." In *Arabica* 39 (1992): 183–206.

Taylor, Charles. *Hegel*. Cambridge, UK: Cambridge University Press, 1975.

Taylor, Richard C. "Averroes on Psychology and the Principles of Metaphysics," *Journal of the History of Philosophy* 36 (1998): 507–23.

Walbridge, John. *The Leaven of the Ancients: Suhrawardi and the Heritage of the Greeks*. Albany, NY: SUNY Press, 2000.

Walzer, Richard. "Alfarabi's Theory of Prophecy and Divination." In *Greek into Arabic*, edited by Richard Walzer, 206–19. Cambridge, MA: Harvard University Press, 1962.

Wasserstrom, Steven M. *Religion after Religion*. Princeton, NJ: Princeton University Press, 1999.

Watson, Gerard. "Imagination: The Greek Background." In *The Irish Theological Quarterly* 52 (1986): 57–58.

———. *Phantasia in Classical Thought*. Galway: Galway University Press, 1988.

Watt, W. Montgomery. *Islamic Philosophy and Theology*. Edinburgh: Edinburgh University Press, 1985.

Wolfson, Harry A. "The Internal Senses in Latin, Arabic, and Hebrew Philosophical Texts." In *Harvard Theological Review* 28 (1935): 69–133.

Yusuf Ali, Abdullah, trans. *Qur'ān*. New York: Tarikhe Tarsile Qur'an, 2001.

Index

Action: framing by appeal to moral rules, 43; right, 10
Adamson, Peter, 56, 99
Aesthetics (Hegel), 73
Al-Akiti, Muhammad Affifi, 85
Alchemy of Happiness (Ghazali), 115
Alexander of Aphrodisias, 100
Alfarabi, 2, 103, 104, 114, 120, 137*n42*; account of happiness of the true philosopher, 47–49; appropriation of Islamic ethics by, 41–45; *The Attainment of Happiness*, 40; *Book of Letters*, 67, 84; on classification of internal senses, 75; *Commentary on the Nicomachean Ethics*, 101, 102; cosmology and, 13; defines religion, 136*n40*; distinguishes between parts of soul, 54; on ethical cultivation of self, 40; foundation for postclassical political programs and, 13; on human perfection, 62; intellectual insight of, 65; Islamic prophetology and, 45–49; notion of prophecy and account of perfection of man by, 51; perfected imagination of philosopher-lawgiver and, 45; *On the Perfect State*, 13, 47, 51; on philosophical inquiry, 41; places life of contemplation above that of the political, 53; poetic prophecy and, 66; *The Political Regime*, 13, 51; political thought, 13, 52, 53; privileging of practice of spiritual exercises, 54; on relation between philosophy and religion, 44, 45; synthesis of Platonism and Aristotelianism by, 53; theoretical knowledge and, 10; on virtue, 41, 46; virtue ethics and, 13
'Alī (ibn Abī Ṭālib), 46
Altmann, Alexander, 50, 146*n19*
Aminrazavi, Mehdi, 147*n33*, 153*n5*
Amir-Moezzi, Mohammad Ali, 46
Ammonian synthesis, 101
Aquinas, Thomas, 26, 106, 113, 151*n50*, 152*n52*; authority of the church and, 107; rejection of separate Active Intellect, 107; *Summa Contra Gentiles*, 106
Arabic, 16, 17, 35, 40, 127*n47*
Arabism, 16
Arendt, Hannah, 139*n64*
Aristotle, 51, 61, 101, 104; on Active Intellect, 49–52; *Book on the Pure Good*, 66; claims body as instrument used by soul, 100; cultivation of the soul and, 18; *De Anima*, 49; on dreams, 83; on infinite number of souls, 103; *Metaphysics*, 49, 104; *Nicomachean Ethics*, 53; on imagination, 75; *phronimos* and, 31; *Politics*, 53;

Aristotle *(continued)*
raising status of poetry, 66; on second nature, 30; on thought thinking itself, 18; view of soul, 96, 97, 100
Arnaldez, Roger, 2
Art: classical, 73, 74; different forms of, 73, 74; symbolic, 73, 74
The Attainment of Happiness (Alfarabi), 40
Authenticity, 26, 27, 58, 130*n12*; attainment of, 28, 34; call of conscience and, 108, 109; cultivation of, 109, 110; as cultivation of taste, 72; of Dasein, 34; as *existentiell* matter, 34; prospect of, 109
Averroes, 81, 103, 107, 113, 114, 120, 125*n26*; on art of wisdom, 91; *The Decisive Treatise,* 89; reply to Ghazali's charge of heresy, 89–94
Avicenna, 2, 17, 77, 98, 103, 104, 125*n26*, 127*n47*, 128*n53*, 136*n34*, 140*n75*, 144*n54*; account of ethical training for philosophy, 76; account of thinking, 56; accused of heresy, 92, 93; on achievement of personal perfection, 54; commentary on *Theology of Aristotle,* 56, 58; commitment to non-Greek sources, 17, 18; concept of astonishment, 77; conditions for cultivation of conjunction with Active Intellect, 4, 53; departure from Aristotelian tradition, 99; distinguishes between parts of soul, 54; distinguishes between philosophy and poetry, 76; *Eastern Philosophy,* 17, 98–100, 148*n8*, 149*n10*, 149*n11*; *Fair Judgment,* 56; *Healing,* 55, 60; on human perfection, 62; on illumination of soul through prophetic insight, 116; imaginative symbolism and, 4; on intellectual prophecy, 60–63; interpretation of prophetic symbols and, 86–89; on justice, 54; Metaphysics of Rational Soul, 99, 149*n19*; on philosophical felicity, 53–60; on poetic cultivation of imagination, 75–79; poetic prophecy and, 66; *On the Proof of Prophecies,* 60, 61, 88; prophecy of future events and, 84, 85, 86; as proponent of prophetology, 19; *Provenance and Destination,* 78; on psychological processes preparing soul for intellection, 55, 56; *Salvation,* 55, 60; soul as form of body and, 96; soul as subject of self-awareness and, 97; on theoretical wisdom, 55; theory of miracles, 146*n13*; view of soul, 96, 98, 100
Awareness: direct perceptual, 29; of self, 11, 97, 104

Baier, Kurt, 9
Becoming like God, 114, 132*n38,* 133*n2*, 135*n28*, 153*n3*
Being and Time (Heidegger), 24, 26, 27, 34, 95, 105, 108, 130*n11,* 130*n12*
Being-one's-self, 109
Being-towards-beyond-death, 22, 36, 95, 96–105
Being-towards-death, 22, 36, 75, 95, 110
Beliefs: justification of, 29, 30; perceptual, 29, 30; production of, 30; rejection of mythological justification of, 29; relation to each other, 29; sensory experience and, 30
Black, Deborah, 143*n43,* 151*n47*
Book of Letters (Alfarabi), 84
Brethren of Purity, 102, 150*n37*
Butterworth, Charles, 10
Buyids, 93

Chittick, William, 44, 132*n2*, 134*n18,* 135*n28,* 153*n3*
Christianity, 15
Commentary on the Nicomachean Ethics (Alfarabi), 101, 102

Common sense, 56, 75, 78
Conscience: call of, 108, 109, 139*n64*
Corbin, Henry, 4, 8, 35–37, 95, 99, 106, 112, 118, 127*n47*, 132*n39*; contrasts to Heidegger, 36, 37; on divine Essence, 135*n25*; *History of Islamic Philosophy*, 45, 51, 114; identification of inner solitary dialogue by, 57; link between modes of being and understanding in, 23, 24; *The Man of Light in Iranian Sufism*, 37; on phenomenology, 23–24, 35–37; on the Pleroma, 110; on prophetic experiences, 36
Cosmology: Alfarabi and, 13
Critique of Judgment (Kant), 71, 72, 144*n52*, 144*n53*

Dandyism, 11
Dasein, 130*n11*; appropriation of phenomena by, 27; authenticity of, 26, 27, 34, 108; as being of man, 26, 107; as being-towards-beyond-death, 22, 36, 95–105; as being-towards-death, 22, 35, 75, 95, 105, 110; dealings with the world, 108; defining, 132*n34*; disclosedness of, 25; existence as ground of essence of, 35; hermeneutics of, 27; individual, 105; inner solitary discourse of, 58, 105; intelligibility of, 105; ontico-ontological priority of, 26; resoluteness and, 109; self-understanding of, 26, 34; traditional understanding of, 109; understanding of being, 34, 130*n11*
Davidson, Arnold, 11
Davidson, Herbert, 135*n30*, *136*n34, 136*n35*, 138*n51*, 151*n50*
De Anima (Aristotle), 49
The Decisive Treatise (Averroes), 89
The Deliverer from Error (Ghazali), 82, 85
Dialectical method, 90, 91
Discourse: abstract rational, 3; apophantic, 24, 25; comparison to thinking, 57; hermeneutic, 24, 25; inner solitary, 58; interpretation and, 24; Orientalist, 1; philosophical, 8, 13, 14; rational, 16, 18, 81, 93, 111, 112, 113, 127*n47*; reticent, 58; silent, 57, 105; theoretical, 10
Divine: experience of, 4; intimacy with, 46, 47; law, 45; revelation, 4, 48, 90–93; solitude to contemplate, 53; will, 43
Dreams, 81, 82–86, 113; dormancy of senses and, 83; sent by God, 83; that foretell future, 83; veridical, 82, 83, 146*n19*
Dreyfus, Hubert, 29, 30, 31, 32, 33

Eastern Philosophy (Avicenna), 17, 98, 99, 148*n8*
Ego: empirical, 73; thinking, 73
El-Bizri, Nader, 132*n30*, 132*n34*, 138*n49*
Elementatio Theologica (Proclus), 66
Empedocles, 37
Empiricism: appeal to presuppositionless sensory foundation, 29; criticisms of, 29
Enneads (Plotinus), 51, 99
Entelechy, 96, 101
Epicureanism, 11
Estimation, 56, 75
Ethics, 133*n5*; act-centered, 9; agent-centered, 9; Aristotelian, 18; centrality of, 9; contemporary, 9; correspondence between Islam and philosophy at level of, 15, 16; Islamic, 41–45; recognition of primacy of, 39; relationship with virtue, 10; theoretical foundations, 10; virtue, 9, 10, 13, 18
Existence: as ground of essence of Dasein, 35; human, 120; light and, 120; ontological structure of, 34, 35; possibility of, 109
Existentialism, 120

Experience: conceptualized, 30–33; divine, 4; human, 113; and imagination, 63; mystical, 12; necessary for understanding, 36; phenomenological, 22; prophetic, 36; sensory, 30, 63; spiritual, 39, 113; of the sublime, 74, 75; surrogate, 69; theoretical, 5; understanding and, 24

Fair Judgment (Avicenna), 56
Fārābi, Abū Naṣr Muḥammad. *See* Alfarabi
Fāṭima, 46
Fatimids, 93
Fear of God, 43
Felicity, philosophical, 41, 45–60, 102, 103, 104, 128*n56*, 151*n45*
Flying Man argument, 95, 96, 97, 100, 104, 148*n3*
Forms: as intelligibles, 50; mediation of, 61; sensory, 56, 61
Foucault, Michel, 10, 11, 124*n19*
Foundationalism, 3, 29, 111
Frede, Michael, 97

Gabriel (angel of revelation), 51, 55, 57, 68, 87, 88, 116
Gerson, Lloyd, 100, 149*n24*
Ghazali, 17, 62, 113, 114, 115, 119, 121, 127*n47*; *Alchemy of Happiness*, 115; attack on Islamic Peripatetic Philosophy, 81, 89–94; *The Deliverer from Error*, 82, 85; denial of intellectualism, 89; on dreams, 82–86, 113; on illumination of soul through prophetic insight, 116; *The Incoherence of the Philosophers*, 85, 89, 90; interpretation of prophetic symbols and, 81, 86–89; on 'Islamization' of philosophy, 85; *The Niche of Lights*, 86, 87, 88; privileging dreams over intellect, 81; on veridical dreams, 146*n19*
Ghazzālī, Abū Ḥāmid Muḥammad. *See* Ghazali
Given: bare, 31; meaningful, 31; resuscitation of, 31
Gnosticism: as anti-rationalism, 16; Persian, 16
God: existence of, 90; fear of, 43; intimacy with, 46; in Islam, 42; likeness of, 53; obedience to law of, 44; surrender to, 42
Good: absolute, 53; diffusion of, 62; in itself, 54; knowledge of, 10; objective, 76; perceiving, 31; sublimity of, 43; unconditional, 59; universal, 54
Gutas, Dimitri, 60, 71, 99, 127*n47*, 140*n75*, 152*n53*

Hadot, Pierre, 3, 8, 10, 124*n19*, 128*n56*; account of ancient philosophy of, 8–12; on marginalization of philosophy, 14, 15; on philosophy as way of life, 21; spiritual exercises and, 10, 11, 18, 112
Happiness. *See* Felicity
Ḥaqīqa, 42, 45
Hasse, Dag Nikolaus, 55, 85, 138*n51*, 142*n27*
Healing (Avicenna), 55, 60
Hegel, G.W.F., 4, 73, 74; *Aesthetics*, 73; on the sublation of sublime in the beautiful, 5, 74
Heidegger, Martin, 4, 8, 54, 72; account of public space, 108; on authenticity, 5, 108, 109; authenticity as *existentiell* matter for, 34; *Being and Time*, 24, 26, 27, 34, 95, 105, 108, 130*n11*, 130*n12*; being-towards-death and, 22; on call of conscience, 57, 105, 106, 108, 109, 139*n64*; contrasts to Corbin, 36, 37; criticisms of philosophy of, 23, 105–110; critique of traditional philosophical psychology, 39; cultivation of self and, 33; defining phenomenology, 35; on divide between mind and

the world, 110; existential sight and, 33; hermeneutics of the soul and, 26; involvement with Nazis, 35; on mind/world divide, 3, 4; notion of philosophical hero, 108–110; phenomenology of, 3, 5, 24–35, 112; on philosophical inquiry, 41; rejection of traditional account of intellection, 54; on the sublime and the authentic possibility for being, 75
Hermeneutics, 23, 24; Corbin's definition, 23, 24, 36; of Dasein, 27; history of principle of, 37; phenomenological, 24; prevalence in ancient philosophy, 37; of prophetic symbols, 36, 86, 89, 116; of the soul, 26; spiritual, 4, 23, 24, 46, 47, 89, 91, 114, 132*n38*, 132*n39*, 135*n28*; unveiling and, 24; as unveiling of what is happening within, 36
Hermes, 36, 50, 57
Hermeticism, 37, 55, 57
Hermetico-Pythagoreans, 17
History of Islamic Philosophy (Corbin), 45, 51, 114

Ibn 'Arabī, Muhy al-Dīn Muḥammad, 118, 119
Ibn Buṭlān, Abu-l-Ḥasan Mukhtar, 101, 102, 105
Ibn Rushd, Abū al-Walīd. *See* Averroes
Ibn Sīnā, Abū 'Alī Ḥussain. *See* Avicenna
Iḥsān, 44, 134*n15*
Illuminationism, 18, 37, 53, 114, 116
Imaginal world, 5, 116, 119, 154*n12*, 154*n15*
Imagination: animal, 68; capacity of, 5; as cognitive, 116, 153*n10*; creative function of, 63; disciplining, 65–79; drawn to Active Intellect, 78; Greek views of, 12; of heavenly bodies, 85, 146*n19*; imitation of intelligibles by, 66, 67, 84; impregnation by Active Intellect, 48, 65, 67; intellectual heresy and, 81–94; interaction with intellect, 81; involvement with divine intellect, 67; Islamic theory of, 4, 68; liberated, 78; of multitude, 67; need for mediation of intellect for prophecy, 71; objective, 78; perfected, 5, 48, 65, 68, 69, 86, 116; poetic cultivation of, 5, 75–79; prophetic, 62, 65–71, 67, 68, 81, 82–86; religious, 45, 68; representation of divine intelligibles by, 61, 66; spiritual exercises for cultivation of, 119, 65; sublime and, 4, 5, 144*n53*; survival of, 119; transcendence and, 113; transformation of intellectual truths by, 66, 67; in veridical dreams, 62, 82–86, 146*n19*
Imām, 43, 44, 135*n25*
Imitation, 12, 66, 139*n66*; artistic, 66, 69; direct, 66; of divine intellect, 67; imaginative, 69, 84
The Incoherence of the Philosophers (Ghazali), 85, 89, 90
Intellect: acquired, 52, 59, 60, 61, 86, 104; actual, 55; conjunction with Active Intellect, 65; correcting sense perception, 87; cosmic, 50; cultivation of, 52; discursive function of, 82; divine, 67, 79; habitual, 58, 88; heavenly, 57; interaction with imagination, 71, 81; perception of theoretical intelligibles, 82; philosophical, 60; potential, 58, 59; practical, 78; prophetic, 60, 61; restrictions of, 113; separate, 50; stage beyond, 82; theoretical, 4, 54, 57, 58, 101, 112, 113; thinking activity of, 100; as thought thinking itself, 52; uncultivated, 58, 76; valorization of, 110

Intellect, Active: access to intelligibles of, 52; activity of, 49; as angel of revelation, 50, 51, 57, 83, 107, 115; as bestower of intelligibility, 69; conjunction with, 60, 61, 86; as divine being, 50; emanations from, 52, 84, 116, 117; happiness and, 48; as Holy Spirit, 57, 107; imagination drawn to, 78; imitations of things supplied by, 66; impregnation of imagination by, 65; intellectual emanations from, 48, 59; internalization of, 107, 151*n50*; intimacy with, 65; mediation of, 48; perfect man as intimate of, 51; poetic symbolization of emanations of, 79; reception of relevant intelligibles from, 55; as separate intellect, 50; Thomistic interpretation of 106; transcendent, 48, 49, 50, 115, 136*n35*
Intellection, 54, 115, 120; effort and training in, 55; processes of preparation of soul for, 55, 56; of secondary intelligibles, 59
Intellectual: cultivation of imagination, 119, 144*n54*; inner dialogue, 62; insight, 65; intuition, 85, 86; knowledge, 115; prophecy, 84, 85; self-identity, 115; soul, 103, 104; truths, 65, 68, 69
Intelligibles: abstracted, 52; enmattered (intentions), 54, 55, 56, 58, 59, 75, 76, 77, 116; ethical, 47; philosophical contemplation of, 52; poetic statements imitating, 66; potential, 55; practical, 69; primary, 55, 59, 76; secondary, 59, 61, 76; theoretical, 84; transcendent, 47, 53; unconditional, 59; understanding, 47; universal, 59
Iran, 114, 117, 121, 149*n19*
Isfahan, school of, 94, 117, 118, 121, 154*n16*
Islam: alignment of philosophy with, 44–49, 90–92; ambiguity of, 43; ascetic practices in, 43; as association of theory and practice, 18; attainment of balance in, 43; committment to dynamic concept of society in, 16; cultivation of soul in, 4, 42–44; as expression of perennial wisdom, 18; levels of human existence in, 44; misrepresentation of, 1; paradigm of religious development in, 44, 45; philosophical corruption of, 93; reconciliation with Greek philosophy, 3, 49–52; reflection of Muhammad's qualities, 46; ritual practices of, 42; Shi'i, 16, 46, 93, 117; state of virtue in, 43; Sunni, 93; surrender to God in, 42
Islam: Religion, History, and Civilization (Nasr), 42
Islamic Philosophy from Its Origin to the Present (Nasr), 117
Izutsu, Toshihiko, 42, 43, 120

Al-Jabri, 'Abed, 16
Judgment: moral, 73, 142*n34*; reflective, 71, 72; of the sublime, 73, 74, 77; of taste, 71, 72, 144*n52*

Kant, Immanuel, 4, 72–73, 144*n54*; on Copermnican revolution in philosophy, 72–73; *Critique of Judgment*, 71, 72, 144*n52*, 144*n53*; empiricism of, 29; on judgment of taste, 71, 72, 144*n53*; on moral principles, 142*n34*; on the sublime, 4, 5, 71, 72, 75, 77, 143*n37*, 114*n53*; "Transcendental Deduction," 73
Al-Kindī, Abū Yūsuf Ya'qūb ibn Isḥāq, 3, 40, 67, 123*n14*, 133*n2*, 136*n39*

Kindness, 32, 33
Knowledge: claims to, 3, 73; discursive, 25, 119; as dispensation of Active Intellect, 55–63; ethical, 3, 10, 31, 33; "givens" as ground of claims to, 22; intuitive, 118; Kant's account of, 72–73; object of, 73; as perfection of existence, 115; of the physical world, 58, 76; prophetic, 55–63, 70, 82, 83; rational, 15, 16, 17, 89, 111; of self, 115; sensitivity as, 3, 28, 33; of spiritual world, 37, 50, 58, 146*n10*, 153*n10*; theoretical, 10, 22, 37, 69; as transformation of the self, 4, 36, 115, 154*n21*
Kraemer, Joel, 15

Lacoue-Labarthes, Philippe, 74
Law, Islamic (*Sharī'a*), 92; cultivation of self by, 43, 108; foundations of, 51; images of the real in, 91; obedience to, 44; starting point for moral excellence, 42; submission to, 43, 46, 47
Lawgiving, 62; prophetic, 69; religious, 67
Leaman, Oliver, 14, 16, 17
Light: divine, 87; dominating, 116; existence and, 120; heavenly, 87; managing, 116; meaning of, 87, 88, 89, 116, 120; positive state of, 49; propagation of, 120; as self-manifesting reality, 87, 120
Logic, 11; priority of, 133*n5*
Luther, Martin, 36

Mahdi, Muhsin, 1, 2, 13, 81, 112; on production of rational knowledge, 16
The Man of Light in Iranian Sufism (Corbin), 37
Marmura, Michael, 2, 104
Massignon, Louis, 23
McDowell, John, 29, 30, 31, 32, 33, 34, 130*n19*, 131*n25*
Meaning: of being, 34; of light, 87
Medieval scholasticism, 14, 106–107, 151*n50*
Meister Eckhart, 37
Memory, 40, 56, 75, 76
Meno (Plato), 50
Metaphysics of the Rational Soul, 99, 149*n19*
Mind: conforming, 49; intuition and, 60; movement of, 60; passive, 49, 50; productive, 49
Mind and World (McDowell), 29–30, 124*n17*, 131*n25*
Miracles, 84, 85, 146*n13*
Mohaghegh, Mehdi, 120
Moral: intentions, 58, 59, 76; judgment, 29–30, 73; law, 73; principles, 62; rules, 43; sensibility, 31–33, 77
Morality: prephilosophical, 40, 133*n5*
Muhammad, Prophet, 87; attributes of, 45; belief in prophecy of, 51; bringing the faithful closer to God, 45; as conveyor of divine law, 45; intimacy with God, 45; revelations of, 4, 68
Mulla Sadra, 5, 117, 118, 119, 120, 121, 149*n19*
Murdoch, Iris, 73, 143*n37*
Mysticism, 11, 14
"Myth of the Given" (Sellars), 29, 30, 31

Nasr, Seyyed Hossein, 17, 23, 35, 118, 127*n47*, 128*n53*; characterization of Islamic tradition, 42; defining Islam, 18; on Islamic law, 134*n20*
Neoplatonism, 67, 100, 101; cosmological dimensions of, 11
The Niche of Lights (Ghazali), 86, 87, 88
Nicomachean Ethics (Aristotle), 53, 62

Nubuwwa, 45, 46, 48

On the Perfect State (Alfarabi), 13, 47, 51
On the Proof of Prophecies (Avicenna), 60, 61, 88
Orientalism, 1, 7–19; philosophical, 12; predicament of discourse in, 1; rejections of, 16; root of quandries in, 2; superiority of Western culture and, 12

Perception, 31, 87; intellectual, 45, 50, *54*, 144*n54*; of present-at-hand, 28, 33, 34
Persian, 16, 35, 57, 74, 117, 118, 119, 121, 127*n47*
Phenomenology, 21–37; access to things in, 21, 22; authenticity and, 27, 35; cultivation of self and, 21; Heideggerian, 95–110; overcomes partition between practical virtue and knowledge, 22; overcoming divide between reason and nature, 21; parallels with Islamic Peripatetic Philosophy, 21–37; Perso-Arabic equivalent, 35; saving the appearance while unveiling the hidden in, 23, 24; spiritual exercises and, 21; unveiling in, 23, 35
Phenomenon: insight into, 46; luminous, 88; phenomenological sense of, 22, 23, 35; seen as they are in themselves, 23; spiritual, 46, 81; unveiling of, 35, 36
Philosopher: counterfeit, 40, 41; false, 40, 41; as prophet, 48; solitary journey of, 51; true, 41, 47–49; union with the divine, 51; vain, 40, 41
Philosopher-prophet-king, 49, 66, 84
Philosophy: alignment with Islam, 45–49, 89–94; ancient, 7, 8, 21, 41; autonomy of, 7, 15, 17; criticism of modernist scholarship on, 8–11; as handmaid of theology, 14, 15; as mere rational discourse, 82; mutilated, 40; Oriental, 12; phenomenological, 24–37; as practice of spiritual exercises, 3, 8–11, 40, 91, 114; prior to religion in time, 52; as production of rational discourse, 3, 12, 14, 15, 16, 93, 127*n47*; reconciliation with authority of the Church, 113; in Safavid dynasty, 16, 114, 117, 121, 155*n36*; spiritual focus of, 93; theoretical, 40, 41; as way of life, 8, 17, 21, 92
Philosophy, Islamic Peripatetic, 2–3; account of public space, 108; Active Intellect in, 49–52; in Baghdad, 101, 102, 105; combines Islamic and Greek philosophical paradigms of excellence, 110; compared with Heideggerian phenomenology, 95–110; divine favor and prophetic insight in, 47–49, 60–63, 65–71, 83–85; Eastern, 98–100, 105, 148*n8*, 149*n10*, 149*n11*; encounters with spiritual beings in, 39; Ghazali's charge of heresy and, 89–94; imagination and, 65–71; immortality of soul in, 96–105; impact of Aristotelian ethics on, 18; impact on later Islamic philosophy, 106–107, 111–121, 151*n50*; importance for modern Western philosophy, 111–113; mind/world dualism and, 4, 39–63, 112–113; notion of soul in, 96–105; philosophical cultivation in, 37, 39–60; as premodern rationalism, 2; primacy of ethics and, 39, 40, 41, 43, 52, 54, 89; prominence of prophetic religion in, 22; reception of notion of Active Intellect in, 49–52; reconciliation of ancient philosophy and Islam in, 15;

relation between religion and philosophy in, 108–110; spiritual exercises in, 5, 7, 65, 93; standard readings of, 11–19
Philosophy as a Way of Life (Hadot), 8
Philosophy of Illumination (Suhrawardī), 114
Phronēsis, 31, 32, 47
Phronimos, 31, 32, 62; perception of, 32
Pines, Shlomo, 101, 102
Plato, 10, 50, 51, 101; defining soul, 97; Demiurge of, 50; distinguishes between parts of soul, 54; on divine kingdom, 61; knowledge of good and, 10; *Meno*, 50; *Protagoras*, 50; *Republic*, 13, 40, 50, 53; *Sophist*, 57; *Statesman*, 134*n19*; *Timaeus*, 50
Pleroma, 110
Plotinus, 37, 50, 51, 97, 136*n34*; allows direct imitation, 66; discursive thinking and, 56; view of soul, 97
The Political Regime (Alfarabi), 13, 51
Politics (Aristotle), 53
Positive science, 24, 28, 129*n10*
Practice of spiritual exercises: in alliance with theory, 18, 19, 110; ancient philosophy focused on, 3, 8–11, 18, 40; as core of philosophy, 3, 8–11, 40, 91, 114; and cultivation of practical virtues, 10; for cultivation of the soul, 115; ethical function of, 10, 15, 53, 54; and the hermeneutic principle, 37, 91, 114; human existence and, 120; imagination and, 4, 75–79 89, 119; in Islamic Peripatetic Philosophy, 5, 7, 37, 40, 95, 110, 127*n47*, 147*n33*; knowledge of self and, 115, 116; phenomenology and, 21, 35–37; and politics, 53; prophetology and, 118, 121; Stoic physics as, 11
Proclus, 66
Prophecy: of future events, 48, 70, 82–86; imaginative, 62, 70, 83, 84; intellectual, 60–63, 85, 86; lawgiving, 46; of messengers, 67; pedagogical aspect of, 140*n75*; as philosophy for the multitude, 69, 136*n39*; poetic, 61, 66, 67, 69; as working of miracles, 62, 84, 146*n12*, 146*n19*
Prophetology, 19, 22, 118, 128*n58*; philosophical appropriation of Islamic, 45–49, 85
Protagoras (Plato), 50
Provenance and Destination (Avicenna), 78
Pythagoras, 61

Qur'an, 51, 68, 85, 90, 120; ethical perspective of, 42

Rahman, Fazlur, 42, 43, 97, 134*n19*
Rationalism: academic, 7–19; crisis of, 2; genuine form of, 2, 81, 112; modern, 2, 111–113; premodern, 2, 112
Rāzī, Abū Bakr Muḥammad ibn Zakariyā, 40, 133*n3*
Realism, 29
Reason, 77; and attainment of self-consciousness, 73; discursive (dialectical), 56–57, 82, 90–92, 114, 119, 131*n25*; forgotten magnificence of, 73; independent, 72; modern, 111, 112; practical, 47, 48, 73, 76, 112; productive activity of, 72, 73; pure, 72; and purposiveness without purpose, 73; theoretical, 10, 47, 48, 58, 76, 128*n56*
Reductionism, 111
Representation, 75, 76; imaginative, 44, 45, 66, 69, 76, 77, 79; possibility of, 2; truth as, 2
Republic (Plato), 13, 40, 50, 53
Resoluteness, 34, 58, 109
Revelation, 4, 48, 90–93

Risāla, 45, 49
Russell, Bertrand, 125*n26*

Safavid dynasty, 16, 117, 121
Said, Edward, 1, 2, 12
Salvation (Avicenna), 55, 60
Self: awareness, 96–104; in cosmic whole, 11; cultivation of, 16, 21, 22, 28, 33, 40, 81, 130*n13*; free, 62; knowledge of, 115–116; Socratic care of, 10; transformation of, 3, 4, 7; uncultivated, 9; understanding, 28, 34
Self-consciousness, 97; methodological, 2, 112; reason's attainment of, 73
Sellars, Wilfrid, 29, 30
Sharī'a. See Law, Islamic
Shīrāzī, Ṣadr al-Dīn Muḥammad. *See* Mulla Sadra
Socrates, 61, 124*n19*
Sophist (Plato), 57
Soul: awareness of own essence, 104; and being in-the-world, 26; brute, 99; capability for achievement of conjunction with Active Intellect, 56; care of, 22; co-dependence on body, 101; corruptibility of, 99; cultivation of, 10, 18, 39, 47, 66, 76, 87, 105, 115, 132*n39*; differences in disposition of, 103; as first actuality of body, 100; of heavenly bodies, 70, 71, 84, 146*n10*, 146*n19*; immortality of, 23, 90, 95, 96–105, 107, 114, 115, 119; intellectual, 103, 104; pre-existence of individual, 103; preparation for intellection and, 55, 56; rational, 58, 76, 99, 101, 106, 136*n34*; as subject of cognition, 97; traditional accounts of, 26; transformation of, 17, 36, 75; transparency of, 26; uniqueness of, 26
Space of reasons, 30, 31
Statesman (Plato), 134*n19*
Stoicism, 11, 66, 134*n19*
Strauss, Leo, 14, 15
Stroumsa, Sarah, 15, 79
Sublime, 4, 74, 75, 77, 143*n37*; and the beautiful, 5, 71–72, 144*n53*; historicizing of, 5, 74
Sufism, 35, 57, 85, 118, 174*n18*
Suhrawardī, Shihāb al-Dīn Yaḥyā, 5, 23, 107, 113, 114, 117, 118, 120, 149*n19*; Illuminationism and, 18; on illumination of soul through prophetic insight, 116; *Philosophy of Illumination,* 114; restoration of Islamic Peripateticism by, 115, 114; on wisdom, 114
Summa Contra Gentiles (Aquinas), 106
Symbolism: hermeneutics of, 4, 86–89, 116; imaginative, 4; Jewish, 73, 74; prophetic, 74, 78, 86–89; of the sublime, 73, 74

Taqwā, 43, 44; as state of accomplished believer, 42
Ṭarīqa, 42, 45, 47
Ta'wīl, 4, 23, 24, 46, 47, 89, 91, 114, 132*n38*, 132*n39*,135*n28*
Taylor, Richard, 127*n47*, 151*n44*
Theology: appropriation of philosophy by, 14, 15; Islamic, 16, 119
Theology of Aristotle, 51, 56, 58, 99, 100, 136*n34*
Thinking: as activity, 49, 104; and *dianoia,* 56, 57; discursive (dialogical), 56, 58, 69, 82; intuition and, 60, 104, 140*n75*; as inward dialogue, 57; rational *vs.* animal, 55, 59, 76, 139*n66*, 152*n53*
Thomism, 106, 110, 151*n50*, 152*n53*
Timaeus (Plato), 50
Truth: being in, 26, 42, 58, 106; correspondence theory of, 25; divine, 18, 42, 46, 48, 91, 92, 93;

esoteric side of, 46; imagination and, 45, 66, 68, 69, 134*n19*; intellectual, 65, 68, 69; primary intelligibles and, 55, 58, 76; religion and, 45, 46, 62, 67, 92, 134*n19*
Ṭūsī, Khawja Naṣīr, al-Dīn, 117, 118

Veyne, Paul, 10
Virtue: appropriate responses and, 33, 131*n25*; cultivation of, 10, 37, 53, 78, 89; deliberative, 10; Islamic law and, 42; practical, 10, 22, 55, 69; relationship with ethics, 9, 10, 13; religious cultivation of, 41; theoretical, 10, 69; training in, 77, 84, 88, 110

Walāya, 45, 46, 48
Walzer, Richard, 12, 13, 51, 67
Watson, Gerard, 66
Wisdom: acquisition of, 3, 7; art of, 91; discursive, 114, 118; divine, 51, 87; intuitive, 114, 118; practical, 30, 54, 59, 66, 76; prophetic, 87; revival of perennial, 18; theoretical, 54, 55, 66; training for, 8
Wisnovsky, Robert, 100, 101
World: conceptuality of the experience of, 30–33; impact on senses, 30; infused with intelligibility, 39, 50; representations of, 29, 30; without a beginning in time, 90